IN THE HOPE OF NIBBANA

IN THE HOPE OF NIBBANA

An Essay on

THERAVADA

BUDDHIST

ETHICS

WINSTON L. KING

OPEN COURT

Established 1887 • LaSalle, Illinois

Library of Congress Catalog
Card Number: 62-9575

IN THE HOPE OF NIBBANA

© 1964 by the Open Court Publishing Company

Printed in the United States of America

AUTHOR'S FOREWORD

This present volume was begun while the author was visiting professor at the International Institute for Advanced Buddhistic Studies (Kaba Aye, Ragoon, Burma) under a grant from the Ford Foundation. It was originally comprised of two chapters in a prospective volume of essays on Theravada Buddhism, but at the suggestion of Dr. R. H. L. Slater of Harvard University, who felt that there is an almost total lack of contemporary material on Buddhist ethics in English, I began to consider the possibility of a more systematic and comprehensive treatment of the subject. The more I studied Buddhist ethics the more fascinating it became. The following volume is the result, which I hopefully dedicate to filling somewhat of the gap of which Dr. Slater speaks, at least in the Theravada (Southern) Buddhist area.

Several facets of the ethical structure of Theravada Buddhism intrigued me in particular, and I here present them as questions to which I attempt to provide at least partial answers in the following chapters: (1) What is the relation of ethics to the total structure of Buddhist doctrine and practice, particularly with regard to the definition of moral values, their metaphysical status if any, and the nature of ultimate sanctions? (2) How does the Buddhist ethic relate itself to the Buddhist psychology, particularly that of its doctrine of *anattā* or no-self? (3) What is the effect of the Nibbana-Kamma (Nirvana-Karma) polarity of emphasis upon ethical value? Or to put it otherwise: In what respects is Buddhist ethic absolute and in what relativistic? (4) How does Buddhism practically and specifically analyze ethical goodness and badness in the area of concrete action? (5) Is there a genuine social ethic in Buddhism, and if so, what would be the form of the ideal Buddhist society? (6) What if any new ethical developments or emphases are to be found in contemporary Theravada Buddhism, which has so long and persistently adhered to its conservative traditionalism of scripture, doctrine and practice?

A word of explanation may be in place with regard to the title. It is actually a translation of words often found upon printed invitations to an anniversary or festival "breakfast" meal (anytime before noon) sent by Burmese to their friends. Early in the morning nearby monks, or special friends among the monks, are fed; then beginning at about eight o'clock the other invited friends (laymen) arrive for a good social meal together. Now all of this, the invitation assures the invitee, is done "in the hope of Neban," i.e. Nibbana or Nirvana. Thus does the ordinary Buddhist himself, far, far from Nibbana or even direct Nibbanaward striving, honor those who *are* thus striving, and humbly hope that even his modest charitable efforts will somehow, perhaps by the process of kammic multiplication, add up to a nibbanic sum in the end. Such words thus seem eminently fitting as a motif by which to characterize the total Buddhist ethical endeavor.

The obligations which I owe for materials herein are numerous. First on the list must be U Hpe Aung, Director of the Institute (noted above), to whose interest in my interest in Buddhism I am primarily indebted for the opportunity to study in Burma and of whose willingness to talk to me about Buddhism there was no end. Appreciation is also extended to the whole staff of the Institute who at all times were most helpful, in particular U Hla Maung, Deputy Director, who answered many questions about things Buddhist and Burmese, U San Myint Aung who helped with the materials of Chapter IV, and U Han Htey who translated some portions of the policy speeches of the Honorable U Nu into English for me.

Outside the Institute staff the Venerable U Thittila and Professor U Aung Than, both of the University of Rangoon, gave me generously out of their busy schedules, time for repeated lengthy conversations. In teaching the Venerable U Pyinnya Dipa something of the history of religions I learned as much in return about Buddhism. Dr. R. L. Soni of Mandalay was most cordially helpful to my efforts to understand Buddhism; and from my association with Thray Sithu U Ba Khin of the International Meditation Center I gained some further awareness (I trust) of the inner dimensions of Buddhist experience. Especial thanks are due to Myanaung U Tin for his good advice at a difficult time and for his reading over the pages concerning what I have called the "Buddhist Socialism" of the Honorable U Nu. To the Honorable Justice U Chan Htoon I express thanks for two interviews and his presentation to me of the copies of two of his addresses on Buddhism given in the United States. Nor should I fail to mention the gracious hospitality of Yogi U Tin and the Buddhist Men's Breakfast-Discussion Group which met at his home, in including me as a guest and speaking English for my benefit; nor the patience of many other persons, both laymen and monks, who sought to enlighten me with regard to their religious practices and faith, acting as guides, interpreters, and friends. And to my wife I am grateful for many side-lights gained from her study of the Burmese language.

Appreciation is expressed to authors and publishers who have given permission to quote from their works. Titles and names of authors and publishers are duly acknowledged in footnotes and bibliography. Thanks of a different sort are due to those friends in India, Dr. and Mrs. B. P. Hivale, and Principal and Mrs. Thomas Barnabas of Ahmednagar College, who provided me with sanctuary in exchange for such duties as still left me time to complete the writing of this manuscript, and provided for me the services of a typist, Mr. D. D. Patole.

For such mistakes of fact or interpretation of Buddhist thought as there may be herein I take full responsibility; I plead only the ignorance which remains after all too short a time for my study as the excuse for such mistakes, not the lack of my will to understand. I do not expect my Burmese friends to agree with all that I have said when it comes to my analysis of the Buddhist ethic; but I trust that they will believe that there is neither ill-will nor desire to search out failure or weakness involved here, but only the desire to interpret Buddhism to the West (and to myself) in terms that are meaningful to us.

One concluding word may be said with regard to the use and spelling of Buddhist terms. Even though the Sanskrit forms are usually more familiar in the West, e.g. Karma, Dharma, Nirvana, I have in all cases used Pali terms (correspondingly Kamma, Dhamma, Nibbana, etc.) because it seemed singularly inappropriate in writing about Buddhism of the Pali tradition to use other than its own traditional terms. And further, in a kind of East-West compromise which may not commend itself to the scholar's scholar in this field, I have anglicized these same terms without remainder, except in their first appearance, or in case of very infrequent appearance. Thus rather than *Nibbāna*, it is Nibbana. Pitaka rather than *Piṭaka,* Sila rather than *Sīla,* and so forth. In this latter case there is no perfect way to secure the correct pronunciation (See-lah) automatically by spelling it in any Pali form, but Sila seems somewhat better than *Sīla*. In order to avoid either a hybrid Pannya or grossly mispronounced Panna for *Paññā,* I have used the compromise form Pañña which I trust will serve its purpose adequately.

CONTENTS

PART I

Background and Framework

CHAPTER I

1. Buddhism and Ethics

Any one who has read even a very little in the early Buddhist Scriptures is aware that from its beginning Buddhism has been centrally concerned with the moral discipline of life.[1] Ethical language abounds in the discourses of the Buddha. Over and over again we see him portraying the Good Life in these terms: the avoidance of violence, harsh language, and all anger; the tethering of riotous emotions; reduction of the scale of one's desires; restraint of the sense-life; control of the self by its own inner power; the purification of the mind; the eradication of such evil dispositions as greed and hatred for example, that lead to evil action; the cultivation of a serene and benevolent mind capable of compassionating all beings without distinction. Not only so, but he presents in the same passages a systematic methodology of ethical discipline and culture by which one may achieve such virtue; ethics here is obviously not merely a matter of pious exhortation to be righteous or a species of emotionally inspired heroism, but the steady pursuit of a rationally conceived goodness.

It is likewise true that metaphysics and religion are largely bypassed, at least in the usual sense of those words. Metaphysical questions, those having to do with the ultimate origin of the universe, for example, are classed as questions whose discussion has no ethical or religious value—as well as being intrinsically unanswerable. The Buddha remained metaphysically agnostic

---

[1] (See Bibliography for full data on PTS (Pali Text Society) translations of Buddhist canon.)

throughout his career, turning rather to a humanistic and ethical way of life whose main interest was psychological analysis and ethical culture rather than metaphysical theory. Likewise the Buddha turned away from the religious practices of his day. He criticized the priests for their overweening pride and false pretensions to revealed knowledge; their elaborate rituals he ridiculed as useless for man's improvement; he undercut the socio-religious caste structure by redefining a Brahman or high caste person in terms of character rather than birth and opening the Order of monks and nuns to men and women of any caste; and the Brahmanical gods he gently lampooned and put in their place of not-so-wise and not-so-important minor spirits.

This has inspired many Western interpreters in particular to conceive Buddhism as purely and simply a moralism. We shall have occasion to note many times later that Buddhism is no "mere morality" since it aims at goals which completely transcend the ethical and always places its ethic in that transcendent context. But for the moment we may say that there is indeed a very central and major ethical concern in Buddhism which contemporary Theravadins (Buddhists of the "southern" or Pali Canon tradition) continue to emphasize. Indeed the Theravadin is not always agreeable to having Buddhism called a religion, or faith; and if he does allow or use such a description of his way of life, he is always insistent upon restating *his* use of it. Buddhism, he will say, has no dogmas, supersititions, necessary rituals, mediating priests, or blind faith in an unknown (and unknowable) God. But "if by religion is meant a system of deliverance from the ills of life, then Buddhism is a religion of religions."[1a] Or it would be congenial to most Theravada Buddhists to have the Dhamma (Teaching of the Buddha) described as a "clear, logical, coherent and scientific ethico-philosophical doctrine of spiritual liberation."[2]

[1a] Venerable Narada, "An Outline of Buddhism," *Buddhist Supplement* of *The Burman*, August 4, 1958.

[2] Mauno Nordberg, "Is Dhamma a Religion?" *Light of the Dhamma*, Vol. I, No. 3, (April, 1953), 40–41.
Interestingly enough the author of this quotation, a European Buddhist writing in a Theravada Buddhist publication, goes on to criticize the worship of Buddhist relics found in Theravada countries as "shocking to us

It is also true that now and again Buddhism is reaffirmed in a social-ethical context reminiscent of its earliest form. One of the most interesting of such restatements is that of the late Dr. B. R. Ambedkar who, taking along with him several millions of fellow members of "untouchable" castes in India, recently espoused Buddhism. He says that he found no secure or honorable place for his people in caste-ridden and religious Hinduism; therefore he turned to moralistic and rationalistic Buddhism. There follows his characterization of the two faiths:

> Hinduism is characterized by the particularity of not being founded upon morality. Indeed the morality of Hinduism is not an integral part of its doctrine but appears as an entirely distinct system, a force supported by social necessities and not at all by dogmatic obligations.
>
> Contrarily the religion of the Buddha *is* morality; morality is the veritable root of the religion, and Buddhism would not exist without it. This is due principally to the fact that Buddhism does not believe in a God which it presents for the adoration of the faithful and because, specifically, it is morality itself which in Buddhism plays the basic role taken by the deity in other religions.[3]

Thus Dr. Ambedkar retains the name of religion with regard to Buddhism but makes it almost completely a moral discipline. And though Theravada Buddhists might not agree completely with Dr. Ambedkar's interpretation of Buddhism—an earlier book of his was criticized in Burma as being quite defective doctrinally—in the main they would approve his central moral emphasis, and assert that ethical development is an intrinsic part of the Buddhist way of salvation.

But this is not quite the end of the matter. One cannot go on directly and simply from the proposition that morality is central

---

European Buddhists," because it is much like Roman Catholic practice. The editor in a note corrects him: the homage which Buddhists give to images and relics is "totally different" from Western varieties of the same practice! Obviously even Theravada Buddhism is not solely a moralism, no matter how strongly ethical elements are emphasized.

[3] Free translation from "Le Buddha et l'avenir du Bouddhisme" in *Présence du Bouddhisme*, France–Asie, XVI (Saigon, February–June, 1959), 552.

to Buddhism to describe its ethical teachings, after the manner of Western moral philosophers. For before the concrete ethical precepts and practices of Buddhism can take their place in the proper perspective necessary for their understanding, we must observe what the Buddhist philosophy seems to mean by the ethical category and to consider the total context to which it is relevant.

2. Self-Development as the Context of Ethics

The ethic of Buddhism may be described in general as an ethic of self-development, though the nature of the self and its development must be carefully examined. It can be called self-development in two basic senses: First as a process of the development *of* the self in terms of its inherent capacities; second, as a development of the self *by* the self. Both of these aspects are strongly emphasized as integral to the Buddhist way, though in somewhat different contexts. Thus in the first sense ethical progress, toward and including the perfection of the saint (*arahat*) and the Buddha, is not a matter of receiving an infusion of supernatural virtue, or a renewal of the moral nature by a work of divine grace; it is the development of those capacities inherent in human nature to their absolute maximum. Every man is a potential saint; Buddhahood is Perfect Manhood. And in the second sense, this development even to the maximum degree of Buddhahood, or perhaps especially Buddhahood, comes about only by one's own efforts. Buddhas are *Self*-Perfected Ones.

Leaving aside momentarily the exact analysis of the Buddhist meaning of "self" we may note that the conception of ethics as consisting essentially of the perfection of the self by the self places the center of interest, the ultimate goal, and the means of development of the self unto perfection, squarely within the individual. Environing social customs and the cosmic status of human ethical values may be largely left out of account—even though not quite so much as seems to be the case at first glance. Thus ethics rather than being a matter of separate interest or independent status comes to be a division of the psychological realm and most of Western-style ethical theory is by-passed as of secondary value. "Ethic" for Buddhism is psychological analysis and mind-control, not the search for a foundation of ethical principle, a hierarchical arrangement of ethical values, or an inquiry into their objectivity.

This makes the analysis of the "self" of primary importance, of course, for any essential understanding of Buddhist ethic. But this process has its necessary limitations; it is perhaps both impossible and undesirable of accomplishment for the Western reader, in full Buddhist style at least. For one thing this analysis has already been carried to encyclopedic proportions of elaboration and refinement in the third division of the Pali Canon, the Abhidhamma, and in the commentarial literature thereupon. Thus the mere enumeration of the constituents of mental states, the varieties of states of consciousness, and possible mental-moral attitudes is an exhaustive labor in itself; and the drawing forth of the logical possibilities of this already intricate material has been a major preoccupation of Buddhist monks for at least 1500 years. Even could it be done by some genius, which the present author is not, it is doubtful whether the statement of Abhidhammic ethical theory would be of much use or significance to the Westerner. Attempts in this direction up to the present are not particularly promising. The usual result seems to be a vocabulary and system of distinctions almost completely foreign and meaningless to the Western mind, in which the ethical element, in the Western sense, is lost sight of in an unfamiliar maze of Buddhist psychological terminology.[4]

---

[4] We may give an example of this mingling of categories. Thus: "The following fourteen psychic factors are immoral: (1) Dullness and deception. (2) Impudence. (3) Shamelessness. (4) Distraction. (5) Greed. (6) False view. (7) Conceit. (8) Hate. (9) Envy. (10) Jealousy. (11) Worry. (12) Sloth. (13) Torpor. (14) Perplexity. . . .
"The following nineteen factors are essentially present in all the types of 'good' consciousness:—(1) faith, (2) mindfulness, (3) prudence, (4) shame, (5) self-sacrificingness, (6) good-will, (7) balance of mind, (8) calmness of the psychic factors, (9) calmness of mind, (10) buoyancy of psychic factors, (11) buoyancy of mind, (12) pliancy of the psychic factors, (13) pliancy of mind, (14) fitness of work of the psychic factors, (15) fitness of work of mind, (16) proficiency of psychic factors, (17) proficiency of mind, (18) rectitude of the psychic factors, (19) rectitude of mind.

Secondly it may be questioned whether an exhaustive survey of such elaborations and enumerations is essential to a basic understanding of the Buddhist ethic, either for a Buddhist or a non-Buddhist. Confessedly Abhidhamma is the elaboration of those central themes present in the popular dialogues or Suttas. Indeed if one must learn all the scholastic distinctions of Abhidhammic philosophical psychology before the essence of the ethic comes clear, he would be strangely like that man parodied by the Buddha in a famous discourse, who, though sorely wounded by an arrow, must needs know all about the kind of arrow which has wounded him, the nature of the bow that shot it, the appearance of the shooter of the arrow, and so forth, before he will submit to the treatment of his wound. The main outlines and essential quality of the Buddhist ethic can indeed be known apart from the complete Abhidhammic analysis.

a. Analysis of the Self

(1) *No-self doctrine*
The central Buddhist doctrine about the self, according to Theravadins at least, is its compounded and temporary nature. The empirically observable human being, and "empirical" observation for the Buddhist includes introspective analysis, is com-

---

Lobha [greed], *Dosa* [hatred], and *Moha* [delusion] have a blinding and agitating influence upon the person, under which he loses his self-consciousness and the reasoning faculty. He forgets himself and feels stiff . . . Quite opposed to that in a 'good' consciousness, the subject is fully awake and mindful, for the types of 'good' consciousness are light, calm, and peaceful." Bhikkhu J. Kashyap, *The Abhidhamma Philosophy,* (Buddha-Vihara Patna, India, 1954), pp. 48—50.

It may be observed that even the author of the above passage evidently recognizes the rather unusual usage of the ethical term "good" by putting it in quotation marks. And well he might in a list in which greed, hatred, conceit, envy, prudence, sacrificingness, and good-will are put side by side with pliancy, distraction, balance, buoyancy, perplexity, and proficiency of mind and the whole lot defined as either "immoral" or "good" with no middle category allowed.

It is interesting to observe also that even that great evil trinity of basically wrong attitudes—greed-hatred-delusion—are "immoral" largely because of their disturbing and depressing effect upon one's mental powers. The "good" mind-state is primarily the skillful or efficient one rather than the ethically pure one.

posed of five groups of elements called *khandhas*. The full or exact meaning of these terms is difficult to grasp in translation, but they may be listed as follows:

(1) The *Rūpa* or corporeality group. This is sometimes called "form" or "matter" as well, and roughly represents the physicality of the sentient being or person. This rupa is capable of successive refinements until it becomes almost immaterial in the case of the higher beings, however.

(2) The *Vedanā* or feeling group, including both physical and psychical sensibilities. This obviously includes the five ordinary bodily senses, insofar as they are identified with their experience-potential rather than the mere physical sense organs; and it adds a sixth, or mental, feeling recognized by Buddhism as a separate and independent sensibility. This group is thus physical-sensation potential plus more generalized feeling overtones.

(3) *Saññā* or perception. Roughly this is the power which is, or produces, perception of physical objects within the human psyche. In some contexts it is equivalent to the total power of consciousness.

(4) *Sankhāra*, translated as mental formations or mental factors. Later Buddhist psychologists divided this category into fifty-odd formations, some of general psychological nature such as mental impression, volition, vitality, concentration, conception, discursive thinking, interest, intention etc., and others of a moral nature such as faith, mindfulness, moral shame, tranquility, and their opposites.

(5) *Viññāṇa*, or consciousness. This is consciousness in the full personal sense of the word, that consciousness which binds the varied sense and feeling elements of the individual—physical awareness, bodily feeling-tone, and mental constructs—into a personalized unity.

This five-fold grouping is sometimes divided otherwise. It may be considered in terms of one physical and four mental factors; or as one physical aspect, three mental aspects, and consciousness per se, in which case the latter is the most important of all and was considered by some early Mahayana schools as the essence of a kind of super-self.

We must be careful how we understand these five factors, however. In a real sense they do represent an entity: the individ-

ual human being of ordinary human experience who is obviously
a genuine unity of some sort, possessing a certain special identity
which he shares with no other being. Buddhist writers insist that
they do not discount the reality of this individual at a certain level
of experience. But this is a relatively low level of experience,
and the individuality known herein is actually of a very temporary and illusory sort. As we shall note in more detail at a later
point, the prime quality of that Ignorance which is the basic force
binding man to rebirth and preventing his enlightenment, is the belief in and the emotional attachment to the idea of the reality of
this temporary selfhood.

This five-element self is temporary when considered in any
one of two or three contexts. There is the obvious brevity of human life; a few short years and the five-fold compound dissolves
in death. And Buddhism with its doctrine of *anattā,* or no-self,
holds that the dissolution of death is a complete dissolution so
far as any distinctive physical and/or mental-personal identity
is concerned. The individuality of the individual is lost; there is
no self or soul of any sort which carries on to another life, only
an impersonal residue or impulse of kammic energy which is
transmitted to a new sentient existence. That energy, to be discussed at a later point, is neither personally conscious nor identical with the deceased self, however.

But more importantly the individual is temporary even in the
course of one human lifetime. He changes, i.e. "dies" and is
"born," from moment to moment. He is literally a different man
from what he was a few moments, hours, months, or years ago.
It is only the rapidity of the change, and the scale on which it
takes place—infinitesmal changes at infinitesmal intervals—which
make it imperceptible to ordinary understanding and give the
illusion of the sameness or identity of a self from moment to
moment. For the body is subject to atomic change in its physical
particles just as the rest of nature; one's whole body is entirely
other, in this sense, after the passage of a few years, though the
tiny individual changes themselves take only the billionth part
of a lightning flash. If the rate of change in the physical element
is this rapid, how much faster are the changes in the mental elements! Buddhism holds that the "mental moment," i.e. mental

unit, is of much shorter duration than even the billionth-of-a-second-long physical unit, and is besides divided into seventeen successive sub-moments. Thus the mentality of the observer, his consciousness itself, is changing more rapidly than the physical element of his body; "I" am not the same, either physically *or* mentally, as "I" was a few short moments ago. As an individual, "I" am a pattern of physical-mental flux whose only existence is in the present moment. The past "I" is no more; the future "I" is not yet.

With regard to the mental pole of this chain of flux that is the "self," Buddhists believe that their viewpoint is increasingly confirmed by many interpretations of personality made by recent Western psychology. Their version of a chain of waxing-waning thought moments that compose the individual "mind" is often linked to the "stream of consciousness" theories of William James and others. The contemporary psychological and philosophical tendency to deny the separate existence of a self apart from the content of its own mental states is enthusiastically endorsed by Buddhist writers. The so-called "self" *is* the content of its awareness, no more, no less; as this content changes so does the "self." Hence there is no enduring self-identical person or soul to be found behind or beyond individual thoughts and feelings. And one of the main purposes of the meditative discipline is to bring the ordinary consciousness, which cherishes the illusion of its own separate and substantial identity, to the full and direct knowledge of its own emptiness and unreality.

It should be noted at the same time, however, that Buddhism rejects categorically those "materialistic" theories of human selfhood that trace the rise of consciousness from certain states of matter (or energy), or its particular organization in special patterns. Consciousness as we know it empirically does not represent a separate self, independent of related physical elements and indestructible; yet neither is it a mere by-product of atomic arrangements. Buddhism indeed gives the reverse answer as the rule—that physical form is the result of mental powers or states. For "mind is the leader" or formative factor of all existence; and achievement of the higher powers makes it possible for an individual to totally change and reform his physical constitution at will.[5]

We may look at the human life of feeling and consciousness in still another context, but one which also emphasizes its changing and temporary nature—though again with a certain sort of continuity. This is the conception of *Bhavanga*, sometimes translated as the Subconscious. It is that which flows along as an "undercurrent forming the condition of being or existence," whether in sleep or waking. It is this stream in which

> All impressions and experience are, as it were, stored up, or better said, are functioning, but concealed as such to full consciousness, from where, however, they occasionally emerge as subconscious phenomena and approach the threshold of full consciousness, or crossing it become fully conscious. This so-called "subconscious lifestream" or undercurrent of life is that by which might be explained the faculty of memory, paranormal psychic phenomena, mental and physical growth, Karma and Rebirth, etc.[6]

This stream flows on during our unconscious periods also— because Buddhist psychology holds that even in sleep or coma the individual is not completely unconscious. He sinks down to the primordial level of sentience, completely in the Bhavanga sphere. This is, so to speak, the minimal and basic level of a person's existence as sentient being. But when stimuli are present, whether of the ordinary five-sense kind or the purely mental sixth sense recognized by Buddhism, they interrupt the smooth flow of *bhavanga-sota* (or the Bhavanga stream) as though it encountered resistance. The result of this interruption is actual sensation and explicit consciousness. But it should be noted that though in one

---

[5] There is strong strand of absolute idealism in Buddhism—a recurring suggestion that All is Mind. Certainly the physical world revealed by the senses is not the real one, and somewhat in the Kantian sense the space-time world is "created" by the sensing individuals therein, so far as its forms are concerned. Theravada Buddhism has never quite settled the matter, having veered away from Hinayana views of the substantial reality of constitutive elements of physical and mental being but halting this side of an absolute idealism.

[6] This and the following quotation are from Mahathera Nyanatiloka, *Buddhist Dictionary* (Colombo: Frewin and Co., 1956), pp. 29–30, 77.

sense the Bhavanga or subconscious flow of sentience constitutes a *kind* of continuous selfhood, selfhood at the level of full consciousness, where alone we may speak meaningfully of a genuine self, is not a separate knower that sees-hears-feels-knows through the organs or senses. It is simply a compound cause-effect affair. Conscious selfhood, or self as consciousness, is thus not a primordial entity but the composite result of the Bhavanga-stream conditioned by stimuli. Without either Bhavanga or stimuli there would be no consciousness; and the five khandhas or self-elements are only characteristics of the mental-physical event called a sentient being. To quote again from the above author in the same vein:

> This so-called individual existence is in reality nothing but a mere process of those mental and physical phenomena. . . . These five groups neither singly nor collectively constitute any self-dependent real Ego-entity or Personality *(attā),* nor is there to be found any such entity apart from them. . . . These five complete groups have no real existence. . . . Feeling, perception and mental formations, for example, form merely the various aspects of those single units [mental moments] of consciousness which, like lightning, flash forth at every moment and immediately thereafter disappear again. They are to consciousness what redness, softness, sweetness, etc. are to the apple, and have no more reality than these things.

The five khandhas may be considered, in a word, not as entities, nor constitutive of an entity together, but as functional aspects of sentient existence.

This resulting "self" then seems to be no self at all in the traditional Western-Christian, or even Eastern-Hindu, manner of speaking. It is not, whatever appearance to the contrary, truly a thinking, knowing, feeling individual possessing personal unity and identity; it is rather a congeries of functions or collection of qualities without substance, formed entirely by the conjuncture of elements whose own nature and separate existence are problematic. And this is the essence of the Buddhist doctrine of anatta—no-self, no-soul, non-self, no self-nature, no true substance, as it has been variously translated. (It originates, of course, from a negative particle *an* prefixed to *attā,* or the Hindu *ātman,* i.e. undying and unchanging self.) While this non-substantial quality applies to all entities in the space-time world of experience, it especially and most importantly refers to sentient "selves." There are various classical passages in the scriptures which give a basis for the anatta doctrine. A few examples follow:

> Then the Lord addressed the group of five monks, saying: 'Body, monks, is not self. Now were this body self, monks, this body would not tend to sickness, and one might get the chance of saying in regard to body, 'Let body become for me, let body not become thus for me.' But inasmuch, monks, as body is not self, therefore the body tends to sickness, and one does not get the chance of saying in regard to body, 'Let body become thus for me, let body not become thus for me.'[7]

The passage goes on to extend the same formula to feeling, perception, consciousness, and habitual tendencies. None of these can be called self because of its impermanent and uncontrollable character. Of each of these one must say: "This is not mine, this am I not, this is not myself." Another favorite, though not canonical, passage which even more pointedly and unambiguously affirms the non-reality of the atta or self is found in *The Questions of King Milinda* in the famous chariot analogy. King Milinda (Menander) is unable at first to believe that there is no self. Nagasena, his monk-tutor, likens the concept of the self to a chariot. What constituted the chariot in which the king had come to see him? Are wheels, yoke, tongue, axle, and so on, the chariot? Obviously not. Indeed when one analyzes the concept chariot into its constituent parts and takes them away one by one, nothing is left. "Chariot" is merely a name for an empty concept including a number of particulars; it has no substantial reality, either as a whole or part, but is a linguistic convenience only. So, says Nagasena, is it with the self.

We may note in passing that the exact significance of some of the anatta passages in the scriptures is a matter of dispute. It was with regard to this point, as well as others of course, that Mahayana Buddhism divided from Hinayana, the ancestor of Theravada Buddhism. The former has tended in many of its branches to give a more substantial role to consciousness as the dominant

---

[7]*Vinaya-Piṭaka, Mahāvagga* section, *The Book of the Discipline,* (P.T.S.), Part IV, p. 20, Text 6:37—44.

aspect of self. A contemporary British Buddhist, Christmas Humphreys, in a recent volume of Buddhist studies, uses language reminiscent of Hinduism: the small narrow self, the higher Self, and the great universal SELF. The first is evil and illusory, the second is to be developed, and the third is to be realized. Some contemporary Indian scholars, in partial agreement with Mrs. Rhys Davids, believe that in the first quoted and similar passages Buddha indirectly asserts the existence of a greater Self (maybe God?) by refusing to identify self with body, consciousness, feeling or any other partial and lesser reality. Now and then a somewhat heretical Theravadin will assert that Buddha never actually denied the self—and becomes known as an "atta Buddhist" in consequence.

For Theravada Buddhism, however, this anatta or no-self assertion has become what is possibly its most distinctive and central doctrine, particularly with regard to its human application. "No anatta doctrine, no Buddhism" is the way in which it is often put today. Thus:

> I would like to emphasize the fact that the fundamental doctrine of Egolessness and Emptiness is not, as some misinformed Western Buddhists assert, only taught in the Southern school of Buddhism, roughly Theravada Buddhism, but even in the so-called Mahayana schools it forms an essential part. Without this teaching of anatta, or Egolessness, there is no Buddhism; and without having realized the truth of egolessness, no real progress is possible on the path to deliverance.[8]

The last sentence of the above quotation shows that the fundamental concern in anatta doctrine is not so much with its metaphysical truth—though this too is asserted with great confidence—as its experiential religious value. The basic reason for the continued and even aggressive assertion of the anatta doctrine is the conviction that only as individuals realize the essential unreality or emptiness of the self-concept and experience, primarily with regard to their own personalities and secondarily with regard to all other persons and entities, can they free themselves from bondage to the realm of suffering and impermanence,

---

[8] Mahathera Nyanatiloka, "Egolessness," *Light of the Buddha*, III, No. 1 (January, 1958), 4.

i.e. achieve *Nibbāna* (Sanskrit *Nirvāna*). For the illusion of the substantiality of the personal self, that "I" am a real unitary being, and the illusion of the substantiality of the "selves" that "I" love or "things" that "I" desire, are what prevent my liberating enlightenment.

Not only so but this self-illusion is the root cause of greed and hatred and all their bitter fruitage. Because we instinctively believe in a self and grasp possessively at other selves and things, we become greedy for more possessions and hate those that oppose us. (Here we have the Buddhist equivalent of the Christian conception of original sin or congenital depravity.) But anatta, and the related truth of *anicca* or the impermanence of all selves and things, come as the sunlight of the true knowledge of "things as they are" and dispel this smothering darkness of self-delusion. These truths are the sharp sword of rational analysis which cuts the bonds of attachment to things and selves by demonstrating the essential unreality of all factors of attachment—of the things one is attached to and of the one who is attached! First apprehended as doctrine, anicca and anatta finally achieve their enlightening and liberating function when they become personally realized experiences of truth.

3. The Dynamic and Continuous Self

We may turn now from this brief sketch of the disjointed momentary aspects of the self, or the no-self, to note that there *is* a more dynamic aspect and a larger degree of continuity in the Theravada self-concept, than anything noted heretofore might suggest. It may be said at the very beginning, however, that the dynamism and continuity resident in the self, or at least in its possible experience, tend to be largely implicit or even to be explicitly denied. For in its passion for negative statement Theravada Buddhism gives most frequent expression to anatta doctrine. The positive experience to which the espousal of the doctrine leads, and the positive implications of the doctrine itself, must be read between the lines as it were. But such elements are there when we view the doctrine of the self in its different aspects; and they have important ethical implications.

There is, for instance, the *other* side of the doctrine of the momentariness of reality in all its forms. Is reality indeed, mental or physical, no more than a series of discontinuous, non-enduring flashes of manifested energy, which have neither past nor future? This is one aspect, but not the totality. Actually it is strongly and frequently affirmed that each moment, whether mental or physical, pours the totality of its content or being into the next moment. A contemporary states it in this way:

> Each new state or chapter of life is a link or a phase in an endless chain or cycle of lives. It contains like a book, a complete record of events, life, action or conduct, which has been impressed in each phase or chapter of life. Each rebirth is but the opening of a fresh chapter or a new sequel in the Book of Life, wherein is traced out, written, or imprinted the Karmic record of all lives, activities and events that have occurred. . . . It is reproduced or recorded with photographic exactness and precision.[9]

While this brings in the Kamma-rebirth motif, which will be discussed in the next chapter, there is no essential difference in the above respect between one life and one moment. Each moment (or life) contains all that the previous moment (or life) contains, plus the new element which *it* may contribute. And since each moment backward, ad infinitum, contains all that *its* predecessor had inherited from the past, plus its own contribution, the present moment is the storehouse of all that has ever gone before. Considering my present existence as a psycho-physical event or moment of existence, the momentary present event that is "I" contains all "my" past within it, at least implicitly. All previous moments and all my past countless lives are here stored up.

Favorite Buddhist analogies to describe this state of affairs in which there is both difference and continuity, but not continuing identity, run as follows: Milk changes to curds, and curds change to cheese; or the seed changes into a plant, into a flower, into a fruit, into a seed again. In this series there are both difference, or non-identity of one state with another (Is milk the

---

[9] Samanera U Pandita, "The Nature and Cause of Rebirth," *Light of the Buddha,* IV, No. 4 (April, 1959), 102.

"same" as the ensuing curds?); and sameness or causally conditioned succession—for curds do come from the milk.

There are, however, some qualifications in the concept of the present as the recipient of the totality of the past, though different statements in different contexts vary somewhat in their emphasis. The quotation above seems to imply that the present moment contains all that ever happened in the totality of past lives, that the kammic procession of states is like an ever-growing snowball. The result would be an infinity of content. And sometimes contemporary language about the Buddha states the matter in that way, so far as the Buddha himself was concerned. It is said that in his consciousness was stored up everything that had ever happened to him in millions of past existences; hence in his infinite wisdom he could draw upon experiences of every kind, in short be an absolutely universal genius with an infinite reservoir of knowledge to serve him. Or, stated in terms of recalling past lives to mind, the saints and Buddhas are held to be capable of recalling in detail an infinitude of their own past lives—though apparently the absolute beginning thereof must escape even them, since it does not exist or is unknowable according to Buddhist doctrine. Further all this would suggest a kind of static permanence in which all the past would be fully and explicitly existent in the present—a state of things that would seem to be impossible and go against the central Buddhist insistence on the momentariness of reality.

A better interpretation seems to be that though all the past might conceivably be *virtually* or *potentially* in the present, it is not present in its fullness. Certainly it is not present to ordinary consciousness; only a fractional part of the past remains therein, and only from one's present life at that. And though the saint or Buddha may approximate total recall, even here there are probably limitations. The presence of the past in the present seems rather to be a matter of certain basic or dominant features having indelibly imprinted their quality on succeeding moments. Some elements are dominant, while others are weak or latent; and it would seem that some cancel each other out, or fall by the wayside, or that there is a net loss of *some* elements. Or perhaps better, using the analogy of the conservation of energy, the form changes but the total amount of energy remains constant.

Whether this latter conclusion is correct or not, it remains true that Buddhism rejects the iron determinism of that fatalism suggested by a present which has lost *nothing* of the past. Buddhists are most insistent upon this as the ground of ethical and religious hope: the present *can* be changed; new elements *can* be added; the past and its effects wear themselves out, i.e. even kammic (Sanskrit *karmic*) debts are finally paid off, or can be diverted, by-passed, or "burned up" by proper spiritual strategy. Thus:

> Admittedly we are born to a state created by ourselves. Yet by our own well-directed efforts there is every favorable possibility for us to create new favorable environments even here and now. . . .
>
> Is one bound to reap all that one has sown in just proportion? The Buddha provides an answer:
>
> 'If anyone says that a man *must* reap according to his deeds, in that case there is no religious life, nor is an opportunity afforded for the entire extinction of sorrow. But if anyone says that what a man reaps *accords* with his deeds, in that case there is a religious life, and an opportunity for the entire extinction of sorrow.'[10]

This brings us to what we may call the *dynamic* element in the self situation. It has two bases: the changing flexibility of the nature of the self, and the power of the self to change itself (just alluded to) that every Buddhist takes for granted. With regard to the doctrine of the changing self we have thus far noted only one aspect of it: that Buddhism conceives the self to be essentially a non-entity, at least on one level. But this is not a doctrine of despair, or chaotic flux pure and simple, as it might seem to be. *For the very changeability of the self means that it is not eternally fixed in one mold, and is alterable in its very essence.*

Indeed the Buddhist looks upon the Hindu doctrine of an immutable spiritual essence or soul as either a contradiction in terms or else a doctrine of moral hopelessness, or perhaps both. If the self or soul is already perfect, then what meaning has the seeming moral struggle? The evil fought against is an illusion or

---

[10] Narada Thera, "The Buddhist Doctrine of Kamma and Rebirth," *Light of the Dhamma*, III, No. 1, (June, 1955), 45.

pretence. On the other hand, if the soul is immutable, a doubt is cast upon its improvability. There is no need for its perfection. Thus on moral, as well as philosophical grounds, Buddhism rejects the doctrine of an unchanging or identical soul.[11] Contrarily the "soul" both does change, and can be changed, at every moment.

But if the doctrine of change is to be one of moral hopefulness as well, the second factor must also be present: *The power of the self to change itself.* In other words, there is in some sense a factor or quality within the self-situation of somewhat greater stability than the momentary-analysis suggests, on whose basis or by whose power change can be directed and discerned. Otherwise there *would* be only meaningless, directionless flux or a complete determinism. What the nature of this stability is, and what we shall call it, is a very difficult question. It involves again the matter of whether the Buddhist, even while he is strenuously denying the reality of any self by means of the anatta doctrine, actually believes in or implies a hidden self behind it all. And again, what is it that passes from birth to birth in the kammic process?

These questions, debated within and without Buddhism for nearly two thousand years, cannot be discussed in their entirety here. But we may say that even though Theravada Buddhism steadfastly rejects the idea of any higher or more permanent spiritual self which remains identical in any sense through its succeeding moments or lives, it *does* allow within the five-khandha compound that constitutes a human being, the power of some elements, which we might call intelligent will-power, to direct the others. The human being is only a combination of elements, but a "very unusual combination of elements" as the Venerable U Thittila puts it. According to the scriptures "the self is lord of the self" and can give to the self-event a definite direction, ethical in nature.

---

[11] Whether identity means immutability in respect to personality may be questioned. Charles Hartshorne in his *Man's Vision of God* conceives personal existence as being the *only* kind of being which can be subject to change and yet retain identity. This indeed is precisely the defining characteristic of such existence.

Given, then, the flexibility of self-process and the will-power that resides within the process to alter itself from within, it is evident that the Buddhist conception of personality is fully dynamic and coherent, even if logically unsatisfying. At some point within the series of seventeen sub-moments which comprise the basic "thought-moment," i.e. the complete intellectual act of awareness-conception-with-feeling-tone, there are a few sub-moments in which the "self" chooses what its reaction to the presented stimuli will be. Or to put it another way: Since the mind deals with only one item at a time, according to Buddhism, thought may discipline itself by excluding all but the (ethically) desirable element from consciousness and incipient action, moment by moment. Such is the purpose of the whole meditative discipline.

Or to put it in still another way: The present moment, the psychological "now," is the key point in moral progress and discipline. Its proper use contains the hope of ethical perfection and ultimate liberation in Nibbana. The past cannot be altered, for Kamma carries every thought, word, or deed to its ultimate fruition, good or bad; and to a great extent my present existence is filled with and determined by my past. Yet each moment is also new and contains elements of freedom within that newness. The present moment indeed is the *only* moment in which kammic process can be directed or ultimately escaped. And since all past Kamma was once present Kamma, every man has the power to achieve his own perfection lying within his control for the full length of his life as a human being; every new moment of existence presents a new opportunity to build good future kamma.

Not only is the Buddhist conception of self flexible and dynamic; practically, it is also *organic* in nature despite its atomistic conception. It may be that conceptually the individual *is* only a group of five elements; and that these in turn are nothing real or permanent, but can be further analyzed and reanalyzed until they vanish into an infinite flux. Yet at any given moment of experience, body-mind represents an intimate organic unity. For though Buddhism recognizes a polarity between the mental and physical constituents of sentient beings, it never sharply divides them but on the contrary strongly emphasizes the close relation of all mental and physical states. The Cartesian dualism is quite foreign to Buddhism in this context; mind cannot be abstracted from matter nor matter separated from mind in any but the very highest of the thirty-one planes of existence, the abodes of heavenly beings. There is ordinarily no physical state without a mental cause; nor any physical state without mental consequence. The two elements shade off into each other, or perhaps better, thoroughly interpenetrate each other to such a degree that the physical can almost be transmuted into the mental at times, as we shall note later.

The Buddhist "Middle Way," balanced between asceticism and indulgence on either hand, is the practical expression of this sense of mental-physical organicism. For bodily abuse weakens the mental powers; the Buddha found that it did not lead to enlightenment, for whose attainment he needed the full force of both mind and body. And sensual indulgence corrupts the intelligence and makes the higher levels of knowledge impossible of attainment.

For ethical purposes important consequences follow. One is that the ideal good, or for that matter any genuine full-bodied good, is for Buddhism a balanced body-mind good. There is no true spiritual good attained at the expense or harm of the body; nor can the fullest bodily good be attained without spiritual health or a balanced mind. The true good is always in terms of harmonious body-mind correlation. For the heightening of the innate mental powers of man up to the level of supramundane capacity, the body must be in a condition of such health as to make it capable of assisting the spiritual quest, rather than hindering it by calling attention to its own pains and troubles. The meditating individual is to be "zestful" (in mind) and "at ease" (in body) at the same time. This does not mean physically indulgent ease or a health-conscious athleticism, but such simple, healthful care of the body as will enable it to function easily and naturally. The healthy and relaxed body is indeed a near necessity for the success of the spiritual quest since its condition and posture affect the depth and clarity of mental insight.

On the other hand, genuine moral purity and the resulting increase of mental insight purify and renew the body. There is a basic conviction in Buddhism that most bodily ills spring from mental-moral impurity and are fundamentally to be treated from within. Indeed it is difficult to separate mental from physical impurity. For the Buddhist they are only differing aspects of the same basic imbalance or internal disturbance, though in general the physical distress is the symptom of the mental impurity. Hence the meditational discipline, which is essentially a mind-training process, is considered to be physically therapeutic as well as spiritually valuable.

Buddhism demonstrates its sane balance in this connection, in some contrast to particular Hindu vagaries, by refusing to suggest that an individual's body can be immortalized by mental-spiritual disciplines. Nor does it maintain the good man will never suffer bodily ill or distress; indeed the Buddha himself even after his enlightenment suffered some bodily pain and injury. In fact until one reaches Nibbana, which is completely beyond the dualism of body-mind, he will always be *embodied* to some extent, even in the Fine-Material Spheres.[12] And embodiment in general, and individual bodies in particular, represent the power of Kamma; they *are* the results of our past Kamma in many respects. But by and large the good man is the healthy man and moral purity casts out disease; and the healthy man can more easily practice the spiritual disciplines than the unhealthy.

Even though this psycho-physical balance represents the Buddhist idea of true goodness in the embodied state, it must be said that even here the mental is actually the more important of the two poles. And further, it becomes increasingly dominant in direct proportion to one's progress upward in the scale of perfection. It might be more nearly correct to say that the greatest practical good on the embodied level is psycho-physical balance; but that the ideal good as found in the life of the saint, and supremely in Nibbana, is clearly of the mentalistic sort.

This is evident in two or three connections. On the layman's level the importance and necessity of physical goods are clearly recognized. It is legitimate for him to strive for such things with-

---

[12] There are some of the highest Immaterial Realms in which there is mind only in existence. Yet these are exceptions of no importance for the present context; and even here there remains a slight residual desire for embodiment or existence as an individual in some form—embodiment in desire if not in fact. When their good Kamma is exhausted even the residents of the Immaterial Realms will descend to new physical embodiment.

in the limits of morality and without lapsing into religious forget-fulness. And he may *rightly* hope and strive for a happier and more fortunate rebirth. But for the monk or would-be saint these things must be put aside until ideally he has no physical concerns beyond the minimal one of keeping healthily alive on the care provided by others, and strives only for rebirth-transcending Nibbana.

Or again, as one cultivates the higher mental powers and nibbanic frame of mind his body becomes increasingly subject to the control of the mind so that it may even be made to fly through the air or take on different forms.[13] Bodily atoms can be altered or reformed at will. And upon physical death those who have attained these higher psychic powers in a human life will be re-born in the refined-material. or even immaterial, spheres where mind is dominant, or is all; or if he has reached perfection as an arahat, he will go directly to Nibbana upon bodily death. And though Nibbana may not be describable it is certainly nearer the mentalistic than the physical pole in nature.

4. The Moral Quality of Human Nature

Thus far we have described the Buddhist concept of the hu-man self both in its momentary unreality and in its dynamic con-tinuity and "substance" and noted that it does have the capacity in its free-will potential to direct itself toward goodness or evil. What then is its predominant bias or innate moral tendency? Is the self good, or bad, or neither? The difficulty in answering such questions in such terms is obvious. Given the non-substantial and atomistic quality of the human body-mind, and the fact that "human" nature can become another nature in a flash upon the moment of death, it is perhaps impossible to state the matter neatly. What does it mean to say that "human" nature is intrin-

---

[13] Today there is some qualification of the literalism of these results of the higher psychic powers. Some persons would speak of the projec-tion of an "astral" body, not the real physical one, through space, even in the case of the Buddha who in the night hours is recorded to have gone to visit souls in need throughout the universe. But others would hold some-what more literally that *if* one cultivates the higher powers, literal defiance of space-time conditions is possible.

sically this or that, when, as the Ledi Sayadaw[14] wrote, "He who today is the King of Gods or a Brahma, endowed with majestic powers, may become tomorrow a dog or a hog, and so on in rotation"?[15] The best that we can do is to say that *some* characteristics are perhaps intrinsic to *all* sentient beings.

But there are also other more specific qualities peculiar to the human situation that importantly affect its *moral* context. The human situation is one that allows for moral action as we have seen, by which the Buddhist means that man possesses free will. Indeed it is *only* on the human level that truly moral action can occur. Other beings lack either the capacity or opportunity for true moral decision. And it is a situation in which moral action, whether good or bad, has lasting effects upon an individual's future, as the discussion of rebirth and kamma will make clear. *"Human nature" then is rather a name for the opportunity and capacity of genuinely ethical behaviour than a description of any intrinsic qualities or specific moral tendencies.*

Yet having said this we may also observe that there are some rather general affirmations and negations about human nature in the Buddhist scriptures and tradition. These statements have served Buddhism in much the same way that various moralistic theories have served in the West, as foundational principles for basic attitudes toward man, philosophies of government and education, and legal patterns for regulating human conduct. We may first note the negative factors, morally speaking, in the human situation.

There is the basic fact that man is a physically embodied creature. While it is true that Buddhism condemns abuse of the body in setting forth its Middle Way; and while it is further true that the Buddhist discipline of meditation employs contemplation on the innate foulness of the human body or its various repulsive stages of decay after death *only* as a curative discipline for the sensually-minded—rather than indulging in a body-hating

---

[14] An eminent Burmese monk and writer of the first decades of the 20th century.

[15] "Manual of Cosmic Order," quoted in part in *Light of the Dhamma*, IV, No. 3 (July, 1957), 5. The editor kindly explains that "Brahma" means "God-Almighty."

morbidity; nevertheless the body and all its senses are viewed as a primary source of many of man's most serious temptations. Various analogies are used to make the situation clear. The bodily senses are bonds of greedy attachment to sense life and pleasures; they are doors through which manifold dangers to man's purity of inner life may come into him; and in one of the most telling analogies, the body, with all its senses, is called a "wound," through which the truly good life of the mind is drained away or endangered.

But perhaps the best known of all such analogies is that of the Fire-Sermon:

> All things, O priests, are on fire . . . The eye, O priests, is on fire; forms are on fire; eye-consciousness is on fire; . . . whatever sensation, pleasant, unpleasant, indifferent, originates in dependence on impressions received by the eye, that also is on fire.
> And with what are these on fire?
> With the fire of passion, say I, with the fire of hatred, with the fire of infatuation; with birth, old age, death, sorrow, lamentation, misery, grief, and despair are they on fire.[16]

The passage goes on to apply the same analogy to the other sensibilities—ear, nose, tongue, and body or tactual sense—and even to the mind, that sixth sense.

In another similar passage the meaning is roughly the same but the basic analogy is changed. Mara, the evil one, appears before the Buddha as a giant plowman and taunts him by saying that to him, Mara, belong the eye and its sight, the ear and its sound, the nose and its smell, the tongue and its taste, the body and its touch, even the mind and its ideas. Hence it is impossible even for the Buddha to escape his clutches; that is, there is no existence possible apart from such activities. To exist at all is to exist under Mara's control. The Buddha agrees that all these do indeed belong to Mara—but claims that there *is* a way, a type of living, which is beyond the power of all sensibility and discrimination and hence free from Mara's power.

---

[16] *Mahā-Vagga* from *Dīgha-Nikāya (Dialogues of the Buddha)*, quoted in H. C. Warren, *Buddhism in Translations* (Cambridge, Mass.: Harvard University Press, 1953), p. 352.

The interesting point here is that the Buddha *agrees* that all sense life is within the power of Evil. This indicates more fully the quality of human (or sentient) nature's weakness. It is not merely or even primarily that this life is partially physical in essence, even though the physical life *is* a great source of spiritual danger to the ordinary man. But the life of emotion and the rational faculties too is a danger, of a still more subtle sort, that may continue to threaten even that man who has control over his body. More correctly we may say that the true affliction or wrong bias in all sentient nature is its *individualization*. As individualized body-mind formation, as a personalized center of sensation and awareness, man has in his very constitution destructive attachments and an innate tendency to immoral attitudes and actions. As it is stated in the *Majjhima-Nikāya:*

> For, Malunkyaputta, if there were not 'own body' for an innocent babe lying on his back, whence could there arise for him the view of 'own body'? A leaning to the view of 'own body' indeed lies latent in him. Malunkyaputta, if there were not 'things' for an innocent baby boy lying on his back, whence could there arise for him perplexity about things? A leaning to perplexity indeed lies latent in him. Malunkyaputta, if there were not 'habits' for an innocent baby boy lying on his back, whence could there arise for him clinging to rites and customs?[17]

The passage further specifies the same with regard to sense pleasures and malevolence—that there is an innate tendency in human nature in particular, and perhaps in sentient nature in general as individualized in separate beings, to cling to sense pleasures and express itself in malevolence.

We may then sum up the negative or evil side of the human constitution in some such terms as these: Man, as an individualized body-mind being, is temporary and impermanent by nature, yet passionately tied to the world revealed to him by his senses and mind—even though that world is as impermanent as he. Every sense, every mental activity of discrimination or judgment, every physical activity, attaches man to his life and its environment. This attachment may be given a general name, that of

---

[17] Sutta 64, *Middle Length Sayings,* (P.T.S.), Vol. II, Text I, 432–3, pp. 102–3.

taṇhā, or craving, or lust for existence. (This is the deep root from which spring *specific* appetites and desires, and to whose nourishment the objects of sense and thought contribute.) And this craving for existence produces the illusion of the permanency of the self or ego, as well as expressing itself in greed for the pleasant and hatred for the unpleasant experiences and sensations of this present life. Thus is man a blind mass of ignorant craving, incapable of purity of mind or heart in his ordinary state, and unable to purpose purely or reason truly. Indeed his perverted reason makes the case even worse for him than for the animals or beings in the hells, for it persuades him that the irrational is rational and the evil is good.

In this context one may sometimes find statements in contemporary Buddhist writings which speak out strongly about the corruption of "human" nature:

> It has been observed that the human consciousness is rooted in greed, hatred, and delusion.[18]
> The Buddha taught that the hearts of ordinary men are not pure. They are tainted, filled with greed, hatred, and delusion.[19]

But this is the extreme limit of the "condemnation" of human nature to be found in Buddhism. And even so, there are important differences to be noted between this and some strains of pessimism about human nature found in the West. There is here none of the sharp dualism between the physical and the spiritual-mental that occurs in some varieties of Greek and Christian thought. The body is not conceived to be an impure prison of the pure spirit; both are the product of a causally conditioned flux of impersonal events. Hence there has never been a disposition in Buddhism toward mind-warping or body-destroying austerities.

In accord with this most Buddhists consistently reject such adjectives as "depraved" when applied to human nature as such—and the above quotations are no real exception. It is of course true that the human individual, by virtue of being a human indi-

---

[18] U Tha Kyaw, "Supremacy of the Human Consciousness," *Light of the Buddha,* III, No. 1, (January, 1958), 29.

[19] Luang Suriyabongs, M.D., "Peace," *ibid,* III, No. 4 (April, 1958), 71.

vidual, is subject to many inherent imperfections and evil tendencies. Yet he is not radically, incurably evil; he is ignorant rather than evil. And there are roots of goodness in him as well as roots of evil, which may be awakened to life and strength by the proper methods. Indeed it could almost be said that human nature is intrinsically good, though not quite in the full Confucian sense as interpreted by Mencius; for the Buddhist holds that in view of the extremely flexible and changing nature of the "self" it can be radically worsened as well as bettered. It is neither a fixed amount of goodness nor of an invariably good quality.

But in any case man has it within his power to alter his own nature; he is not fated to pursue evil, even though one man's birth and environing conditions may make it harder for him to pursue good, or put a lesser good within his reach, than for his fellow. And there is an innate capacity in him, rooted primarily in a kind of primordial or essential purity of mind, that can be developed to an almost unbelievable degree. For men are gods in disguise; and a Perfect Man is far above all the gods that are in existence. Thus in a contrasting and more usual vein:

> According to the teachings of the Buddha anybody may aspire to that supreme state of perfection, Buddhahood, if he makes the exertion. The Buddha does not condemn men by calling them wretched sinners, but, on the contrary, He gladdens them by saying that they are pure in heart in reality. In His opinion the world is not wicked, but is deluded by ignorance.[20]

This passage is not fundamentally contradictory to the ones which speak of the impurity of heart. For the third evil, delusion, is the key element. Dissipate man's ignorance and the basis for moral impurities will be destroyed. To truly know, in the Buddhist sense, is automatically productive of moral purity. Man needs an enlightenment of the mind rather than a change of heart. Thus it is that Buddhism often protests against the over-moralized, sometimes vindictive, conceptions of human moral depravity, and the proper remedies therefor, that are to be found in the

---

[20] Venerable Narada, "Buddhism in a Nutshell," *Light of the Dhamma*, III, No. 4 (August, 1956), 11.

West. Human nature in all its weakness is to be gently illumined, not rigidly and violently coerced.

5. The Ultimate Goal of Self-Perfection

The above discussion of the goodness or badness of human nature has been something of a digression from the direct line of development of the original turn of thought. Yet it seems to be a necessary digression for the Western reader who tends to think in such terms because of his native religious tradition. The Buddhist, on the other hand, is less concerned with the specifically and analytically ethical approach in such matters because of his organic conception of human nature and his subordination of the explicitly ethical to the psychological or to the psycho-physical wholeness of man. And precisely because of this difference in approach, it has seemed the more important to try to relate the two approaches to each other in some meaningful way. But having made the attempt we may go on to inquire: What is the *nature* of that perfection which the Buddhist ethic seeks through self-development?

When we consider the Buddhist ideal of human perfection in terms of self-development, we encounter two related problems that in turn grow out of the contrasting ways in which Buddhism considers the self—as a momentary unreality and as an integrated spiritual character capable of Buddahood. The first of the problems we may call a *two-level approach to perfection*.[21] The content and practical tensions inherent in this dichotomy will be discussed in the chapters on the actual practice of Buddhist ethic; but here we must note the existence of the problem and observe its form. Briefly stated the situation is this: There is first that

---

[21] It may be questioned whether we have here a genuine duality between Buddhism and Christianity, or rather one between an intellectual and a religious approach to knowledge and morality. Intellectualism, including intellectualistic religion, is sure that men can "know" the good and not do it; religion, especially of the mystical sort, is quite sure that "knowing" equals being and doing. To know the truth is to serve it, otherwise one does not know it. Indeed something of this may also be found in Jeremiah: If one "knows" God he will do righteousness. Yet historically Judeo-Christianity does put its emphasis upon the evil will and Buddhism upon the unenlightened mind.

lower level or first stage on the road to perfection called *sīla*. Sila means roughly, morality, and refers primarily to those external standards of behaviour that represent minimal Buddhist morality for the layman. The core of sila is the Five Precepts which approximate the Judeo-Christian Ten Commandments and the Moslem Five Pillars in content and religio-social function. They serve as a basic moral code for the individual and his society. They are primarily concerned with the prohibition of anti-social actions (killing, stealing, lying, sexual aggression, and intoxication); and if positively adopted as principles by an individual they make him a sober and responsible member of family and community groups. These basic principles may of course be "inwardized" into attitudes and further extended by the addition of those more positive ethical qualities such as compassion, loving kindness, and sympathetic joy.

It should be observed here that in Buddhism "moral" and "ethical" connote only the lowest and most primary level of self-development. It is not that ethical behaviour is forsaken at the higher levels, or that morality is essentially "inferior." For the highest states of mental attainment and self-development must be solidly based on good ethical character; and final perfection, as we shall note, may be considered in one sense, at least, to be the inward *ethical* perfection of the saint. Yet to avoid confusion it must be kept in mind that such is the connotation of these terms; and that explicit ethical analysis in Buddhism is confined almost exclusively to matters of external behaviour and standards. The higher levels of attainment are spoken of in non-ethical, or only implicitly ethical, terms of psychic development, with religio-mystical overtones. We may consider them ethical in the wider and Buddhist sense of full self-development, already noted; but specifically the Buddhist often talks of "rising above" the merely ethical, both in his analysis of self-development and in his practice of the way of perfection.

The specific terms which are used of these higher-than-ethical stages bear out this interpretation. Above sila stands *samādhi* or the power of mental concentration, the attainment of one-pointedness of mind. And above samadhi stands *paññā* (Sanskrit *prajñā*) or insight and wisdom as the crown of the perfected life. The Perfect One is called the Enlightened One (a Buddha, possessing *bodhi*) rather than the Holy One. So that while concentration of mind and insight may not be opposed to, or exclusive of, ethical goodness, they are somewhat other. And again this distinction is borne out by the structure and practice of the Good Life's discipline. For the higher levels of samadhi and pañña are difficult if not impossible of attainment by the man engaged in active family and social life as a layman. It is only the monk as the rule who can expect to achieve these higher levels of the ascent to perfection, the way to Nibbana; his life-pattern as contained in the rules of the Order is specifically designed to that end.

Even though the Buddhist approach to perfection, especially on its higher levels, is different from Western and Christian approaches, we may draw some analogies which will perhaps be helpful. We might say that the highly developed "good" man in the Buddhist context becomes an "inner-directed" person who is able to choose and follow on to his chosen spiritual goals unswayed and undiverted by outward circumstances and pressures. Perhaps, even better, he may be called an "autonomous" man who makes his decisions, not on the basis of inflexible principles or dogmatic rules, but from within his own free and intelligent perception of each situation that he confronts. In more specifically Christian turns we may think of Buddhist sainthood as similar to the higher Christian life: The fulfilling of the whole externalized apparatus of outward rules is turned into the inward desire to love God and man; the natural growth of goodness in the outward life is found to stem from the inward goodness of one's being; the higher life is a putting off of the old man or carnal nature, the "crucifixion" of the flesh with its lusts and the putting on of the new man, the resurrection of the spirit into freshness of power and aliveness to God. Or we may liken it to the less scriptural rule that if a man love God supremely he may then "do as he pleases."

Functionally speaking then, Buddhist sainthood is like all other sainthood in its vision of the perfect life as a life of *spontaneous goodness*. It is one in which the good or right way of living is as natural as breathing itself, an integral part of the saint's being. The sharply moralistic struggle between good and bad motives, uncertainty about the ethical desirability of alternative courses of action, the personal inability to do the good that one recognizes as being good—all this is a matter of the past and lower levels of development. Without deliberate thought or consciously controlled will, the perfect man performs the good as a natural function of his purified self. Thus writes the Honorable U Nu about one of the lower stages of sainthood, that of *Sotā-panna* or Stream-Enterer:

> It becomes *absolutely impossible* for a man who has reached this state to kill or to take other's property not given to him or to utter falsehood or to drink alcohol or take drugs.[22]

The very existence of this higher level produces a tension with respect to the lower level of ordinary living. To one on this latter level the saint may seem to be indifferent to the ordinary conventions, or to be strangely uninterested in those ethical questions that concern the average man and his fellows most directly. This is a normal religious tension. But the Buddhist version of the perfect life seems to complicate the situation further, at least in the way it states the matter. For one of the most persistent notes is that of the saint's complete transcendence of the moral order, or his transmuting those moral qualities which have previously characterized his life into something quite different. One practices loving-kindness, then compassion, then rejoices in the joy of others, and finally as the highest expression of all these qualities achieves equanimity, or as it is sometimes translated, (emotional and intellectual) neutrality. Or again in another context: There are morally good deeds and morally bad ones, and these have fitting consequences in terms of character and destiny. But the *perfect* deed that brings one to liberation or full perfection, has no such results, either good or bad; it is the detached thought, word, or deed which has no kammic consequence. Hence the highest life seems to be a complete escape from, or transcendence of, the ethical sphere. Or to put it in Buddhist terms: *merely moral practices will never bring a man to sainthood or Nibbana.*

---

[22] "What is Buddhism?" *Light of the Dhamma,* III, No. 2 (January, 1956), 2.

Another complicating factor is that type of consciousness which is achieved at the higher levels of self-development, namely a *non-individualized* consciousness. At this level the moralistic attitudes of loving kindness, compassion, and sympathetic joy are progressively extended from those nearest and most friendly to us, even to those furthest and most hostile to us, until our compassion and loving-kindness include every being in all the universes without distinction. The mark of sainthood or full development is the ability to universalize, generalize, or depersonalize such attitudes, both in quantity and quality; not only are they to include all beings in their scope, but they are to be experienced with no distinction at all, either intellectual or emotional, between one's own self and any other self. The individual self of the saint, save as it is embodied in a separate body, knows no difference in feeling between own-self and other-self. Do we not have here then a complete transcendence of the ethical, at least in the usual sense in which a distinction between persons and mundane situations seems essential? Or is there here a kind of super-morality that only appears to transcend the ordinary ethic of "right" and "wrong" by raising these terms to an absolute context and actually reflecting a transforming power upon the lower levels?

There is a second main problem or area of tension here. It is related to the Buddhist conception of the self. We have noted already that there is a divergence, perhaps a fundamental one, in this area. One set of terms, those most frequently used and most insistently emphasized in Theravada Buddhism, treats only of the momentary and atomistic nature of the self. This is of course the no-soul or anatta doctrine, whose experiential realization is held to be the essence of man's highest attainment.

Yet on the other hand, there is an implicit emphasis upon the active, unitary, enduring characteristics of the self. Occasionally this comes to explicit contemporary expression as in the following passage:

> Certainly the practice of this path [the central Buddhist discipline] gives one great material benefits in the present in the

integration of the personality on an intellectual and ethical basis; and in the future, in happier lives.[23]

But this emphasis, modest though it be and on a very mundane level, is not often found. Usually it is present only by implication. (Indeed, in the quoted article it had already been declared that there is "no experiencer" of Nibbana, that highest goal of "self-development.") This does not make it the less important, to be sure. But in any case one is told to rely upon himself for his own salvation—though commentators carefully explain that this is "self" only in the conventional sense; one learns to control himself; he guards his own senses; he perfects his innate or at least potential powers of mind until he is able to achieve supernormal feats of insight and body control. He is less and less under the control of sense impressions; indeed, as the Buddha claimed in the Mara-ploughman account, he may even achieve a realm of being where he is completely beyond the reach of such impressions. And finally even Nibbana, that apparent end of all self, is often called the "deathless."

How do these two aspects of the self relate to the two levels of spiritual life—the ethical striving for a better rebirth and the super-ethical striving for Nibbana? On first sight it might seem that the relationship is a simple one-to-one affair: The unitary dynamic aspect of self is that emphasized in the life of the ordinary active man busily engaged in the tasks of self-improvement and social betterment, while the not-self emphasis is to be found in the higher life of the monk who aspires to become a saint. And to some extent this is true. The ordinary man, according to Buddhism, seldom questions the reality or permanence of his own self; he considers that he is a dynamic, integral person who thinks, acts, and experiences. It is only after prolonged meditation that he can apprehend the truth of no-self and become prepared to give up his attachment to self and its values.

But there is a paradox here. For it is precisely in this "higher" life of the realization of the truth of no-self and its detachment that the *truly* dynamic and unitive quality of the self appears. For here only does the self achieve liberation from the

---

[23] W. F. Jayasuriya, "Introduction to Abhidhamma," *Light of the Buddha,* III, No. 4, (April, 1958), 21.

tormenting and betraying sense-world and become master in its
own house, i.e. become integrated on a super-temporal, super-
sensible basis. Here alone is it able to independently and freely
chart its own course, completely free from greed, hatred and
delusion and all other impurities—save alone the remaining bond
of the final physical embodiment. It is in the saintly life that the
mental pole gains almost perfect control, even of the bodily nature. To state the paradox fully: Only by the full realization of
the truth of its own non-existence does the self—or should we say
the non-existent self?—become completely itself, i.e. *attā,* or that
which is fully self-controlled and not in any sense other-controlled.

Thus, as it seems to the author, we come to realize the basic
tension within Buddhist ethic: the tension between the "positive"
and "negative" views of selfhood. This tension presents problems,
produces conflicts and logical inconsistencies; and provides dynamism within the total Buddhist ethical scheme and its practice
when it is not compartmentalized into separate contexts. To the
further description, and hopefully, to the elucidation of the concrete expressions of this dynamic imbalance, the rest of our
chapters will be devoted.

1. Kamma and Rebirth

The Buddhist conception, or conceptions, of the self sketched
in the foregoing chapter, in a one-life context for the most part,
is not *fundamentally* altered when we place it in the Kamma-rebirth context which in Theravada Buddhism is so central. Even
when it is a matter of an infinite succession of lives rather than
moments that is involved, both aspects of self-hood are still present. In fact the Kamma-rebirth context tends to intensify them
if anything, both in their intrinsic quality and in their opposition
to each other.

On the one hand the assumption of a series of lives does not
change the explicitly stated quality of the self as a series of individualized moments always in flux, without permanent reality
or character. This series is simply extended to infinitude in both
directions from the present moment; and even what we call lives
or existences become only "moments," as it were, in such an infinite perspective. On the other hand, if we think of the contrasting aspect of the dynamic, progressive unity of self-development,
this too is fully present in the kammic context. Indeed it is here
that it comes to full-scale power and glory. For in a one-life context the process of self-development is bound to be in a more
implicit and understated form; there is not scope for it to achieve
full expression. But when the self-life continues, not only through
a few short years but through a multitude of lives of cumulative
development, then the whole concept of development gains vast

depth and power, though the basic nature of that development remains the same as in one life.

This wider context of the self-life then becomes of great importance, both religiously and ethically speaking, precisely because it does extend the temporal perspective to such immense proportions. In one way of viewing it we may say that it is the Kamma-rebirth context that gives to the doctrine of self its essential *religious* dimension, rather than leaving it as a psychological moralism pure and simple. For Kamma and rebirth introduce factors of a metaphysical nature and of ultimate destiny into the context of self development. Or, if "metaphysical" be objected to, at the very least the age-long context of spiritual development, with Nibbana as its hoped-for consummation, vitally affects the Buddhist ethic itself by the introduction of those special proportions and depths into the ethical situation which give to it its distinctively *Buddhist* quality.

For purposes of clarity we shall briefly sketch the Kamma-rebirth doctrine, though it is one of the best-known (and most misunderstood, say Buddhists) of all Buddhist doctrines. Theravada Buddhism teaches that existence or being at any level, animate or inanimate, microscopic or cosmic, is a beginningless series of momentary states. The absolute beginnings of the will-to-be, which expresses itself in craving or desire *(taṇhā),* remains a mystery so far as Buddhism is concerned, though *logically* speaking the situation seems to call for a statement of some sort. Buddhism in the Hinayana-Theravada tradition has more or less consistently rejected speculations with regard to absolute beginnings as being totally inconclusive and religiously unprofitable, even harmful. One can, and should, say only: This present observable process of momentary states of being, both on the physical and the mental planes, is all that can be known empirically. But by logical projection from the present, *every* present state must have had a previous state from which it sprang,[1] and by the traditional records of the saints' and Bud-

---

[1] In an ingenious approach a contemporary writer offers to give an absolutely irrefutable proof of the rebirth doctrine from the structure of conscious experience itself. That is, no experience can ever exist without being rooted in or presupposing a past experience. To be conscious at all

dhas' memories of their own past states of existence, we know that the process has been going on for many ages, perhaps from infinity itself. But of any absolutely First Cause or primordial beginning, either of the chain of successive world orders or individual beings, we can know nothing.[2]

Thus for practical purposes Buddhism views the universe as eternal process in which worlds, and individuals in them, rise and pass away in endless succession and in infinite numbers. Every successive universe and every successive moment of reality in every universe delivers its full cargo of fact and meaning over to the next moment, life, or epoch. Hence present reality is the only reality. It is the fullness of reality, the sum of all that has gone before—though some of the elements remain latent for long ages. Thus a present circumstance or happening is sometimes explained as the result of some deed a thousand or so lives in the past; and the memories of past experiences remain hidden almost forever, until the individual develops his powers of insight sufficiently to bring them to the surface of consciousness. But generally speaking the present moment of reality, whether considered physically or psychically, on small or large scale, is a kind of chemical blend into which have been mixed all the states and elements that have ever been, from infinity. And to this blend each new moment or event will add its own quota of new fact and deed, mental and physical.[3]

---

is to be conscious of a past. Hence there are no absolute beginnings. And this applies to successive existences as well as to successive moments in one existence. See Nyanavira Bhikkhu, "Sketch for a Proof of Rebirth," *Light of the Dhamma*, IV, No. 2 (April, 1957), 37–42.

[2] The Buddhist view of the world as process, rather than static or substantive reality, might seem to have much in common with the process-philosophy of A. N. Whitehead, both in general and in some particulars. Thus Whitehead's "pan-psychism" and his depreciation of human self-consciousness as a totally distinctive or unitary type of experience—being rather composed of several psycho-physical elements—would seem to be congenial to Buddhist teachings about self. But Whitehead has not been discovered by Theravada Buddhism yet. Perhaps his organicism would prove too positive in any case, for Theravada Buddhism usually emphasizes its doctrine of process mainly to undercut the categories of substance and individuality, not to provide a sense of cosmic unity.

[3] The question of absolute beginnings on the grand scale and *de novo* additions to process along the way is thus left unresolved. There

In this totality of momentary flux-in-process there is no discoverable central purpose or goal, but only uniformities and tendencies. Existence does indeed take on certain uniform patterns, causally conditioned and intimately interrelated; and it has characteristic rhythms of development and dissolution on the grand scale, governed in great part by the kammic quality of the beings existing in this or that universe. But generally speaking the constitutive elements-in-flux are more real than the totality of the process itself; and any meaning or value which is found in the cosmic process is only projected into it at various points by its constituent individuals. Thus in common with atheistic humanism Buddhism proclaims that there is no metaphysical backing for moral values nor any great overall purpose by which man should be guided and to which he should conform his ways. Such at least is the orthodox statement, though the role of Kamma presents a possible exception here as we shall see, and now and then other apparent exceptions come to view.

Within this total flux-process, however, we must distinguish special chains that are themselves continuously fluxing processes, yet each an indissolubly joined linkage that possesses an eternal individuality which is never crossed, confused, or blended with any other chain or process. These are sentient beings—whether "souls" in the purgatories, animals, human kind, or spirits resident in earth and the heavenly spheres (devas, nats, et al). Each one of these beings, or chains of process, has existed from all

---

seems to be a dilemma here: If the new element that a new moment adds comes into existence at that moment, then it is creation on the spot; and this would be congenial to the Buddhist doctrine of free will. But it also would break into the uniformity of causal sequence which Buddhism also espouses. If, on the other hand, all elements of all present moments have always existed—perhaps only rearranged now in different ways—then there is nothing new in any absolute sense either in the "beginning" or along the way. The iron law of causality is upheld, but free will seems impossible and novelty a mystery.

The usual explanation is that since being is infinite, the infinity of elements in it can combine in an infinity of "new" ways that give the impression of novelty. And with regard to free will, one's "free" action is outside the *present* causal order but conditioned or caused by some remotely past deed. Kammic cause thus sometimes leaps over the intermediate states in seeming disregard of the causal series.

eternity. It has passed through countless existences of infinite variety, from highest Brahma spheres to lowest hells (purgatories), but has remained continuous and separate, something like a tube or channel hermetically sealed from pollution or interference by any other stream of being.[4]

As suggested in the beginning of the chapter, when the self is thus set in an infinite series of rebirths, both of its qualities-intension are intensified. On the one hand it becomes more than ever like a succession of bubbles each of which disappears into nothingness when its moment is past; or like an infinite series of numbers, each of which can in turn be divided into an infinity. And for "moment" one can read "life" or "aeon" indifferently. But on the other hand there are the iron-bound continuities of separate units or chains of existence, called sentient beings, that are never confused or merged with each other no matter how many times their destinies crisscross. It is indeed a common Buddhist tradition that husband and wife, parents and children, or close friends in any given existence may well have been thus associated in past existences also and may hope for such close relationships in future lives as well—unless they are set upon reaching Nibbana directly. But let it be emphasized that however close or frequent such association of the "same" selves has been, their kammic individualities and destinies remain forever separate from each other.

Here is a curious paradox of extremes, then. The "self" is not an entity per se, but only a stream of energy or channel of force whose composition changes at every moment. Yet on the other hand there is an age-long, irrevocable individuality that no power, save the power of salvation in Nibbana, can ever break. The series of moments or lives that has produced the present psycho-

---

[4] This raises the question as to whether the number of beings in the universe has a fixed upper limit, since no new beings ever come into existence. Theoretically it does so fix the number; and since some beings are achieving Nibbana through the ages, and are thus removed from the causal process, perhaps in the end all beings will so achieve, "existence" will disappear, and Nibbana be all. However it is said that since beings are infinite in number, infinity cannot be exhausted even in infinite time; so there will always be a universe of striving beings or *samsāra*, the realm of rebirth and death.

physical event called "I," is more tightly and intimately tied together than any other series. There is an internal connection of
the strongest sort which can come to remember its own past
states and that can only be altered by "its own" inward self-
caused action. In a word "I" have always been "myself" through
countless ages, "I" am a super-individual of indestructible
proportions.

What is it then that passes on to another life? This is one of
the great basic Buddhist intellectual puzzles that has been volu-
minously debated for centuries. Here we shall sketch the Buddhist
answer only to such an extent as is relevant to the ethical problem.
It is *not* a soul or permanent self, insists the Theravada Buddhist,
as he carefully distinguishes his view from the parent Hindu view
of transmigration of souls. Just as there is no permanent self
which remains the same from moment to moment, or is "behind"
or "beyond" the content of present consciousness, or exists in addition to the sum of one's present mental states, so also is it between successive *existences*. The dying of physical death is not
qualitatively different from the perpetual "dying" which takes
place at every moment in every individual. To repeat what was
said in the previous chapter: There is indeed continuity between
states, but not continuing *identity*. Just as a flame (the "same"
flame?) is passed on from candle to candle, or the "same" vibra-
tion from tuning fork to tuning fork, so the "self" which passes
from life to life is only a continuing stream of energy, or a persist-
ing impulsion that carries its own propulsive energy with it, feed-
ing on changing conditions as it goes. The most that Buddhism
will concede with regard to this force is that it is a current of
"personality-producing energy."[5]

---

[5] It may be noted that this raises logical and metaphysical problems
and seems to be an instance of such excessive addiction to negative terms,
"no-soul" in this case, that difficulties are glossed over. The personal
self may not be a real entity in the ultimate sense; yet its illusory form
persists through countless births and deaths, and the whole Buddhist effort
is directed toward its salvation—from itself. And though only occasional
children, and the mind-developed saints and Buddhas, can remember their
past lives, obviously the "personality-producing energy" which persists
through insect, subhuman, animal, human, and superhuman forms, carries in itself the memory of even minute details of all these past lives, as

It is in connection with this passage of personality-producing energy from life to life that we must come to a closer examination of the law of Kamma. Or perhaps more accurately this energy might be called "sentient-being-producing energy" since all living beings have the same sort of life-force in them.[6] But the distinction is essentially unimportant since animals presumably have "personalities" too, though some personalistic characteristics may be in temporary abeyance. In any case the passage of this energy is governed by the law of Kamma, or action. The law of Kamma is that every action (mental, vocal or physical) or intention or tangible activity, has its absolutely inevitable result in the ensuing moments or lives of the acting individual. Kamma is part and parcel of the general pattern of causality regnant in the world order; it is the intrinsic tendency of each state to pass its essence on to an ensuing one. It is essential to observe, however, that the law of Kamma is not merely a general expression of causal consequences or a mechanical succession of states in which each state is the "cause" of the succeeding one and the "effect" of the preceding one. Kamma represents a *very special* kind of causal order, and is the dominant one in the universe.

It is the Moral Law of cause and effect that rules the whole universe; it is the very law which metes out justice with promptness and exactitude to the noble as well as to the wicked. It shows no frown or favour. It knows no pardon. It needs no propitiation

---

well as distinctive moral, mental, and personal characteristics. (In the *Jātaka Tales,* the quarrelsome, generous, clever, or envious person has been that same way a hundred births before, whether as man or animal.) Genius is thus explained as a kammic inheritance from past lives, which has little to do with present parents and their capacities.

Thus mere "personality-producing energy" seems to be a potential or virtual self, whatever name is given to it, that possesses memory, moral character, special talents, and personal characteristics, all of which are passed on from life to life in at least potential form.

[6] Occasionally, and rather surprisingly for Theravada Buddhism, one finds a suggestion that there is a kind of subconsciousness even in plants. Thus: "It was the Buddha who discovered sensation and subconsciousness in plants and trees. The Buddha, therefore, enjoined on the Bhikkhus to abstain from cutting trees and branches and severing their leaves." Umesu Chandra Mutsuddi, "Buddhism's Contribution to World Culture," *Light of the Buddha,* IV, No. 2 (February, 1959), 22.

nor any intercession whatsoever. It is inexorable in its execution and no one can stop it. In the end it is one of the universal Laws that reign supreme. They are immutable, everlasting.[7]

The key word here, of course, is "Moral." The evil deed brings evil, i.e. painful or unpleasant, results; and the good deed brings good, or pleasant, results to its doer, in this life or in another future life.[8] My present character, social situation, economic status, and many psycho-physical characteristics are the result of the moral quality of "my" past deeds. And if one asks what are the moral standards by which Kamma itself is governed in exacting its penalties and adding its blessings, the reply must be that they are those of basic Buddhist morality. Kamma punishes those who kill, lie, steal, commit sexual immoralities or take intoxicants, with appropriate deformities and calamities. Or to state it more Buddhistically: these sins inevitably produce such results; for the Buddhist would say that one is punished *by* his sin rather than *for* it.

In *The Questions of King Milinda,* post-canonical but quite "orthodox" in viewpoint, we have the following statement of the working of the law of Kamma:

> Why is it, Nagasena, that all men are not alike, but some are short-lived, some are long-lived, some sickly and some healthy, some ugly and some beautiful, some without influence and some of great power, some poor and some wealthy, some lowborn and some highborn, some stupid and some wise?

---

[7] Venerable Narada, "The Buddhist Doctrine of Kamma and Rebirth," *Light of the Dhamma,* III, No. 1 (June, 1955), 45.

[8] The use of such terms as "moral" and "justice" raises some problems in the kammic context. In order to avoid any suggestion of a Moral Order or Lawgiver of theistic proportions, Buddhism seeks to make Kamma mechanical in its operation and equate justice with mathematical inevitability or impartiality. Theoretically correct as this may seem, its concrete delineation demonstrates its essential illogic. Evil in the *moral* sense, produces evil in the *hedonistic* sense, that is, unpleasantness or painfulness. And *good* character results in beauty, health and prosperity. Clearly there is no mere mechanical causality working here, nor even alone the natural worsening or bettering of character, but a force which adds pleasantness to virtue and pain to vice. Here is a sort of hidden God-force or rewarding and punishing Providence.

And Nagasena replies that just as different vegetables are produced by different seeds,

> Just so . . . are the differences you have mentioned to be explained. For it has been said by the Blessed One: Beings, O Brahmin, have each their own Karma, are inheritors of Karma, belong to the tribe of their Karma, are relatives by Karma, have each their own Karma as their protecting overlord. It is Karma that divides into low and high and the like divisions.[9]

Nor should it be thought that such an explanation belongs to the classical past of "original" Buddhism alone. It is a vital principle of contemporary Buddhist faith; Buddhism would not be Buddhism without Kamma and rebirth, in the eyes of the Theravadin. Thus one Prime Minister of Burma, distressed to discover the widespread ignorance of the basic Five Precepts among his own countrymen, set forth at length the concrete kammic results of the observance and non-observance of the Precepts:

> A person who steadfastly and continuously observes the Five Precepts can gain the following beneficial results:
> (1) he can gain great wealth and possessions;
> (2) he can gain great fame and reputation;
> (3) he can appear with courage and confidence in the midst of a public assembly;
> (4) on the point of death, he can die with calmness and equanimity, without falling into lethargy;
> (5) after his death, he will be reborn into the world of the Devas, [i.e. radiant, happy, god-like beings.]

And if we take each Precept in turn, its observance or non-observance has very specific results. For example take the First Precept's prohibition of killing any living creature whatsoever:

> The person who vigilantly and steadfastly observes the precept of refraining from taking another being's life reaches the world of *Devas* on his death. When he expires in the world of the *Devas* and is reborn in the world of human beings, he is endowed with the following qualities: no physical defects or deformities . . . swift in movement . . . well proportioned feet . . .

---

[9] Volume X, *Sacred Books of the East,* Chapter III, Section 2. Cf. *Majjhima-Nikāya,* Sutta 135 (PTS *Middle Length Sayings*) and *Anguttara-Nikāya,* Sutta 197 (PTS *Gradual Sayings*).

pleasant figure, gentleness, cleanliness, courage, strength, ability
to speak well and smoothly . . . the object of affection and regard by others, having a united following . . . being free from
harm at the hands of others, not subject to death by others' weap-
ons, having a large retinue . . . a beautiful golden complexion,
handsome appearance, free from disease and illness, anxiety and
grief, being able to associate with loved ones always, being long-
lived.

As might be expected the results of *breaking* any Precept are as
*un*desirable as its keeping is desirable. For example:

> The person who takes intoxicants is extremely likely, on his
> death, to reach one of the four lower planes of existence, and
> after that, if he should be reborn in the human world, he is liable
> to suffer from madness, or psychopathic complaints, or he may
> be a deaf and dumb person.[10]

We may pause here to expand somewhat further on the theme
of the good and bad results of good and bad Kamma with a view
to appreciating the almost astronomical range of possibilities
within the rebirth realms according to the Pali scriptures. First
we shall note the glories of rebirth into the deva-worlds as the
result of good deeds. In this case a woman is born as a glorious
devi because of a gift of food and money to the Order of monks:

> Through the power of her merit there appeared for her a
> great mansion that could travel through the sky, beautiful with
> many pinnacles, with park, lotus and the like, sixteen yojanas in
> length, breadth, and height, diffusing light for a hundred yojanas
> by its own radiance. And when the devi went (anywhere) she
> went with her mansion and with a retinue of a thousand heaven-
> ly nymphs.[11]

The physical dimensions of the deva-world itself are conceived
in proportion to the above mansion. Thus wrote a near-contem-
porary Burmese Buddhist monk:

> In the Happy Course of Existence the size of the Devas and
> Brahmas is three gavuttas. By Burmese mileage four and a half

---

[10] Honorable U Nu, "The Five Precepts," *Light of the Dhamma*, V,
No. 2 (April, 1958), 39–51.

[11] "Monastery Mansion," *Minor Anthologies of the Pali Canon*, Part
IV (Luzac, 1943), p. 76. A yojana is about seven miles in length.

Burmese miles (or 9 English miles) mean three gavuttas. As regards the mansions in the planes, they are 12, 15, 20, 30, 60 yojanas and so forth wide. Any one of these mansions is greater than either the town of Alon or Dipeyin township in our country of Burma. Even the mansion of the Sun alone is greater than Burma.[12]

At other times the splendors of these splendid realms are described in related terms: Abundance of food of all sorts, unbelievable riches, great powers, and of course immensely long life, stretching into the millions of years, according to human standards. The further one rises in the scale of splendid beings, the longer the term of existence there—though the highest realms are completely immaterial and the product of developed mind-power rather than mere good works.

But at the other extreme are the hells or purgatories. As with life in the heavens, so also life in the hells is of immense length but not eternal. And here are agony and suffering as intense and terrible as life in the heavenly worlds is beautiful and desirable. Thus we find it written in *Jātaka Story* No. 530 *(Saṃkicca):*

Who so from greed or hatred shall, vile creature, slay his sire,
In Kālasutta hell long time shall agonize in fire.
In iron cauldron boiled till he shall peel,
The parricide is pierced with shafts of steel,
Then blinded and on filth condemned to feed
He's plunged in brine to expiate his deed.
The goblins 'twixt his jaws, lest they should close,
Hot iron ball or plough share interpose,
These fixed with cords his mouth so firmly prop,
They into it a stream of filth can drop.
Vultures, both black and brown, and ravens too,
And birds with iron beaks, a motley crew,
Rending his tongue to many a fragment shall
Devour the quivering morsel, blood and all.

The passage goes on to describe other equally gruesome torments: Being ploughed on the back with deep furrows, drinking one's own blood, being eaten by enormous worms with iron mouths, impaled on foot-long red-hot thorns on a flaming tree,

---

[12] Ledi Sayadaw, "Kammathana Dipani," *Buddhist Supplement* of *The Burman,* December 15, 1958.

having one's tongue pulled out, and being beaten with clubs—yet never dying.[13]

There is yet another factor here that increases the already sharp contrast between the hells and the heavens even more, if possible:

> So the Happy Course of Existence is very extensive in area, but the number of its inhabitants is very scanty. . . . But Maha-Avici is the lowest of the eight Hellish countries, each of which is ten thousand yojanas wide. . . . The reason why it is called Maha-Avici is because the commentaries call it Avici on account of the reason that the Hellish male and female beings are packed in to overflowing, just as mustard seeds are compressed in a bamboo-hollow.[14]

And what is the reason for such disparity of numbers? Presumably because it is harder to be "good" than to be "bad." One contemporary writer states flatly:

> The Buddha explained, unequivocally, that the man who takes a life of even one insect goes to hell for quite a long time and that once one reaches one of the four lower stages, it is a matter of aeons of time and the utmost difficulty to regain man's estate.[15]

To be sure there are also some passages (in the same scriptures quoted with regard to the Heavenly Mansions) in which a very small good deed, particularly if done to the Order, is productive of magnificent good in the next life.

But these are of the later stratum of scriptures, written possibly with a view toward encouraging more munificent gifts to the Order. And though the Order or Sangha does still hold a very privileged position with regard to the benefits of good deeds done to it, nonetheless the traditional Buddhist emphasis seems to be rather on the ease with which one descends to sub-human births and the difficulties of escaping them, than on the ease of attain-

---

[13] PTS Edition, V, 138–9. *Cf.* H. C. Warren, *Buddhism in Translations* (Cambridge, Mass.: Harvard University Press, 1953), III, 51a, quoting *Anguttara-Nikāya*, Text iii, 35.

[14] Ledi Sayadaw, *ibid.*

[15] U Ohn Ghine, "Five Precepts," *Buddhist Supplement* of *The Burman*, October 6, 1958.

ing deva-birth. Indeed, logically speaking, it might seem absolutely impossible to escape at all, since, as Ledi Sayadaw goes on to say about the individual in a nether (sub-human) plane:

> He is getting farther and farther from meritorious deeds, existence by existence, and getting worse and worse by freshly committed kammas [deeds].[16]

For it is held that when an animal such as a tiger kills, it acquires more evil Kamma because it has killed; and the being so incarnated has been thus incarnated because his grievous sins call for such punishment—a truly vicious circle. Nonetheless even such bad Kamma finally is exhausted, for punishment in the hells is not eternal, as has been already observed.

One further feature of the Kamma-rebirth situation fills out the picture: Man's estate is both crucially important and a rare privilege. It is crucially important because only on the human level can one achieve liberation, with one partial exception.[17] Those in the higher-than-human spheres are too engrossed in the pleasures of their long lives to realize that existence is impermanence and suffering. And those of the lower than-human levels (ghosts, beasts, dwellers in hells) are so overwhelmed by their miseries, so lacking in opportunity to perform good deeds, and perhaps so limited in their intelligence, that their hope is very meager. Thus for one reason or another it is only on the human level of mixed bliss and woe that one can realize that existence is suffering and yet have the capacity to take advantage of this realization to gain liberation from existence.

---

[16] *Ibid.*

[17] The one exception, and not a genuine one at that, is the *anāgāmin* or non-returner, the saint who is just one stage below the *arahat.* He has rid himself of all the fetters which bind him to rebirth except the attenuated forms of the desire for continued individual existence in some form or other, self-esteem, restlessness, and ignorance. Though he does not go directly to *Nibbana,* as does the arahat who has completely destroyed *all* fetters, he does not return to human birth but ascends to the highest immaterial planes from which he goes on to Nibbana. Yet the real work of his salvation has been done on the human level. *Other* inhabitants of those spheres, who are there because of the development of high mental powers, must return again to human or other embodied forms.

Man's estate is also a rare privilege because of the astronomical unlikelihood of being born into human estate. The seemingly large number of human beings should not blind us to the fact that they are only a relative handful when compared to the totality of beings in all the universes, most of them in animal or purgatorial form. This rarity of human estate is expressed by several striking analogies. It is said, for example, that there are as few human beings in proportion to the total number of beings in existence as there are grains of dust that can be put on one's fingernail compared to the dust of the whole earth. Or again one is as likely to be born a human being as is a turtle to put his head through an ox-yoke under the following conditions:

> There is, O Bhikkhus, in the ocean a turtle both of whose eyes are blind. He plunges into the water of the unfathomable ocean and swims about incessantly in any direction wherever his head may lead. There is also in the ocean a yoke of a cart which is ceaselessly floating about on the surface of the water and carried away in all directions by the tide, current and wind.[18]

And finally if we consider the likelihood of being born as a human being in a *Buddha* era, or one in which a Buddha's teachings are still known and practiced to some extent—and this is the only condition under which even in human status one may achieve salvation—then the chances are even more unlikely. It is as likely to happen to a given individual, or perhaps to any individual, as it is that a needle tossed from the top of Mt. Meru (the great 84,000 leaguehigh central cosmic mountain) into the earth Island a million leagues or more away across the six intervening seas should strike point to point with another needle there.[19] How then can one possibly overestimate his good fortune in being born in this era of the Gotama Buddha's teaching, and especially being born in a Buddhist country?

It may well be inquired in passing whether in fact the above portrayal of the kammic course of sentient life represents the actual view of a contemporary Theravadin? This is as difficult to answer as the question: Does a Christian believe in a literal

---

[18] Ledi Sayadaw, *ibid.*

[19] Capt. Henry Yule, *Court of Ava* (Smith, Elder, and Co., 1858), p. 237.

heaven of hymning angels and a hell of leaping flames? That depends on the Christian. So here it depends upon the particular Buddhist in question. There can be no doubt of the technical orthodoxy of the above views, of course. They are those found in the Pali Scriptures which are accepted by all Theravadins without much concern over what is an "early" and what is a "later" stratum, since the whole canon is considered to have come directly from the Buddha. And Ledi Sayadaw was one of the most eminent Buddhist expositors in Burma in the last generation; his works are even now being translated into English as some of the best writing Theravada Buddhism has to offer. So also contemporary pagoda art keeps stressing hellish tortures, which are naturally more picturable than the transcendent peace of Nibbana.

Yet most of the writing, for foreigners at least, emphasizes the positive rather than the negative. Good rebirth and ultimate liberation, or the inner peace of the higher life, are held up for inspiration. Their non-attainment, i.e. wandering in the less fortunate realms of *samsāra,* still subject to rebirth, is held to be a tragedy. But the negative results, though mentioned, are not so specifically described as by the Ledi Sayadaw; more often spoken of are the dissatisfactions of craving, the fever of hate, the general unhappiness attending the unspiritual life, and somewhat general and cautious references to possible rebirth in "the nether planes." And Burmese friends have told me that nowadays the gruesome tortures of the hells are neither so much preached about nor believed in by the younger generation, as by their fathers.

2. Ethical Results and Implications

Having thus sketched out the Kamma-rebirth context in which the human self functions, we may go on to observe some of the specific ethical emphases and proportions that seem to result from this context. We shall note three aspects:

a. *A Tendency to a Mechanical and Externalized Interpretation of Morality, as Expressed in the Doctrine of Merit*

The word "merit" has appeared in one or two quotations thus far. And this is not surprising for it is one of the most ubiquitous

words in Theravada Buddhism. Briefly, merit may be described
as follows: It is the favourable balance in one's kammic account
produced by past good deeds. (Of course *de*merit, though the
word is less often used, is the precise opposite in all cases.) It is
the totality of one's accumulated or stored-up goodness, which
will manifest itself in good fortune of various kinds, both in this
life and lives to come. Pleasures, success, health, friendships,
those surprising items of good fortune which come unexpectedly
like God's grace, and above all, *happy rebirths,* are the direct
consequences of meritorious deeds. It may be considered to be
the accumulated beneficial kammic force that virtuous actions
and attitudes create and of which no man may have too much.
It is the only coinage of any worth in paying one's passage to
better existences in the future, and carrying him on toward
sainthood.

It must be further emphasized that essentially one's merit is
one's own, i.e. belonging to that particular stream of kammic
force that has resulted in the present "me," and no one else's.
Both responsibility for, and fruitage of, merit rest squarely upon
each individual in himself and by himself. Strictly speaking one
cannot share the basic result of his merit or demerit, even though
there is a doctrine of merit-sharing in Buddhism, as well as some
suggestions of a collective or group merit and demerit that produce good or bad societies and finally produce and destroy
whole universes. With these aspects we shall deal later; but they
tend to be peripheral rather than central in the actual ethical operation of the doctrine of merit.

The logical and actual result of merit doctrine is that every
action of every sort is rated in terms of its merit-producing power.
The total realm of morality, or sila, is completely permeated
with merit-awareness. The standard way of praising the good
deed is to call it meritorious; and there is a good deal of sharp
calculation of the various grades of merit-potential as between
given types of deeds. Indeed it is almost second nature, as natural
as breathing to the Theravadin, to speak of every action in such
terms. Merit creeps into the language of hospitality, in whose
words the family offers the anniversary breakfast to the guest
"in the hope of (the host's) Nibbana." It divides the area of good
deeds into common and preferred varieties by the doctrine of the

better, i.e. more profitable, "field of merit"—traditionally confined to the Buddha (images), the Order of monks, and the building of pagodas. This quantification of religious and moral worth
also creeps into the more spiritual matter of religious exercises,
such as the telling of beads, recitation of scripture verses, saying
of pagoda "prayers", and even into that most inward of all Buddhist disciplines, meditation—by counting the merit produced by
each meditative hour.[20]

Some of the concrete manifestations of questing for merit will
be considered in more detail later. Here we may consider some
factors, both built-in and traditionally present, that qualify the
seeming crassness of the merit doctrine in the direction of greater
altruism and spirituality. One of these factors is an intrinsic part
of the doctrine itself, that of *merit-sharing*. Merit-sharing is giv-
en a prominent place in some portions of the Pali Canon—though
these on the whole are later ones it must be confessed. In the
Peta-Vatthu (in *Minor Anthologies)* are related several instances
of human beings sharing the merit of their good deeds, especially
almsgiving, with the disembodied spirits *(petas)* who wander mis-
erably about over the earth. The effect is such that some of them
are instantly transferred to the heavenly realms as devas.

In Burma in particular, where the merit doctrine has taken
such a strong hold, there is a very ancient and specific tradition
of merit-sharing. It is an institution in its own right, so to speak.
Even with regard to the multitudinous pagodas of Pagan, the
translator and editor of *The Glass Palace Chronicle of the
Kings of Burma* observe:

> It is significant that the kings left us, not stately palaces as
> monuments of their earthly greatness, but magnificent pagodas
> as a proof of the sincerity of their faith. Their reward is merit.
> Yet to say that king built a pagoda from a selfish desire to gain
> merit would be doing him an injustice.

---

[20] After ten days in a mediation center, during which he had spent a
hundred odd hours in actual meditation, a devout young Buddhist re-
marked: "This will certainly create a great deal of merit." When chided
by a co-meditating non-Buddhist for such a quantitative view, he readily
conceded that the degree of inner calm and strength gained was of
more real importance. But his first reaction was clearly the natural one.

'By this abundant merit I desire
Here nor hereafter no angelic pomp
Of Brahmas, Suras, Maras; nor the state
And splendors of a monarch; nay, not even
To be pupil of the Conqueror.
But I would build a causeway sheer athwart
The river of *saṃsāra,* and all folk
Would speed across thereby until they reach
The Blessed City.'[21]

So prayed Alaungsithu at the dedication of the Shwegugyi Pagoda in the eleventh century; and such also has no doubt been the motivation of many of those who have built pagodas and supported the Order of monks in the centuries since. Indeed merit-sharing still retains a prominent place in Burmese Buddhist thinking and practice, being celebrated in many a public ceremony and symbolic action.[22] There is of course the consoling thought that none of one's merit is *really* lost by the sharing of it. Certainly the *total* quantity of merit in the universe is thus increased. In this connection Buddhaghosa, the great fifth-century commentator in Ceylon, likens merit-sharing to the lighting of a thousand unlighted lamps from an already-lighted one. Is the light of the original lamp (merit-sharer) lessened thereby? No; and the total amount of light in the world is greater. It may even be that the merit of the *sharer* is actually increased by such sharing, as many hold.[23] This perhaps has some slight spiritual kinship with the Christian statement that love increases through loving.

---

[21] Pe Maung Tin and G. H. Luce (trans.) *The Glass Palace Chronicle of the Kings of Burma* (Oxford: The University Press, 1953), p. xi.

[22] Most notable is the merit-sharing formula which ends nearly every Buddhist meeting of the formal sort. As specified individuals pour out water drop by drop from glasses or cups into a basin or pot, the congregation repeats a wish-prayer that the merit of gifts given and noble deeds done at that meeting should bless all living creatures—and call the earth to witness this sharing. Likewise the symbolism of the struck gong is the sending out of waves of good-will and benevolence to all creatures from pagoda, temple, or religious procession.

[23] The *ne plus ultra* of all conceivable calculations for both giving and receiving maximum merit is (historically or facetiously?) related by Maurice Collis as having been produced in Burma long ago: "At some time an ingenious lordling had invented a method of increasing the merit

To be sure there are limits to merit-sharing. Animals and those in the purgatories cannot be helped to a shortening of their suffering by such means. Nor can one *essentially* alter the kammic destiny or nature of another, so completely is one the product of his own deeds. Yet merit-sharing is in deep harmony with a fundamental Buddhist hope of achieving higher and higher states of more and more universal good will, at whose maximum level the saint extends absolute good will to absolutely all beings.

There is a second merit-qualifying factor that is sometimes stressed, though it too seems to move in a kind of circle which comes back in the end to oneself and his own benefit. This is the statement that the best quality of merit can be gained only by *truly* unselfish deeds, and by what may or may not be the same thing—depending upon what one calls ultimately the supreme good—dedicating the meritorious deed to the attainment of Nibbana rather than securing better rebirth for oneself.

In this connection we may observe that there is absolutely no question but that those deeds done for the specific purpose of achieving a more fortunate rebirth are effective. This is an axiomatic implication of the law of Kamma. But it should also be observed that Buddhism tends always to temper human lust for even the deva-worlds, let alone merely more fortunate human births, in two ways: It points out that the desire for sensual gratification is impossible of satisfaction. As in one of the *Jātaka Tales*, even though one lives for millions of years as one of the highest gods, he can never satisfy his desires, for his desires increase in direct ratio to his powers. Secondly, even such glorious careers end at last; and the ex-deva, his good Kamma or merit

---

which might be normally expected (from pagoda-building). It was the practice to set up a dedication tablet in stone, whereon the donor expressed a wish to acquire the full merit due. The gentleman in question put forward the idea that the donor should ask in the inscription to be allowed to share the merit with a number of other people, say, his uncles and his aunts. The very fact of stating his desire to share merit, rightly his own, was itself an added merit, and it was calculated that the device, without increasing the cost of the structure, doubled the merit that might accrue from it alone. . . . At a later date an even more ingenious person suggested . . . that a maximum merit might be won if the donor, on stone, gave the whole of his merit to others, not even reserving a minor share for himself." *She Was a Queen*, Faber and Faber, 1937, pp. 182–3.

exhausted, comes down to human or animal form with a thud. And a million years *gone* is no longer or better than an hour gone. Besides it may be that a god's day even in its living, though it be a thousand human years long, seems no longer to him (the deva) than a *man's* day is to *him*.

There is also the further consideration already discussed: Nibbana, which is the only final cure for existential misery—even that misery of the deva-worlds, sometimes called bliss—cannot be reached by those who are seeking for more fortunate rebirths *any*where in the realm of individualized existence, be it human or Brahma-world or immaterial sphere. Thus warns the Honorable U Nu in a public greeting to a Buddhist assembly:

> In giving bountifully, in observing moral precepts and in practising Vipassana-bhavana [i.e. mental development through meditation on Impermanence] one should aim at Nibbana only. This is . . . the Right Way.
>
> On the other hand, if one aims at becoming in future existence a rich man, king, emperor or universal monarch, a Deva or a Brahma, he is on the Wrong Way. . . . He will not be able to attain Nibbana. . . .
>
> Dana [liberality], Sila [morality] and Bhavana practised by many people nowadays are mostly in the Wrong Way because they see themselves as powerful beings moving in higher circles and not as renouncing all worldly things and attaining Nibbana.[24]

If this seems to contradict the same author's earlier statement in which the hope of happy rebirths is held up as the proper motivation for keeping the Five Precepts, the contradiction is more seeming than actual. For the earth-bound layman of the ordinary sort must be encouraged to even the minimal moral practices by whatever means; and though rebirth in the Brahma and deva-worlds is not the ultimate goal, yet efforts of an ethical nature to achieve even such rebirth contribute in the end to progress toward Nibbana itself, by enlarging one's spiritual capacities and providing better opportunities for more spiritual living. The sheer hope of Nibbana itself, however, is so remote for the generality of men that some nearer and warmer hope must be found to *start* them on the Noble Path.

---

[24] *Light of the Dhamma*, IV, No. 3 (July, 1957), 62.

One other related quality of the merit conception, perhaps ordinarily more implicit than explicit, is to be noted. This is the interpretation of merit as *moral worthiness*, suggested by Mrs. Rhys Davids. In this context to gain merit means to become increasingly more worthy, to gain more and more spiritual capacity which will enable one to achieve sainthood in the end. Certainly this is implicit in the merit conception, for that benevolent attitude of the saint in which lovingkindness and compassion are shared universally and undiscriminatingly with all beings, is the long-run goal of even the smallest generous or loving deed. Further, Buddhism has always maintained that one is incapable of helping another until he himself has been helped, i.e. has gained abundant good character through abundant merit. And the better a person becomes, i.e. the more saintly, the more he *can* share his goodness with others.

One very practical and human note must be inserted here. Human nature tends to overflow the doctrines of its faiths, both for better and for worse. Certainly in the case of Burmese Buddhism there has been an overflowing of the strict doctrine of kammic merit for the better. For if anything is characteristic of the Burmese Buddhist it is his generous hospitality to stranger and visitor, his willingness to share both food and friendship. While there may be some calculation of merit in the background—and whose motives for doing good are *not* mixed?—the hospitality is too genuine and spontaneous to be *totally* explained thus.[25] And even though a strict interpretation of Kamma might logically lead to complete indifference to another's plight and the desire to avoid the contagion of the unfortunate's misfortune, there is a

---

[25] It is almost impossible to escape from a Burmese home on even a ten-minute visit without the insistent offer of something to drink or eat. And on one occasion the author was fanned by his hostess herself, while he was drinking the hospitable cup of tea.

Of course some of this may be explained by the non-technized state of Burmese society, the easy-going way of life in which time and food are plentiful, and the liking for sociability in general. Nevertheless Burmese hospitality and friendliness are delightfully genuine and spontaneous; and it is likewise quite certain, I think, that the Buddhist doctrines of gentleness and benevolence have contributed importantly to their manifestation.

great deal of *un*organized kindness shown to all such, as well as a growing tradition of self-less community service.

What then shall be our final estimate of the ethical influence of the doctrine of merit? Even with all the qualifying factors taken into account we must say in the end that it has had a quantifying and narrowing effect upon the exercise of moral virtue. In combination with the individualistic interpretation of Kamma and the doctrine that one must help himself before he can help others, the merit doctrine has tended to keep the eye of the ordinary Buddhist fixed on the main chance and sharpened to a careful calculation of the merit potentiality of each deed. And it has kept alive, despite some few iconoclastic reform attempts, the pagoda religion of prayers, beads, and image reverence. On the other hand the concepts of pursuing the good *for* itself and loving others for their own sakes alone, have been of slow growth in Buddhism,[26] largely in consequence of this same merit-Kamma complex of ideas and motivations. And the alternative which the ideal of good-for-itself and love of others for their own sakes has furnished to the West, has been missing on the practical and social ethical plane in Buddhism. The only good-in-itself that Buddhism knows of is Nibbana, which is so

---

[26] One may say that the "good-for-itself" motif only now and then, and rather ashamedly, peeps out in Buddhist thinking. For on the whole it is not highly esteemed. The following quotations will make this clear:

"A Buddhist is aware of future consequences (kammic), and he refrains from evil because it retards, does good because it aids progress to *Bodhi* (Enlightenment)."

"*There may also be some that do good because it is good, refrain from evil because it is bad.*" Venerable Narada, "Buddhism in a Nutshell," *Light of the Dhamma,* III, No. 4 (August, 1956), 15 (Italics added.)

Again:

"The highest motive that Western ethics can conjure up is altruism, which in spite of aims of personal disinterestedness is yet inextricably intertwined with the subtler forms of worldly desires. . . . [This] Western view has spread throughout the world and today, even Buddhists have begun to subscribe to it and have started to show signs of *being apologetic* in their Buddhist faith." N. Sein Nyo Tun, "The Importance of Abstention in Buddhist Practice," *The Open Door,* II, No. 3 (January, 1960), 4. (Italics added.)

far removed from ordinary social concerns that it gives little direct guidance or inspiration therein.

It may be noted in passing that there is perhaps *some* weakening of the potency of the merit-demerit complex of ideas today in Buddhism. As suggested above, it may be that the horrors of the lower planes (purgatories) are less real to the generation under thirty years of age than to their grandfathers; and perhaps the same applies to the glories of the highest planes. In any case merit-gaining tends as a result to lose some of its driving force and merit calculation its sharp edge. This may in the end represent a gain for "higher" religion if this motivational weakening of the merit doctrine is replaced by wider and more positively ethico-social values.

b. *A Combination of Virtue with Pleasure and Material Success to Constitute the Complete Good.*

To this we have already referred in terms of body-mind good, but we must keep it in mind especially with regard to the kammic context. The blending of goods with goodness, inclusive of both physical-material and mental-moral factors, is inevitable. For the logic of Kamma, as we have seen, is that material prosperity, happiness, health and rebirth in the splendid deva-worlds come as the absolutely certain result of morally good deeds. And the absence of such factors, especially in reverse situations, is just as certainly the sign of unvirtuous or immoral deeds somewhere along the line.

Indeed we have here precisely the philosophy of Job's comforters: Sin brings suffering; whoever suffers has sinned. There are differences of course. The sins for which we now suffer, or the goodness because of which fortune smiles on us, may well belong to some past *existence,* the more so if they seem to be unexplained by the present one. Nor is it a God who punishes us after carefully considering our case; it is the inexorable law of Kamma by which our own past evil or good is developing into its end-product of pain or pleasure.

But we must go further to reiterate the important point that not only are material benefits the sign and result of virtue, they are *inseparable from* virtue in the complete good. Purity of character without pleasantness of condition is not completely good in the Buddhist sense; nor of course is pleasantness of condition without purity, completely good either. (Of course average Buddhists tend to put the emphasis upon the pleasant circumstances in their thought of goodness, since it is so often lacking as present virtue's visible reward.) The calm frame of mind, bodily health, and a pleasant situation seem to be viewed as not only conducive to the gaining of superior virtue, but as an organic part of it. The perfect situation, viewed only from the Kamma-rebirth level of estimation, would be that of the high gods who possess unusual psychic and physical powers, almost endlessly long lives, and live amidst every condition of splendor in which every wish can be instantly gratified.

To be sure there are qualifying factors. Even in the Buddhist scheme good fortune is the result of *past* good deeds, not always or often of present virtue. A man's *present* virtue must be nourished in the hope, not the possession, of its reward. And conversely a presently virtuous man may suffer from poverty and disease because of past misdeeds, not present misconduct. So also it must be said that Buddhism is only doing on the installment plan what the Christian does all at once with the concept of Heaven: joining virtue and happiness together in perfect union. For is not the Christian Heaven, whatever variations of portrayal there may be, essentially the adding of just deserts to virtue, *both* to be enjoyed at the same time?

There are besides some of what we may call relatively transcendent elements in the Kamma-rebirth realm itself, apart from the ultimate transcendence of Nibbana. The deva-worlds are not entirely riotously sensual paradises; and the higher Brahma-worlds in particular are more and more rarified in their sense life, representing a mood of serene and rarefied contemplation approaching Nibbana in quality. They are such that some beings, the non-returners to human life, can go directly from them to Nibbana itself.

Perhaps the whole matter of Kamma-rebirth rewards and punishments *might* be spiritualized into an elaborate parable of the Buddhist's central conviction of the fact that virtue and vice carry within them their own rewards which cannot be escaped. But they are taken much too literally for this interpretation in Theravada Buddhism; there *are* tangible rewards for virtue and the thirty-one planes of sub-and super-human existence *do* exist. And in this context of ideation that governs the practical Buddhism of most Buddhists, physical benefit and moral virtues are Siamese twins. Historically this seems to witness to the attempt—begun long ago but representing a perpetual task in Buddhism—to join the layman's pursuit of lower and lesser goods and worlds of Hindu origin to the monk's pursuit of Nibbana in one structure called Buddhism. Thus it is maintained that even the pursuit of the lower goods and the goal of deva-world rebirth ultimately makes measureable progress toward Nibbana. Yet in the meantime the better rebirth in a more fortunate human circumstance or deva-world is the goal *actually* aimed at.

We may mention one other qualifying factor: that of the Bodhisatta type of morality which also manifests itself on the rebirth level. Bodhisattas, destined to become Buddhas by countless lives of virtue, are often portrayed as performing deeds of self-forgetful sacrifice: the sacrifice of individual good for public good, the spending of material resources or even the surrender of life itself, for the sake of others. Does this not leaven the lump of the seeming selfishness of the rebirth type of goodness? It does, and importantly. Yet the Bodhisatta remains a character apart, scarcely human or imitable. Even here the dominant emphasis tends to be upon the superior wisdom, power, cleverness, position, and good fortune of the Bodhisatta as compared with his fellows. In a word, virtue and its rightful rewards—power, superior talents, good fortune, success—are joined together in this figure in *every one* of his existences. He is not the Suffering Servant of the Christian tradition in any sense of the word, in whom present virtue finds not reward but anguish—and hence his *true* virtue.

The result is that the Western Christian finds many of his characteristic moral emphases and distinctions missing in Buddhism. The themes so familiar in his tradition—virtue versus success, intrinsic versus instrumental good, goodness gained through suffering, vicarious suffering of the consequences of another's sins as the highest type of all moral goodness—seldom appear as such in Buddhist morality. And it will inevitably appear to him, as a result, that some important ethical distinctions—especially those rooting in the difference between moral goodness and physical condition or the ideal of seeking pure ethical goodness for its own sake—cannot be made significant in such a context. Neither in clear example nor definition do they appear.

c. *The Quantitative Enlargement and Qualitative Enrichment of the Self*

One of the most significant results growing out of the Kamma-rebirth context, and the most closely related to the nature of the self, is what we may call the quantitative *enlargement* of the self and its qualitative *intensification*. It must be kept in mind that this consequence is seldom explicitly stated in Buddhism, because it is not superficially congenial to the anatta (no-soul) terminology which is almost always used in speaking of the self. This enlargement is not the less genuine, even though implicit, for it is closely related to that dynamic continuity of self-states which was discussed in the previous chapter. Indeed we may say that the Kamma-rebirth context but results in the deepening and intensification of that continuity, with most important ethical results.

By the quantitative enlargement of the self I refer to the long process of character-formation which, according to Buddhism, has preceded the appearance of the saint or Buddha, or for that matter, even the more-than-average good man. One of the profound mysteries of human life is the difference in moral character and personal quality of human beings, even between those that have been reared in the same family. How can saint and pervert spring from the same soil, i.e. be produced by the same parent; or the genius by the most ordinary parents? The Buddhist is not persuaded that the sum of the variations of biological heredity (differences in genes) and environmental differences is sufficient to account for such diversity.

And this is where Kamma and rebirth come in to solve the puzzle. Says Buddhism: Significant personal differences do not arise in *one* lifetime but are the results of age-long past Kamma. Every man has an infinitely long past that explains for the most part, why he is the sort of person he now is.[27] For most men this

---

[27] The Buddhist has the same difficulty in relating kammic determination to the minute circumstances of each life, as does the Christian in

infinite past is not especially significant in the ethical sense because it has been a dreary and inconclusive see-saw of better and worse kammic results that have largely cancelled each other out in the long run, though *now* they may be on the crest or in the trough of their kammic fluctuation between good and evil. Or to change the figure, most men are mixed bags of good and bad kammic inheritance.

But for the truly good or intensely evil man the case is somewhat different. As good or evil he represents not just a momentary lapse or product of happy or unhappy chance, but the end-result of an age-long process of discipline or of willful submersion in evil. In the Buddhist scriptures there are two great opponents of the Buddha: Mara and Devadatta. The former is very roughly equivalent to the Christian Devil, though by no means so strong, so fully personalized, or so completely evil.[28]

He might be considered to be simply the symbolic personification of all the forces of hate, sensuality, fear, greed, deceit, and evil in general. Nonetheless he is the Buddha's chief opponent and his existence in this form would call for a long past of steady evil intentions. So also, on a lesser scale, is it the case with Devadatta, Buddha's human cousin and one of his followers who enviously aspired to be apointed as the Buddha's successor. When the Buddha refused to so appoint him, he created a schism among

---

relating the human will to the Divine activity. Is every smallest personal characteristic, circumstance, and event the direct work of God—or the effect of Kamma? If so then there is no freedom, and a man can blame *all* that occurs upon Divine will or past Kamma and cease to struggle against his fate. Practically, both religions deny this conclusion, allowing for a measure of mechanical chance or instrumentality, some indeterminate factors, and a limited exercise of free will.

[28] Quite interestingly, though Mara's career is full of evil deeds such as tempting Gotama not to persist in his quest of enlightenment and seeking to thwart him at all points in his efforts to enlighten men, he remains in the spirit world as a kind of deva or god. Why, if such status comes only from good Kamma? Because, say some, Mara has in the past accumulated such a store of merit that even his many evil deeds have not exhausted this merit. Or have there been successions of Maras? And are they finally saved? No doubt we have here the incongruity resulting from trying to fit the devil-spirits of Indian mythology into the Buddhist kammic framework.

the Buddha's followers and became Mara's human counterpart, as it were. But according to the *Jātaka Tales* this was not the first time that that being (or stream of kammic force) which was now Devadatta had opposed the being (or stream of kammic force) that was now the Buddha; at countless points in his career as Buddha-to-be, whether in animal or human form, he had been unsuccessfully countered by Devadatta-to-be.

Of course in the instance of the Buddha himself we have the maximum case of the age-long growth of spiritual excellence. The Buddha (any Buddha) is the end-result of countless existences of consistent effort toward self-perfection. It was millions upon millions of years ago when he as a monk came into contact with the then Buddha, and made a vow that he himself would become a Buddha in ages to come. Since that time he had been maturing the vow by virtuous living in successive existences. In those existences he achieved the fullness of moral-spiritual attainment in perfecting the ten *pāramī*'s: charity, morality, patient resignation, vigor, meditation, wisdom, skilfullness in teaching, power over obstacles, spiritual aspiration, and knowledge.

Likewise it is true, in a manner suggesting the Christian doctrine of the Incarnation, that only "in the fullness of time" when everything had been prepared, could the Buddha appear in human form. The degree of elaboration of the theme depends upon the particular scripture involved, but a common pattern is as follows: The Buddha-to-be was in the Tusita heaven. The other glorious beings there approached him and told him that it was time to appear in the world as a Buddha. The only woman fit to bear a Buddha (because of her purity and character) had been selected, and would bear him in virgin birth—after which she would die within a week, since it was not proper that a Buddha's mother should bear other children after his birth. Even the manner of the birth itself, and the first acts of the Buddha, were of a supremely miraculous nature.

However one wishes to interpret such accounts in detail, the main ethical implication is clear: Good character, particularly on the level of sainthood, is not something easily or suddenly come by. It must be continuously and assiduously cultivated through a multitude of successive life-times. Thus when one encounters a saint, let alone a Buddha, he realizes that he is in the presence of an ages-old persistent will-to-virtue. And so it is that the true saint is always to be highly revered, far above the gods who are merely expending all the accumulated good results of past virtue in lazy fashion without adding thereto.

This facet clearly modifies the crassness of the merit doctrine in the direction of a strengthening of the concept of cumulative worth, or intrinsic goodness, as its essential meaning. For when one thinks of ages of meritorious actions that have finally resulted in the worldly detachment of saintly character that is devoid of the desire for rebirth in any form, then clearly such merit is a matter of increasing inner worth rather than outward success. Here the quantitatively infinite has been transmuted into the qualitatively transcendent; the successive multiplication of ordinary virtues, plus the compound interest of the kammic process, has produced the absolute good.

It may be observed in connection with the immensities of time and effort required to produce saints and Buddhas, that though this immeasurably deepens the value and meaning of moral character in general and the saintly life in particular, it also introduces what we may call the slow-tempo, passive-virtue mood into the ethical life of Buddhism. If a saint comes in to being only after a thousand life-times of meritorious living and a Buddha only after countless millions of life-times of one-pointed strenuous endeavor, there will be many who will not find it in their hearts to unduly hasten the process. Sainthood and Buddhahood, so very very far away along the high hard road! Indeed, the more revered they become, the less hope has the common man to arrive where they stand. It is much easier to honor them with reverence, and hope that this reverence will count in the long run to his account, than to take a vow to become a Buddha or begin the long ascent to sainthood. Besides, will not those who are ready to be saints be "called" to that high level of attainment when they are truly ready? That is, will one not feel the urge to sainthood when and if his past Kamma, now beyond his reach, has prepared him for it?[29]

---

[29] There is obviously an interesting parallelism here with some forms of Christian predestination: If one is elected of God to salvation, he will be moved to repentance whether he will or not. For him divine grace will be truly irresistible. So runs one version.

So also a slow-tempo passivity has to some extent characterized the social applications of the Buddhist ethic. Kamma has
often represented the equivalent of the Christian "will of God.'
Just as Christians in some periods have taken the status quo–
which obviously could not exist without God's willing it to exist–
as the divine order of things, not to be struggled against, so Buddhism has often seen in present situations the just results of
Kamma. If a man be diseased, or wicked, or society cruel, no
doubt each sufferer is only reaping his just deserts. Besides, what
permanent improvement can be made in the world of samsara,
or birth-death-suffering? But however much this has been the
flavor of Buddhism in some periods and places, we must not
take it as the only reaction of which Buddhism is capable, ethically speaking. At a later point we shall observe that under
contemporary conditions considerable effort is being made to
reinterpret the kammic ethic in terms of the more active pursuit
of both personal and social good.

We may look at the same matter in another way, in terms of
what may be called the *kammic potential* of the self. Here we
must refer to the earlier distinction of the interpretations of
the self: The momentary, unreal self composed of the five khandhas, and referred to as anatta or no-self; and the long-term self
or kammic continuity that persists in one way or another from
birth to birth as personality-producing potential. If we look at
any man in *cross-section* at any given moment and empirically
analyze what we find, we see only the self of composite nature,
the anatta, that has no real being or substance. But when we take
the momentary self in its kammic context as the embodiment of
some type of *cumulative* continuity and individuality that persists through the ages, then we have added an important dimension to selfhood.

It is this long-term self to which the term "kammic potential"
applies. A man's kammic potential consists in those empirically
undiscoverable elements which are nonetheless attached directly
to the empirically observable man according to Buddhism. To
the concrete historical being who stands before us in visible
form, or whom we know more directly in our own persons, we
must add the invisible but very potent aura of his kammic past,
a margin of unexpected, unpredictable tendency or power for

good or evil. This is the unknown self by which Buddhism explains those strange differences between similarly nurtured individuals; this explains those unexpected, seemingly out-of-character actions, powers, and desires in an individual. They are the basis for all of the apparently sudden transformations of character, of conversions either to good or evil.

As such this adds a tremendously important element to human selfhood. It makes the human self much more substantial and dynamic than the anatta doctrine, taken by itself, would suggest. Here there is a core of solid character, or hidden roots, that may be developed for the future in full confidence, since Kamma will guard and preserve them for us and in us. The ethical implication is two-fold: In ourselves we must nourish and cultivate whatever roots of goodness there may be, by deeds of virtue; and suppress, and finally eradicate, whatever of evil potential lies hidden within. For the Buddhist teaching is that each type of action stirs up and "attracts" the latent power (potential) within one's kammic heritage. There are "forces of purity" within one's past, as one meditation master puts it, that may be called into an active role in one's present life, if he attracts them to him by virtue and by meditation. The same holds for the evil potentialities. But as we have seen, the balance of Buddhist opinion is that human nature tends toward virtue rather than vice; and to parody the Quaker phrase, there is "that of goodness" in every man which is more fundamental than his evil—else how could one *ever* escape from the lower planes?

Whatever the finer shades of interpretation, the situation is clear. The self is not merely the empirical not-self of our direct observation; there is a larger and hidden self which can contribute to our salvation if only we exploit its hidden treasures of power and goodness by appropriate disciplines. The likeness to the Christian teaching of Divine Grace which surrounds us, invisibly but certainly, to strengthen our apparent weakness and in seemingly miraculous fashion save us from disaster, is unmistakable. So also is the necessity of being prepared to receive works of grace. And this the Buddhist sometimes recognizes:

> What others call Grace we name right effort and faculties latent in us only waiting to be discovered, developed, and used.

Only by the application of such hidden forces do we become genuine Buddhists, the followers of the Perfect One.[30]

The difference is that what the Christian calls God, the Buddhist calls one's past accumulation of Kamma, self-produced; but in either case there is the Larger Self inclusive of the invisibilities of moral potential.

The second implication is in respect to our treatment of others. One must not judge them hastily, for they too are possessed of a hidden self of kammic potential that must be taken account of in all reactions to them. There must be a deep tolerance here because of our knowledge that every man is handicapped by some roots of evil in him, shown by his unexpected weaknesses; and at the same time a great faith that there may well be in him deep roots of goodness that will respond to our loving-kindness. In a word, though one may not respect a man for his immortal soul, or because he is made in the image of God, Buddhistically speaking he *must* respect him for his kammic potentiality, the possibility that he may in the long run become a saint, or even a Buddha, no matter how unlikely seeming at the moment.

One final comment: It is of course only at the highest level of sainthood (arahatship) that kammic potentiality for good has become kammic *actuality*. In such an one there are no hidden areas, either of good or bad, in his self-hood; no surprises of grace or depravity within, await him. All evil roots have been totally extracted; all kammic demerit, save perhaps some few results which may manifest themselves in bodily misfortune or weakness, is exhausted in him. But his "forces of purity," i.e. accumulations of past good kamma, plus the Nibbana element (*Nibbāna dhātu*) have combined to transform his psychic nature into pure "goodness" and even affect his bodily structure. That larger and hidden self has now become the real and actual self, as visible as it is possible for ultimate spiritual realities to become in space-time. The pure, the true, human self or mind is now in complete control, i.e. the saint is fully *attā* or self, save for the body; and that will soon pass away.

---

[30] Thera Nyanasatta, "Practical Buddhism," *Light of the Dhamma*, I, No. 3, (April, 1953), 38.

3. Conclusion and Transition

Thus is the sentient self set in the massive beginningless and meaningless cycles of the rise and fall of universes and the infinity of transformations called the "births" and "deaths" of individuals; and all of it from the highest immaterial plane to the lowest hell is governed by impartial, inexorable Kamma. But extensive and universal as this vast realm ruled by Kamma may be, it is not absolutely all-inclusive. There *is* a realm of reality, and a kind of living suited thereto, that are not under the power of Kamma. This is that ultimate Reality of realities called Nibbana; and it is also the saintly life that is "beyond" morality in the kammic sense, even though it is held that good kammic actions lead one Nibbana-ward—though not quite through its gates.

Thus in the end the ethical significance of Kamma is ambiguous. Or perhaps it is better to say that its ethical significance is relative, not absolute. For kammic evils are only temporary evils, and kammic goods only half-way houses on the way toward the truly good. Kammic goodness is the necessary but not sufficient condition for either the saintly life or the attainment of Nibbana. True perfection is transcendent of all kammic values.

Indeed kamma and all that it represents are a bondage and danger to the life of the saint in the final analysis. He must kick away from under him the laboriously built ladder of kammic merit by which he has risen toward sainthood, and take to the transcendental flight on the wings of super-normal (super-kammic) wisdom. By definition the saint is one who has escaped from Kamma altogether. So long as he remains in the slightest degree bound by kammic goods, say even the desire to continue as a glorious being in the highest heavens in a formless state, so long will he be unable to attain to the *Supremely* Highest. The abundance of that good Kamma itself which raises one to such a realm, and the love even of the highest kind of goodness to be found in the realm of Kamma, no matter how much preferable to the love of evil, bind him more subtly and dangerously than before to the realm of time and space, that is, birth, death, and suffering.

Thus everything in the realm of Kamma and rebirth, points to the necessity for a transcendent goal and a transcendent way to it. For as Dr. Malalasekera puts it: "The ethics of Buddhism is prompted by one motive only, the need for release from Samsara, the round of rebirth and death."[31] Nibbana, and the Path to Nibbana or the Way of the Saint, are the Buddhist response to this necessity. For Nibbana is utterly beyond Kamma— in Christian terms, a goal beyond history. It cannot be understood or appropriated in kammic terms. And what is the essential nature of this Goal and its Way? What is the result for Buddhist ethics of its incommensurability with Kamma? How can Buddhism determine its values and the means thereto, with two radically different contexts to work in? Such will be the problem of the next chapters.

---

[31] G. P. Malalasekera, "Buddhism," *Light of the Dhamma,* I, No. 2 (January, 1953), 57.

CHAPTER III

Thus far the Buddhist formulation of ethical values has been considered under two aspects: as an internalized process of self-perfection; and as that same process set in the context of an infinite number of successive rebirths. With regard to each of these it has been impossible to avoid references to that ultimate and transcendent goal of all ethical process and development, Nibbana. For self-perfection attains to Nibbana as its absolute consummation; and the chain of successive rebirths is meaningless unless it leads onward toward the attainment of Nibbana.

Therefore since all Buddhist roads in the end lead to this Supreme Goal of human moral and spiritual endeavor, we must now turn to consider its nature and its relation to all lower goods found in the kammic context of values. And as has been indicated before, it is this very supremacy and transcendency by Nibbana of all time-space realities that constitutes the basic problem for the understanding of the Buddhist ethic, particularly when we seek to relate it organically to the mundane values and concerns of that space-time realm in which human beings actually live. Temporarily the problem of the historical origin and meaning of the tension will be by-passed. The Nibbana-Kamma tension will be considered in terms of the present Buddhist value-structure as it now stands with regard to the ethical influence that the nibbanic concept and experience exercise therein. And first to be considered is the general subject of ethical relativism and absolutism of which the Kamma-Nibbana tension represents the specifically Buddhist form.

1. Ethical Relativism and Absolutism in Buddhist Ethic

It must be said in the beginning that the problem of absolute and relative value in Buddhist ethics is no simple one. For there are strong currents of both relativism and absolutism to be found here, and their intermingling and transposition make their relationship a complex matter. Sometimes one is persuaded that all is relativistic, especially in the Kamma-rebirth context. But again, as we have seen, there is in Theravada Buddhism at least, a strong sense that even the basic Five Precepts are absolute moral laws of the universe. Sometimes, which emphasis prevails appears to be only a matter of the context or level of discourse. And finally we must mention again the ethic-transcending flavor of Nibbana, with an absolutism of its own, that pervades the total situation.

We may begin by noticing first the relativistic statement; and it is very frequent. Most Theravadins will insist, for example, that there is no real metaphysics in Buddhism—though the Abhidhammic schema of the constitution of the self and its various states may be considered a functional substitute for metaphysics, since perhaps the world of the inner mind is the most real world of all. And it must also be added that there is a considerable cosmology in Buddhism which embraces such matters as the rise and fall of world systems and the structure of a complete set of heavenly worlds and purgatorial realms. But with regard to such matters as to whether the physical universe had a beginning in time or not, whether it will come to an absolute end, whether a sentient being exists or does not exist upon reaching Nibbana, and like matters—called indeterminables—orthodox Buddhism refuses to posit any theory at all.

Likewise Buddhism finds no God in the universe, i.e. no supreme Creator, First Cause, Moral Will, or ultimate purposiveness. The universe is conceived to be only an impersonal meaningless process whose ultimate nature—beyond the fact that it is a patterned process and flux—cannot be discerned. Hence there is no ultimate moral structure or pattern by which man may guide his own conduct. A contemporary statement of this general viewpoint follows:

> We must accept the fact that the cosmos is indifferent to human values. The physical universe gives no indication whatsoever of a beneficent deity or a purpose. . . . The life process is a blind satisfaction of desire. . . . In Buddhism the only higher purpose is what man puts into it.[1]

Another slightly different statement emphasizes the relativity and irrelevance of such terms as good and bad in the Buddhist context:

> With regard to 'good' the one question to be investigated is whether or not a religion tends to produce a tranquilized mind working in perefct equilibrium. This is the ideal of Buddhism. . . .
> 'Virtue and Vice' as understood by theists are not found in Buddhism. The closest Buddhist equivalent of these terms may be regarded as beneficial and harmful actions—profitable or unprofitable for deliverance of the mind from craving. From this it must be obvious that they are wholly subjective in their results. . . .
> The question of the objective results of an action, whether there be any or not, does not concern a Buddhist at all at the time of his action. He is concerned primarily with his own frame of mind irrespective of objective results.[2]

Thus both on the cosmic and personal levels we seem to be moving toward a completely relativistic and individualistic ethical valuation. There is no overall moral structure of value in the cosmos to which a man may, must, or should conform; he may project his own values into the situation according to his own fanciful desire, for logically one set of values is as good as any other. And, as suggested in the second quotation, in the moment of concrete action a person need not, indeed should not, have any concern for the results of his actions upon others. To state the seeming logic of the above statements in

---

[1] "Buddhism—The Religion of the Age of Science," an address delivered to the Conference on Religion in the Age of Science, Star Island, New Hampshire, August, 1958, by the Honorable U Chan Htoon.

[2] M. Ninananda Bhikkhu, "The Right Knowledge of the Path to Bliss," *Light of the Dhamma*, I, No. 3 (April, 1953), 7, 12.

its extremest form: To kill another being is "bad," *not* because it destroys another living being or disrupts social order, but because it may destroy and disrupt the peace of mind of the killer and cause his rebirth in one of the hells.

There is the further factor of the ambiguous ethical quality of the kammic process itself. What, indeed, *is* the true meaning of ethical badness and goodness in the kammic context? There seems to be in actuality, whatever the theory of kammic justice, an essential alteration of ethical significance between kammic cause and kammic result as noted in the previous chapter. When "bad" and "good" are used to describe the kammic *cause*, i.e. those actions which produce kammically determined results in the future, they are used in the purely ethical sense of ethically desirable or undesirable actions. But when the same adjectives are used with regard to kammic *result*, i.e. those states or conditions that follow from the morally good and bad causes in accordance with the law of Kamma, *then* they are usually defined in materialistic and hedonistic terms. That is to say: The "good" *result* of an ethically "good" action, such as a charitable deed, is a state of pleasurable existence replete with such *non*-moral, materialistic goods as health, beauty, wealth, fame, good fortune, peaceful old age, many loyal friends or perhaps aeons of existence in the glorious deva-worlds. And conversely the "bad" ethical cause produces a "bad" result whose badness consists in disease, pain, misfortune, disfigurement, poverty, and aeons of existence in the hells.

It is true that sometimes moral results are mentioned. The good deed of a former existence or past period of life produces a good disposition or strengthened character. But as we have abundantly illustrated in the previous chapter, the predominant emphasis in the kammic context is upon the non-ethical results of ethical action. And though we take account of the fact that for Buddhism the physically pleasant is considered to be an integral part of the complete good, the ethical ambiguity present in the operation of kammic justice is not completely cleared away.

Again we seem to be led toward a relativist and instrumentalist conception of ethical good, characterized by hedonistic overtones, that throws suspicion even upon the ethical integrity of the casual elements or actions. For if an action is called "good" because it will produce a materialistically pleasant state of being in the future, and only for that reason, then what does it signify to call it "good," except that it is *good for* producing such results? Hence we must say that charitableness is good, not in and for itself, and hatred bad, not in and for itself, but because each type of attitude in the end produces a pleasant or unpleasant psychophysical state of being in the loving or hating man.

Yet there are several considerations which prevent one from assuming that this is the final and fully valid conclusion. One instantly calls to mind the general moralistic flavor of Buddhist tradition and practice. There is nothing in it to suggest antinomian or libertine tendencies—save perhaps in some Tantric expressions and even these need to be read carefully. Especially in a staunch Theravada country like Burma one may speak even of a species of ethical puritanism which characterizes the Buddhist tradition in most respects. The basic tenets of Buddhist morality are in some sense at least regarded as absolutes even by the ordinary layman, though he may not observe them absolutely. And so also the long historical reputation of Theravada Buddhism as a sober, rationalistic moralism bears witness to the same.

The conviction that the principles enshrined in the Five Precepts are part of the eternal order of Dhamma (as stated by Bhikshu Sangharakshita) does indeed find some explicit expression among Theravada Buddhists at the present time. If one specifically questions them about the Precepts, most will affirm that they embody universally valid moral principles. With regard to the First Precept it might be stated thus: It is always wrong in any situation in any culture in any age in any universe to kill any creature whatsoever.[3] How much more absolutist

---

[3] Such is the substance of an opinion expressed to the author in conversation by Professor U Aung Than, head of the Pali Department of the University of Rangoon. But the nagging question remains: *Why* is killing always wrong? Because killing always results in unpleasant results for the killer? It remains also with regard to what is said below about "intrinsically" good attitudes. Are they intrinsically good because they always result in good fortune?

than this can one be? Or one may push the analysis a little further from the act itself on to the attitude underlying it. Buddhists often affirm that all anger whatsoever, even of the most diluted sort such as is present in mere preferences, i.e. liking one person or situation or food less than another, is wrong per se. Many would say that hatred and greed are *never* good in any conceivable universe; they are *intrinsically* evil. And conversely, lovingkindness, compassion and sympathetic joy as attitudes (though not necesssarily in all their expressions) are always good.

We must also note that there are absolutist portrayals of kammic justice, whatever the ethical ambiguity of kammic rewards. (Perhaps one can say that Kamma operates in absolute fashion, i.e. absolutely impartially and inexorably, whatever we think of the ethical quality of its results.) For though the Buddhist usually avoids calling Kamma a Moral Order, sometimes it *is* so called. Thus rather surprisingly we find the essential moral nature of the Universe strongly emphasized by these very authors who also seem to deny it. To quote from Justice U Chan Htoon again:

> To begin with, it must be understood that in the Buddhist system there is no place for a Creator god. There is moral law and moral order, and these principles are supreme. . . . The moral order works through the continuum of events on the psychophysical level which we call life. It is the spiritual aspect of the law of cause and effect that prevails in the physical universe.

And even more cosmically still:

> Faith in spiritual values is part of the logic of Buddhism. The universe is governed by a moral principle which is self-existent in its causal laws and so forms part of its essential mechanism.[4]

A "moral order" may not be a "Moral Order," but when it is "self-existent" and "governs" the universe, the difference seems negligible. And it seems perilously close to asserting what was so vigorously denied in the previous quotation from the same author—that there is a purpose in the universe. For there

---

[4] From an address to the Sixteenth Congress of the International Association for Religious Freedom, Chicago, 1958, in privately printed pamphlet form, p. 11.

seems on the face of it, at least, to be contradiction in the conception of a universe which is absolutely indifferent to human values and is yet governed at its very center by self-existent moral laws that inexorably "enforce" the maxims of a specific (Buddhist) moral creed. The answer—satisfactory in Buddhist eyes at least—is that one may have a moral law and its order without a Moral Lawgiver or a Moral Purpose in the universe. Or otherwise stated: a mathematically conceived, mechanically operated system of cause and effect is identical with providential, personalized justice in its results and meaning.

Of course one *may* interpret the sheerly quantitative absoluteness of kamma, that it always and in very tangible ways works out its inexorable results, as a kind of parable. The very insistence upon the element of mechanical inexorability and mathematical exactness of good and bad consequences may be Buddhism's way of symbolically affirming the *intrinsic* absoluteness of moral distinctions. Though its materialistic and quantitative garb seems to hide its ethical purity, the doctrine of Kamma is intended to make the majesty of the ethical absolutes apparent to all, particularly the less mature. Mechanical absoluteness is the incarnation of the eternal qualitative absolutes in space-time forms. However this is probably a non-Buddhist fantasy found only in the author's mind; for I have never seen the matter stated thus in Buddhist writings of the Theravada tradition, where Kamma and its results are taken, as the rule, in all literalness. The most that one can say in this context is that perhaps, even in the realm of Kamma and rebirth, there is a kind of absoluteness of moral principle and substance embodied in the doctrine of Kamma itself, and that moral principle is considered ideally to be binding upon the devout Buddhist under all circumstances.

Leaving the Absolutely Absolute (Nibbana) out of consideration for a little longer, it may be of interest to inquire how the Buddhist actually lives with his limited absolutes. How can he bring even the absolutes of non-killing, non-lying, non-stealing, non-hatred, or non-greed into line with the relativities of ordinary existence?

We may of course expect to find in Buddhism, as in Western religion, the all-too-familiar gulf between the ideal and the actuality. Many a religious creed makes absolute denials and affirmations concerning the good life but practically, or even theoretically for that matter, finds a multitude of creed-saving compromises both necessary and possible. Much of this is involved here also. The Buddhist as easily as any other can live alongside his own compromises with absolute virtue with a degree of comfort. But there is an important difference as well between the Eastern tradition in general, and the Buddhist and Hindu traditions in particular, and the Western Christian tradition with regard to ethical absolutes and ethical practices. This we may call the doctrine of levels—levels of ethical situation and moral capacity.

The contrast with the Judeo-Christian tradition in this respect may be stated as follows: Judeo-Christian tradition does indeed recognize that practical compromises with ethical and religious absolutes will occur in human life—and has made many of them to prove its point. Indeed it has been more conscious of the necessity of such compromise, in some respects, than either Buddhism or Hinduism. The strong Jewish sense of history, in which context the believer is always working out some adaptation or manifestation of the absolute in time-space forms, keeps the believer always aware of the gulf between actual and ideal, temporal and eternal; no haze of the infinite distances involved in a view in which only the individual and the Absolute are real, and have endless existences in which to approach each other, hides the sharpness of the ideal-real contrast from his eyes. Hence, *any* approximation of the actual to the ideal is both urgent and difficult. The Christian realizes both the height of the absolute in all its sheerness, and the shortness of time which he has to introduce it into the actual visible order.

Thus he becomes a master compromiser. The method of love is ideal, but some semblance of its fruits must be achieved by the coercive justice of social ordinance. Man ought not to sin, but he does continually do so; some of his most grievous sins indeed are committed by him in his very zeal to achieve the eternal ideal in time-and-space actuality, here and now! Therefore there must be forgiveness both between men themselves, and man and God, to heal the breach between the ideal and actual worlds. Compromise, failure, and evil are the stuff of which historical action is made.

Yet when he has made all due allowances for human frailty and excused his unaccountably "bad" results wrought with "good" intention, the Christian still finds his unachieved absolutes weighing heavily on his conscience. The absolute demand, the wrath of God, the sense of impending judgment, still permeate the situation with a sense of inherent wrongness. Even forgiveness, that balm for the conscience of the compromiser, is itself the recognition of the continuing relevance of the absolute demand to the actual situation. One must be forgiven because he has failed to achieve absolute purity and goodness; and though forgivable, moral imperfection is always guilt-bearing, even in its forgiven form. Even the sometimes elaborate casuistry of some moralists who have conclusively proven that men do not *really* sin against the absolute by their compromises, evidences only a continuingly bad conscience in the matter. And as a result of this persistent awareness of the absolutes in his tradition, even the lapsed Judeo-Christian expresses his disinherited concern with eternal absolutes by creating their non-religious images in absolute rules, principles, laws, and reforms that admit of no exception.

With Hinduism and its offspring, Buddhism, however, the fact of the incapacity of most men to achieve even a reasonable facsimile of moral absoluteness in their lives is frankly and fully recognized. The principle of the accommodation of absolute standards and distinctions to relative situations is not admitted surreptitiously through a side door into the religious edifice, to remain there as an officially unacknowledged visitor, as has happened so often in Judeo-Chistianity. But the principle of accommodation to human weakness is welcomed at the front door as an honored and beloved guest. "Yes," says the Buddhist, "the Five Precepts do represent absolute principles which ideally all men ought to observe in all their absoluteness. But only the saint is actually called upon to do so in actuality, because he alone has the capacity to live according to absolutes." And this is the key to the Buddhist understanding of man's ethical predicament. One can approach the ethical absolutes in practice only so far as his capacity allows him to; the degree to which he has matured his *pāramī*'s or perfections, in past lives, determines his present capacity for approaching perfection. Actual performance in the present is the only genuine evidence which we have for the existence of such kammic potential for perfection. He who *does* not, apparently *can*not!

Of course the Buddhist, like the Christian even of the most predestinarian conviction, continues, as the rule, to exhort the less devout in the hope that improvement may (illogically) come about; that his hidden kammic potential may finally come into action. But the fact remains that the Buddhist extends to the weaker brother a far greater degree of tolerance than the Christian. For how can one know, the Buddhist would ask, unless he be an omniscient Buddha, what lies in the hidden past of another? How can we attempt to coerce him into ethical performance according to one absolute rule which is held to be binding upon all men alike, whatever their capacities? Considering the infinite range of kammic being and past history, such coercion is sheer fanaticism.

There is also a socio-historical extension of this doctrine of levels. Not only does one's past kamma define the quality and level of his present personal capacity, ethically speaking; it tends to cast him into a certain social position at birth. He is born there as the inevitable result of past lives. And this in conjunction with his inner capacities or incapacities, makes it almost inevitable that he shall become a business man, a public servant, a farmer, a professional man, or what have you in the family heritage. And in that profession or position certain duties are incumbent upon him, those that may interfere with his full observance of the moral precepts, as when a head of state or army officer must command and carry out the destruction of human life. Therefore one must not condemn even those whose occupations seem inconsistent with Buddhist moral principles, for such occupations are the result of a man's past Kamma and socially necessary in the world of Kamma.

Do we then have a complete relativity in which no given rules or standards can be considered binding upon anyone, either because of individual variations in capacity or kammically destined situations, or both together? *Logically* it might seem that complete relativism follows from complete tolerance; but *practi-*

cally this is not the case. All due allowance must be made for individual variations of capacity and situation, yet certain basic or minimal laws of human conduct—observance at least externally of the Five Precepts for example—*are* binding upon all, whatever their kammic background. No good Buddhist really excuses laxity here and he countenances social penalties for disregarding such basics. So also a man must fulfill the obligations of his social position or the agreements that he has made, even when these seem somewhat at variance with the absolute keeping of Buddhist principles.[5]

But there remain ways in which the individual may yet serve the Buddhist truth even in socially compulsive situations. Those in public position can counteract the possibly evil effects of their non-Buddhist actions by a kind of compensatory building up of their *pāramī's* (perfections) by the private performance of good deeds, by trying to keep wrong attitudes down to the minimum through meditative discipline, and by a personally disinterested and emotionally detached performance of their official duties.[6] So in a real measure the individual may find a way to serve the absolute principles even in the midst of his compromising social commitments. But if he becomes absolutely convinced that his present calling is dangerously compromising his pursuit of the good life, and feels within himself the power for a contemplative vocation, he may leave the world and enter the Order.

---

[5] A curious, but possibly extreme example of this, is that of the courtesan who, because she is faithful for the agreed-upon time to the man who has purchased her favors, is adjudged worthy of great reward because she has performed an "act of truth."

[6] As it was once expressed to the author by a member of the Buddhist Democratic Party of Burma who was urging the direct application of Buddhist teaching to statesmanship: "The beauty of Buddhism is that a man can always cleanse himself from all his evil deeds"—by means of detachment through meditation and because no sin's consequences last forever. This was said in specific connection with military service. This appears to be approaching the Bhagavad-Gita's principle of "action without attachment." Presumably if an army officer be required to kill, he may do it with a minimum of anger, maintain his inner spiritual discipline of detachment, and thus minimize the evil kammic effects.

2. Nibbana: Transcendent Summum Bonum

But whatever the tensions between more or less absolute elements in the area of kammic morality, or between the actual and the ideal, the most fundamental tension has only been touched on. For in the last analysis, when all the ethical distinctions possible in the space-time world of Kamma have been made, they turn out to be ultimately relative even in their absolutest absoluteness. Even though Kamma is the active principle of absolute justice (the *moral* expression of that Dhamma which is elsewhere expressed in the world-order delineated by science) it is still related to time-space entitles and conditions. And all of the goods and evils found in the realm of Kamma are likewise conditioned and relative. It is only when we confront all grades of ethical distinction and all types of conduct with the demands of the Absolute Goal, Nibbana, that we can speak with assurance about true values.

In what sense we may call Nibbana an *ethical* entity needs to be carefully considered. But even before we come to this examination we can affirm in principle its crucial role in Buddhist ethic. For whatever shade of metaphysical opinion or denial of it, or variety of ethical relativism or absolutism, one may find among Buddhists, certainly all Theravadins agree that Nibbana is the one supremely good and ultimate element known to Buddhist experience; it is the one unquestioned Absolute that allows of no degrees in its reality or desirability.[7] Therefore it is the final destination to which all quest of ethical good finally leads, whether it be ethical per se or not. Because it is that fundamental truth-reality beside which all else is temporary and illusory, it becomes the supreme arbiter of all moral values at every level in the Buddhist ethical structure.

---

[7] Of course some Mahayanist versions of Buddhism, like Nagarjuna's "nihilism" denied the reality of suffering, deliverance from suffering, the Buddha, and the ultimate distinction between Nibbana and the realm of rebirth. But this appears to have been a dialectical play on words whose main purpose was to reduce mere logical reasoning to the futility of inherent contradiction when it dealt with reality, in order to open the door to a kind of experiential absolute of intuitional realization. At the very least this was the introduction of the *un*conditioned *quality* of Nibbana into the conditioned realm of space-time thinking.

If, then, we shall seek for the truly absolute elements in Buddhist ethic, either in history, action, or attitude, we will find that no matter what is said about them in other contexts, their final worth can be judged only in relation to Nibbana. To be sure the relation of such elements to Nibbana is seldom spelled out. If at all, it is usually only in terms of a negative disjunction: "This value may be good in one sense, but it does not lead to Nibbana." Nor can we expect any clear schematized table of ethical values in terms of their nibbanic likeness; such is not the Buddhist approach to Nibbana. But what we *may* hope is to estalish some pattern of priorities; or to discern some lines of force, so to speak, in Buddhist ethical structure, leading from the lower levels to the Highest.

To do this it will first be necessary to answer the basic question: What is the nature of Nibbana itself? Once this is established, we may ask with regard to any action, state of mind, or attitude: Does it partake of the intrinsic nature of Nibbana? Or, if too far down in the scale of values to be thus described, does it conduce toward the final realization of Nibbana *more* than an alternative action or attitude? When these questions can be answered in the affirmative then we can be certain that such actions and attitudes partake of goodness in the absolute sense.

First then we shall turn to the characterization of Nibbana and secondly to the discovery of those elements of experience that Nibbana draws to itself, as like to like.

As with all true religious ultimates, Nibbana is essentially indescribable. Buddhism in all its varieties is especially insistent at this point. Indescribability, whether of sensible or super--sensible realities, is perhaps the mark of ultimacy per se. What can be described in words, be it the color blue, the taste of apples, Tao, God, the Absolute, or Nibbana, is something this side of the ultimate ultimacy of the experience itself, and, of course, of that of which the experience is an experience. And no religion has been more insistent upon the ineffability of the experience and the indescribability of its ultimate, than Buddhism. So it is that concerning Nibbana there are many qualitative implications but few substantial statements—save that it cannot be substantially described. Frequently, indeed, the flavor of the "descriptive" terms is almost entirely negative. Etymologically there is some difference of opinion about the precise root meaning of the term Nibbana, but all the accepted meanings are negative in quality: the going out of a fire for lack of fuel; to blow out; extinction; cessation. And this theme of cessation is writ large in Theravada interpretations of Nibbana, both in their generalized and particularized forms.

Sometimes it is spoken of as the extinction of greed, hatred, and delusion, and that alone, with no further description or metaphysical implication. Or again it may be termed "Freedom from Desire," referring to the final destruction of that mainspring of all continued existence as a sentient being, Craving *(taṇhā)*, or the thirst to be, in some form or other. Still again it may be considered as the absolute end of the delusion of the separate reality of selves, one's own in particular, but also all selves and all physical entities in general. It is the bringing to an end of all this series of nightmarish existences that we call life, which in themselves are only a succession of shadowy body-mind states compounded of momentarily combining elements.

Thus if we take Theravada Buddhism seriously in what it says, or chooses to emphasize from the scriptures, its basic conviction about Nibbana is clear: Nibbana is the consummation of the anatta (no-self) doctrine. Progress toward Nibbana may be portrayed as the progressive realization of the emptiness of all selfhood. First one comes to know and approve the anatta doctrine intellectually; life and selves are not entities but compounded elements that are in continual flux. Then, by the meditational discipline, he experiences its truth first-hand within his own body and consciousness. He directly "'realizes" the changing states within his body and consciousness, the momentary rise and disappearance of his feelings, thoughts, and even consciousness itself. And finally there is the full "going-out" in Nibbana.

Now all suggestion that they do not literally mean what they say when they talk of the utter cessation of individual existence is stoutly resisted by Theravadins. They flatly reject the Mahayanist or Hindu interpretations of anatta doctrine and nibbanic cessation as referring only to the destruction of a "lower" or "'narrow" self while the "higher" or "larger" Self persists on into some kind of Super or cosmic SELF. It is often reiterated that Nibbana is the *full end* of self, the absolute termination of individualized existence, "the graveyard of the mind." Consciousness in all its forms, as that which makes and clings to distinctions and hence creates fictitious entities and selves and lays the foundation for future existence, is utterly destroyed. Thus:

> Nibbana is a single, i.e. uncompounded element, a Real existing in its own right and different from the conditioned phenomena of mind and matter, which exist only as compound states. . . . So . . . neither in Nibbana is there a self apart from this single element. Hence there is no experiencer.[8]

There are other considerations, however, which seem to speak of the transcendence of Nibbana rather than of its purely negative character. There is the constantly reiterated claim that though Nibbana is indescribable, it *is* experienceable. Thus writes a contemporary author:

> Experience and non-existence are both conditional and relative to each other. Nibbana which is "Absolute" cannot be designated as being either existence or non-existence. Therefore Nibbana which is incomprehensible and profound, can only be realized by those who have attained it and have passed beyond both limitations, existence and non-existence.[9]

Apparently it is the full realization of Nibbana after the death of the saint that is spoken of here, i.e. *khandha-parinibbāna* or "full extinction of the elements of existence." Nonetheless it is apparently somehow *experienceable* even after death, for it is qualitatively described. And there is besides the fact that the nibbanic quality of life may be experienced here and now in earthly life—which is Nibbana considered as the "full extinction of defilements" or *kilesa-parinibbāna*. This latter is Nibbana experienced as the extinction of greed, hatred, delusion, and all other desires that bind one to existence; and contemporary

---

[8] W. F. Jayasuriya, "Introduction to Abhidhamma," *Light of the Buddha*, III, No. 4 (April, 1958), 19. For the phrase "graveyard of the mind" I am indebted to Dr. R. L. Soni, of Mandalay, Burma.

[9] U Ba Thaw, "Exposition of Knowledge in the Eightfold Noble Path," Part IV, *Light of the Buddha*, V, No. 1 (January, 1960), 2.

Theravadins are most insistent upon the *present* possibility of this experience of freedom from defilement and attachment. Indeed this hope of an increasing approximation to nibbanic serenity, or perhaps what we might call a this-life participation in Nibbana, is a very moving hope to Buddhists. It represents to them what the livingness of God represented to the Hebrew or the baptism of the Spirit to early Christians—an earnest of fuller glories yet to come.

It may be noted in this connection that even the negative discipline of the realization of the truth of No-self, *may* be interpreted as a technique for the realization of the more positive aspect of Nibbana as the Permanent and Unchanging Reality:

> Then he will meditate on the impermanence of conditioned things so intensely and so long that he sees the opposite . . . of impermanence, the Real Permanent, i.e. the Transcendental Summum Bonum (Nibbana) which causes the extirpation of the greed-lust, anger-hate, and delusion-bewilderment.[10]

And how can meditation on impermanence produce the realization of the Permanent? This is indeed the *via negativa*, but for Buddhism it is a genuine, *the* genuine, way to truth for all that. For before the glory of the Real can be seen, the illusion of the unreal must be dispersed. Only as we come fully to realize the complete emptiness of all things and selves, their absolute impermanence, their sheerly relative goodness, can the true nature of the really Good be identified. The lesser goods are like idols which must be cast aside before the supreme Good (God) can be known. Indeed the more intensely we realize the unreality of self and the world, says the Buddhist, the more surely will we realize the reality of Nibbana. Realization of *un*reality is but the converse of the realization of Reality.

Almost inevitably we have come to metaphysical assertions about Nibbana. Nor is this just a *Western* perversion of Buddhist emphasis; the Buddhist himself, however reluctantly, comes there sooner or later as the above quotation shows. The experiential ultimate—which Nibbana most certainly is, however

---

[10] U Po Sa, "Mind Delights in Evil," *Light of the Buddha,* III, No. 4 (April, 1958), 48.

else it may be interpreted—becomes the metaphysically ultimate in function if not in statement. The "Transcendental Summum Bonum" of experience becomes the "Real Permanent," the one Absolute by which all else in Buddhism, particularly its ethical practice, is determined.

We may note in passing, therefore, that however chary of metaphysical assertions Theravada Buddhism may be, Nibbana as a Real Permanent provides a solid existential backbone for ethical motivation. Somehow or other, "somewhere" or other— even if beyond time and space and not at all like time-space being—it *is*. That is the most unassailable fact about Nibbana— that it is. And, given Nibbana, morality is then no mere pursuit of unrealizable goods nor a merely theoretical structure of beautiful ethical ideals that are completely irrelevant to the human situation. The moral discipline is, rather, a strongly motivated pursuit of the Supremely Real and Good, whose realization depends upon the seeing of things as they are. It is positive and dynamic even though the way to it is paved with negations. As the Buddha stated it:

> Verily, there is an Unborn, Unoriginated, Uncreated, Unformed. If there were not this Unborn, Unoriginated, Uncreated, Unformed, escape from the world of the born, the originated, the created, the formed, would not be possible.[11]

Two corollary propositions flow from this quality of Nibbana as the Real Permanent, both of some ethical consequence. One is that in Buddhist thought, *reality is the complete negation of change*. Nibbana, as the great Primordial Simple, i.e. that which has no parts, no distinctions within it, is eternally the same. This indeed is the only way in which Buddhism knows how to define reality. That which changes, it views as necessarily unreal.

But it is questionable whether the word "static" should be used with regard to the Buddhist permanent. For in Western usage the connotation of this term is definitely prejudicial; what is static has no life and dynamism, and perhaps in the final

---

[11] Quoted from Mahathera Nyanatiloka, *Buddhist Dictionary* (Colombo: Frewin & Co., 1956), (*Udāna*, VIII, 3), p. 99.

analysis, no reality. This is quite contrary to the Buddhist view which finds, not life and power, but death and destruction, in the ever-changing. That which changes is *un*real and *im*potent. The changing manifests not genuine dynamism, but feverish and frustrating agitation. It is rather the unchanging and undifferentiated Absolute that is the center of reality and power. And in practical terms this means that equanimity and serenity, even detachedness, are stronger than frenetic activity because they represent a focus of balanced powers, the possibility of truly realistic and rational action undisturbed by distortive emotions or compulsive necessities. Indeed the essential dynamism of all reality, both human and cosmic, is the immutable.[12]

The other implication of the permanent reality of Nibbana is that it is *impersonal*. Or perhaps, out of consideration for Western connotations, one may say super- or supra-personal; or even better, non- or super-individual. But *any* terms that we may use here are somewhat unsatisfactory in the end. For Nibbana, or at least nibbanic realization in this life, is both a highly personal and individual matter in one sense, and in another it is the negation of all that is personal and individual. Its realization is of course completely inward to the individual; he experiences it in the impenetrable depth of his own being, by his own efforts, only for himself. He can neither share nor describe this realization. It is a state of mind rather than a state of body or sense-experience—though its realization affects the body. And when he enters the ultimate Nibbana, that of the full extinction of all the khandhas, he can take no one else with him but enters by his own private door, so to speak.

Yet on the other hand that higher consciousness (see below) which is the essential prelude to the attainment of Nibbana, and is in some sense nibbanic realization itself, is less and less personal

---

[12] One qualification needs be made here on the metaphysical level. Though Nibbana be true reality, and fully dynamic in experiential terms even to the ending of the cycle of rebirth, it is not *cosmically* creative. In no sense can Nibbana be thought of as that power which originates and sustains the natural order. This is governed by Dhamma (order, law) but since it is a passing order of things, it is entirely different from Nibbana which is eternal and immutable.

and individualized, more and more super-individual and universal, or general. One conditions himself for the higher awareness by the discipline of breaking down the walls of his own separate consciousness and fragmenting the unity of his own mental processes. Emotion and preference are detached from himself and spread to all other beings. His perfection is to become totally unaware of any difference between own-self and other-self in any respect whatsoever.

However difficult this state is to describe, it must not be taken as sheer negation of the personal, or better, of the mental. Some would say indeed, as before noted, that however different Nibbana may be from anything else that we know, it is more like the mental pole of our being than the physical. And like its shadow a strongly positive implication with definitely personalistic connotations always dogs the verbal nihilism of nibbanic definition. Though the self ceases to "exist," and though Nibbana may be "the graveyard of the mind" and the cessation of consciousness, it is nonetheless infinitely desirable, the one legitimate object of man's passionate striving for, with heart, "soul," mind, and strength. It is not an Absolute Zero of Being so much as it is the Ineffable Good and the Indescribably Blissful, that can indeed achieve only *conceptual* nullity but which is in fact *experiential* fullness and perfection.

This positive quality indeed, though usually only implied and sometimes denied, is not without some expression. Rhys Davids has compiled a list of descriptive phrases from the Buddhist scriptures, relative to Nibbana, which are quite impressive in their "'positive" quality:

> the harbour of refuge, the cool cave, the island amidst the floods, the place of bliss, emancipation, liberation, safety, the supreme, the transcendental, the uncreated, the tranquil, the home of ease, the calm, the end of suffering, the medicine for all evil, the unshaken, the ambrosia, the immaterial, the imperishable, the abiding, the further shore, the unending, the bliss of effort, the supreme joy, the ineffable, the detachment, the holy city.[13]

---

[13] *Early Buddhism,* p. 172, quoted in Bhikshu Sangharakshita, *A Survey of Buddhism* (Bangalore: Indian Institute of World Culture, 1959), p. 74.

And despite its generally negative vocabulary, Theravada Buddhism has picked up this positive interpretation of Nibbana as a basic doctrine.

Thus writes a European Singhalese monk:

In Buddhist countries of the East, however, there is as far as is known to the writer not a single Buddhist school or sect that favors now a nihilistic interpretation of Nibbana . . . as mere extinction.[14]

And other writers from Theravada countries back him up in this opinion, both with regard to the ultimate nature of Nibbana and also its proximate nature as present experience. To quote:

The Nibbana element is first and foremost a reality which is most radically different from that of the mundane elements. Yet it is more closely akin to Mind than to matter. Above all it is a state of peace, happiness and deathlessness, which is seen by saints, and had, or identified with, only by the Highest Saint (arahat) at death.[15]

And once again, in a passage that equates Nibbana with liberation:

From the Buddhist standpoint, liberation is not annihilation, on the contrary it is construction; it is also not negative but positive. It is not entering into mere void and emptiness, thereby losing oneself as some Westerners have misunderstood . . . but it is entering into Truth . . . becoming part of the Truth and going out and liberating those who are contented with mere reflection and not the reality.[16]

3. Nibbana and the Scale of Ethical Values

Thus may Nibbana be characterized, as far as it is possible to characterize it. It is actually transcendent of *every* characteriz-

---

[14] Venerable Nyanaponika, "Nibbana in the Light of the Middle Doctrine," *Light of the Dhamma*, IV, No. 3 (July, 1957), 46.

[15] W. F. Jayasuriya, "Introduction to Abhidhamma," *Light of the Buddha*, II, No. 9 (September, 1957), 17.

[16] U Ba Thaw, "The Ultimate Aim or Final Purpose of Life," *Light of the Buddha*, III, No. 4 (April, 1958), 106.

ing phase, being open only to a certain type of experiential realization. Therefore the most that can truly be said about Nibbana is that it is the changeless, timeless, supra-personal, ultimate Good and Goal of all human striving. What then are its effects upon the ethical values of that way of life which is dedicated to reaching it, that is, the Buddhist discipline? Such is the concern of the following pages.

First we may distinguish two aspects of the ethical meaning of Nibbana and its effect upon ethical values. We shall find that there are some values, states of consciousness, and related modes of conduct that can be called *intrinsically* good because they themselves partake of the nature of Nibbana. Naturally such consciousness and conduct characterize the higher ranges of saintly attainment. But there are also what we may call *instrumental* and *analogical* goods, or those deeds and attitudes that lead to Nibbana, or are more like Nibbana than their opposites. For though strictly speaking Nibbana is utterly incommensurable with anything else whatsoever, it *can* be said that peaceableness, serenity and lovingkindness in action are more nearly like it, and their practice in attitude and action more likely to lead to it, than quarrelsomeness, agitation, and hate. Thus whilst the instrumental and analogical attitudes and actions are to be found primarily on the lower levels of ordinary ethical-social life, even here we find *some* genuine likeness to and effect of Nibbana.

The basic drive in the Buddhist ethico-religious discipline of effort is, of course, to rise from the analogical and the instrumental goods to the intrinsic goodness of Nibbana itself. And therefore the whole Buddhist technique of religious living is one of effecting this transformation of the lower into the higher state. Thus it seems most meaningful to describe the effect of Nibbana upon ethical values in terms of this progression. The influence of Nibbana may be seen as a magnetic attraction of individuals up through the various levels of ethical endeavor and inner realization until their lives as saints partake of the nibbanic nature itself. To follow these lines of force in making our analysis, rather than to make clear intellectual distinctions between various levels of goodness in relation to the absolute goodness of Nibbana, is therefore to be in accord with the Buddhist experience itself. For Buddhism holds that to concern oneself overly with analytic distinctions is to deceive oneself, substituting a word-game for the actual realization of what the words refer to.

It may be observed also that this progression from the instrumental and analogical to the intrinsic goods is also a progression from the kammic to the nibbanic realm. For as we have seen, it is in the realm of Kamma that we face the questions of relativity and absoluteness of moral values, and the hand-to-hand encounter with ethical uncertainties and problems. It is there that we need to exercise ethical judgment in the making of careful but dubious distinctions between what is right and good, and what is wrong and bad. But on the nibbanic level this relativity and ethical uncertainty are past. The moral struggle and even the relativistic distinctions of the kammic realm have been transcended. Only the absolute peace and distinctionless awareness of Nibbana remain.

Yet in exactly the same degree that Nibbana and Kamma, and their respective goodnesses, contrast with each other, the tension that characterizes their relation becomes evident and is reflected in their respective ethics. Therefore in the following portrayal of the nibbanic ethical dynamic under five headings we will observe these two characteristics: (1) The progression of the ethical life from lower (instrumental, analogical) good to the higher (intrinsic) goodness of Nibbana as the essential Buddhist Ethic; (2) the everpresent tension between the kammic (this wordly, time-space) values and the nibbanic (eternal, absolute, transcendent) value. This latter aspect will be of especial importance for our later consideration of the concrete forms and tendencies within the actual expression of contemporary Buddhist ethical life, both individual and social.

a. *The Buddhist Ethic Progresses from the Conceptual Knowledge of the Good to its Experience and Realization*

This phase of the ethical dynamic grows out of, is indeed a form of, the Buddhist-Eastern preference for "realization" of the direct sort over the logical analysis of intellectual "knowledge," referred to briefly in a previous chapter. It is a direct result of the ineffability and indescribability of Nibbana itself. And this indescribability in turn is the outward form of the implicitly metaphysical nature of Nibbana as composed of both value and fact, to use Western terminology. For in Buddhist thinking, truth and reality are ultimately one; value and fact are identical on the highest level. When these two elements are separated, except for the temporary purpose of intellectual analysis, it is an indication of a lower and relativistic experience of both truth and reality. So Nibbana in its aspect of ultimate reality is also ultimate truth, or better Absolute Truth-Reality, which must be directly realized to be truly known.

This value-factness of Nibbana has important consequences for Buddhist ethical experience and language. With regard to experience it is held that knowledge and experience must move hand in hand; that each one is function of the other, or perhaps better, each is an aspect of a central progression along the Eightfold Path toward Nibbana. Of course there must be initial indoctrination and intellectual knowledge of the "truth"; and in one sense this must always precede time-wise the *experience* of the truth. But unless this intellectual apprehension of the truth leads on to a first-hand feeling-knowing awareness, it is indeed not knowledge at all in the true sense. And on the ethical side such emotionalized knowledge - in - depth is bound to transform the totality of the person's thought, motive, and action. Thus growth in ethical knowledge is growth in character; to know the truth is to be the truth in oneself. And also oppositely, unless there is the genuine transformation of the person and the enlargement of his capacity, there can be no true inward understanding and further appropriation of even the intellectual truth. The words used may be correct but their interpretation and application will be totally wrong. This of course is an existential and religious approach to ethical truth.

But there is a subtle shift of emphasis as we proceed upward in the scale of ethical growth in Buddhism, as we turn from the kammic level of truth-knowing, or truth-being, to the nibbanic. We tend to leave the inter-personal for the intra-personal good; the realm of historical action for that of mystical realization. That experience which is to be the guarantee and the incarnation of the verbal truth in actual living practice, becomes an end in itself. An *experience* of the truth replaces the experience of the *truth*. "Experience" becomes an idealized entity in itself and as such cuts off its connections with time-space entities one by one, becoming more and more internalized in the experiencing self. Thus it becomes increasingly psychologized and less and less ethicized.[17]

The movement toward experience is reflected in the matter of language. One may say that as Buddhist teaching, whether in scripture, commentary, or contemporary discussion, moves away from the context of Kamma and rebirth toward Nibbana, so also a change in the quality of its language takes place. While difficult to pin-point either in actual term or description, the change is undoubtedly there. Roughly speaking we move from good persons and good deeds toward the higher realization of the impermanence of all entities and the supreme truth of no-self. We change from the direct assertive use of such terms as good, bad, right, wrong, and evil to "good," "bad," "right," "wrong" and so forth, or to a talking about what is only "kammically good." This is the process of "rising above good and evil," or should we say above *mere* good and evil in the usual moral-istic sense. We turn away from the virtue of vigorous affirmative preference for the ethically good over the ethically evil, to the language of non-preference or detachment; we rise in the scale from loving-kindness, compassion, and sympathetic joy to neutrality or equanimity.

Or, if we characterize this change in language quality by descriptive terms, some such as the following may indicate the nature of the change: We move from the concrete and descriptive toward the "abstract"[18] and connotative; from distinction, cate-gorization, and analysis, to a synthesis of feeling-knowing in a

---

[17] This, of course, is the problem of all mysticism—though Therava-da Buddhism rejects that *title*. An ultimate real-and-good, which even in experience transcends the historical and ethical, tends to pull its experi-encers and their experiences ever away from that same historical and ethical context of values.

[18] This is not quite the right term. The *abstractness* here is not that of bare dry analysis as opposed to full descriptive portrayal or emotively conditioned terminology. It is rather abstraction from the concrete ethi-cal-social context, full of particulars of circumstance, person, and deed, to a vaguer, more psychic awareness of attitudes, to intuitive feeling and to mentalistic-mystical generalizations and entities.

more generalized awareness; from the language of a sharply personal consciousness of interpersonal relationship to an impersonal relation to all beings-in-general and an awareness of the infinitude of super-personal states and realities; from sharply positive terminology to neutral; and in the final analysis, from a fullness of speech to complete silence as best conveying supreme truth. In any case, the further language moves from the kammic toward the nibbanic, the less recognizably ethical it becomes.

In passing, it is of interest to note one partial exception to the basic Buddhist movement from words to experience, from the lesser truth of concept to the greater truth of realization. This is to be found in the intense attachment of Theravadins to the *Abhidhamma Piṭaka,* the third and most philosophical part of the Pali Canon. It is often said that in the Sutta literature of the Canon, that is, the somewhat popularized discourses of the Buddha, there is truth only in its conventionally expressed form; but that in the Abhidhamma, which is presumed to have been spoken first in the Tusita heaven by the Buddha to his reborn mother, there resident as a deva, one has a statement of truth in its ultimate form. Indeed from the intense devotion given to the elaboration of Abhidhammic terms, one sometimes gains the impression that these terms in themselves have some sort of metaphysical being, and that knowledge and repetition of them brings salvation per se. However this is scholastic enthusiasm rather than fundamental Buddhist teaching; when pressed, Abhidhammic scholars would readily admit that even ultimate terms do not replace experiences of ultimate truth, but only indicate them. And some Theravadins themselves are critical of this addiction to an "ultimate language" as being to some extent a perverted idolatory of words.

b. *The Quest of the Ultimately Good, Turns Toward Inward States of Realization and away from Outward Action; Resultingly, Ethical Attitude is Considered More Important than Exterior Situation*

There is no absolute dichotomy between action and realization, or physical and mental states, especially on Buddhist premises. For as has been noted, physical-mental, external-internal dimensions of life and action are most intimately conjoined. The pure mind produces health in the body and is conducive to a more fortunate rebirth; the complete good, at least on the kammic level, is one which includes both the physical and mental constituents. Likewise thought and thought-feeling are action just as truly as physical movement, so far as Buddhism is concerned.

Nevertheless as one progresses up the ladder of spiritual maturity, or, what is the same thing, as ethical experience moves through kammic good toward nibbanic good, the mental factors and their development take increasing precedence over the physical factors. Progress toward nibbanic good is essentially the development of innate mind-powers. This does not refer only, or perhaps even primarily, to those psychic potencies of penetrating the thought of others, knowing one's past rebirths, and the ability to create an astral or mind-body, Such powers, and the desire for them, must be guarded carefully since they may represent only the continuation and magnification of the individual self. There *is* a kind of short-cut to Nibbana, much emphasized today, which stresses the discipline of realizing the great negative truths of impermanence *(anicca)*, suffering *(dukkha)*, and insubstantiality or no self-nature *(anattā)*, rather than psychic attainments. Yet these latter are characteristically and usually attached to the higher levels of attainment in the scriptures; the short-cut, while allowed, is the a-typical and somewhat inferior route of the "dry-visioned" one.

But even in the case of "the way without psychic powers" the development of a type of mind-power is likewise central. It is an experience in which one is taught to analyze introspectively his body-process, mental states, and emotional fluctuations from a detached point of view, until he knows them with microscopic exactitude. He—the observing, analysing "he"—becomes more and more master of the processes and factors of his total personal consciousness; more and more he is able to cut himself loose from the "distractions" of sense stimuli and live in a world of his own making, or at least, realizing. It is a world that is shut away from the world of ordinary consciousness—above, beyond, or perhaps within it—whose perfection is found in those moments in which Nibbana itself is directly apprehensible to him.

Such states of awareness are absolutely good in themselves, without qualification.

This may be put in a more personalized and concrete form. What is the ideal of sainthood in Buddhism? The arahat or highest grade of saint is one who has so mastered the powers of his mind, and developed them, that he can at will put himself into a state of complete absorption wherein nibbanic factors, if not the nibbanic realization itself, may be experienced. The moment of nibbanic realization, in which the saint is "dead" to the outside world, i.e. totally unconscious of it and perhaps to all appearances dead physically, is the perfect life arrived at its perfect moment. Yet even in between such moments, when he returns to the ordinary world, the saint can scarely be said to be a full member of it, but is only abstractedly there. Thus it is reported of one of Burma's holiest monks that he eats the foods given to him indiscriminately mixed, without preference and perhaps without sensing their flavor.[19]

This enshrinement of the state of inward (and ideally the nibbanic) realization as an absolute or intrinsic good, explains why the meditative discipline is the king of all Buddhist disciplines. It is thus treated because it is the one and only technique which can bring a person to the realization of nibbanic states in this life and Nibbana itself in the end. Therefore the one indispensable method of achieving the one absolute Good cannot but stand at the head of every hierarchy of disciplinary techniques. This preeminence of the meditative discipline is recognized in the Theravada construction of the Noble Eightfold path as Sila (morality), Samadhi (concentration of mind), and Pañña (insight or wisdom).[20] This, as we have already noted, places the

---

[19] I refer to the Webu Sayadaw who after many years of solitary meditation now receives visitors and makes journeys through Burma. He is a man of unusual sweetness and calm of personal presence.

Some interpreters of arahatship would say that the arahat does indeed *taste* all the flavors of all the foods he eats, perhaps *more* keenly than other men, but he is not attached to any one or any combination of them, hence eats "indifferently."

[20] Theravadins change the usual order of the Eight-fold Path by placing the third to fifth "steps" of Right Speech, Action, and Livelihood on the Sila level; the sixth to eighth steps of Right Effort, Mindful-

moral elements first and lowest. And while there are perhaps elements of all the "steps" or "stages'" present everywhere along the course of ethical development toward perfection, it *is* the *ethical* discipline that is perfected first; and it is the *meditational* discipline which later and more importantly produces samadhi and pañña.

The ethical logic of all this is obvious. The "better" one becomes in terms of Nibbana, the greater the tendency to think of goodness in terms of inward realization rather than social action. Or, as the Buddhist would prefer to put it: As one develops along the nibbanic way he changes his *mode* of ethico-social action. He radiates spiritual-moral health and goodwill to the surrounding community, and even to the universe at large. (As we shall see in a later chapter this is the heart of the Buddhist conception of the ideal society.) So far as he is concerned this is both a more mature and more effective type of "action" than much of the physically strenuous social action that goes on at the lower levels of ethical activity.

And even for those who do not attain to the capacity for such powerful radiation of goodwill as may transform society, there is to be found here a guiding principle: Pay more attention to the "inner" factors in a situation than the "outer." That is, the personal attitudes and qualities of the actors in a social-political situation are more important than stated policies.[21]

Or, again: The most dynamic and effective way to control a social situation is from the psychic inside, i.e. by seeking to change motivation rather than physical circumstance, or by seeking to control the physical circumstances by means of a control of the motivations of the persons involved. Or yet again: the fundamental problem of all problems is not the conquest of the physical factors in the human environment (including outer space) but man's conquest of himself. The similarity of this ap-

---

ness, and Concentration on the Samadhi level; and the first two, Right Understanding and Thought, on the Pañña level. Whether this represents a *uniquely* Theravada development I cannot say.

[21] This is the core of the philosophy of government espoused, and hopefully put into practice, by U Nu in the political regime of Burma in 1961-62. See below.

proach to social ethics in many respects to that of the Moral Rearmament Movement and of the Quakers is striking.

c. *Supra-Individual or Generalized Consciousness is Better than Highly Individualized Self-Consciousness*

Nibbana, considered as the supreme existential reality and the highest of ideal goods, has exerted a tremendous influence on what we may call the philosophy of personal values in Buddhism. It has resulted in a view that is at sharp variance with that of the Greek-Christian West, and we may begin by describing that contrast.

In the Greek-Christian-Western tradition the individual human selfhood, with all the rights and perquisites appertaining thereunto, is highly valued. The proud awareness of the uniqueness of individuality, with its own intimate sense of experiences and cozy selfconsciousness, has been celebrated by many a poet and examined by many a philosopher. The values of individuality have come to be considered an intrinsic part of the good life, Western version. This individualism has had its political expression in the gospel of a democracy of sheerly individualistic freedom from governmental restraint. And religiously there has been the Christian emphasis upon the immortal soul in each man, forever separate from every other soul, and infinitely precious because unique and everlasting in its uniqueness. For although there is an important and substantial mystical tradition in Christianity which sometimes speaks of the absorption of the soul into God as its ultimate salvation, it has never overthrown the central personalistic individualism of Christianity. And the classic Christian "losing" of oneself in loving service to God and man is quite a different thing from what we have in mystical Christianity or in Buddhism.

Turning to the latter we find the values quite reversed. Buddhism sees in highly developed "selfness," of whatever description and on whatever level, the essential evil of human life that binds man to rebirth and prevents him from achieving Nibbana. It is to be avoided and eradicated, not cherished and gloried in. The nourishment of a strong sense of selfhood is evil because it results in a clinging (attachment) to the narrowness of our little selves and to their ideas and emotions, in constant fear of their diminution by circumstance or dissolution by death. And because of this self-attachment, pride, greed, and hatred govern all our actions toward those who seem to threaten the glory or existence of the self. Thus all knowledge, all willing, all motives, and all action, are distorted and poisoned at their very source. We attach false importance even to "things," i.e. entities of ordinary sense experience, clinging to them as to solid realities, attributing to them a physical selfhood or substance, an attribution that only serves to shore up our own sense of genuine individuality and permanence.

Therefore Buddhism seeks to destroy what it regards as the baneful illusion of separate, permanent selfhood by every means possible. Its method is two-fold: a discipline of negation through introspective analysis of the self by the self; and the positive development of a supra-individual type of consciousness which overrides and finally ousts the ordinary individualized consciousness.

We have already referred briefly to the negative discipline in discussion of the anatta doctrine and observed that the fundamental effort in the negative discipline is to bring the meditator —for meditation is its methodology—to a complete conviction of the impermanence of all being, including his own self. The meditator abstains from all vigorous bodily action, thus slowing down the bodily processes and activities to the point where they lose their illusory quality of unity and spontaneity, and can be analyzed into component parts. Likewise the emotions, sense impressions, and thoughts are made to pass by through the narrow gate of bare, detached attention one by one, as it were, so that their component elements and their rise and fall can be closely observed. The end result is a vivid firsthand realization of the ebbing and flowing of selfness in all its aspects; a realization of the fact that self is a composition of elements, not a simple substance; and the final destruction of the illusion of its permanence and unity. Having faced the facts of his own true nature and found the "self" to be only a temporary nexus of elements-in-flux, a man finds that his sense of integral selfhood is forever dissolved, and attachment to it cut off at the root.[22]

But there is also a positive methodology for overcoming the evil of highly personalized self-consciousness. At least it is more positive in form; though in the end it seems to be but the other side of the negative method, concomitant and simultaneous in its operation. For the end-result is the same—the destruction of narrow self-consciousness; and the respective techniques for achieving the result—the meditative and radiative disciplines—are intimately interlocked. Nevertheless there *are* important distinctions between the negations of the anatta doctrine and approach, and the positive development of a universalized awareness.

The possibility of a universalized or supra-personal consciousness grows directly out of the Buddhist conception of the nature of that pure mind which inheres in all mortals. And pure mind is of course good mind, after the analogy of Nibbana. For its nature is not secrecy and self-confinement, but clarity, translucency, and universality; not separateness and inclosedness but the power of penetration and the quality of interconnectedness. The purer and more developed the mind becomes, the greater is its ability to overcome all sense of separateness either in time or space; to enter into and join with the thoughts of others; to overpass the limits of time and space into past lives and other universes; to be aware of the sameness of truth and reality in all places and times and in all beings; to achieve in itself a full universality of awareness (maximum case, the omniscience of the Buddhas); to be pure, unsullied consciousness, an absolutely clear lens for truth's

---

[22] The inversion of values here is most interesting. Buddhism has so much existence, so many lives, on its hands that it is embarrassed by their plenitude. It sees the human predicament as condemnation to life, not death—though of course death always follows birth and makes birth evil. Hence its basic fear is of continued existence, not an ending of it; and thus it talks pseudo-bravely about "facing the facts" of "no-soul" because "no-soul" goes on and on in what we call existence. But the Christian-tinctured Westerner, with only one life at his disposal, is concerned to continue existence and afraid that death is its ending. So Buddhist Nibbana is the cessation of existence as we know it on earth; and Christian Heaven is its enhancement.

passage in either direction, as well as a penetrative mangnifying glass for its discovery.

What the essential quality and content of his supra-personal consciousness actually signify is difficult for the Westerner to ascertain. Certainly for the Buddhist it is not an emotionalized mist of vague luminous awareness—the mist more luminous than any specific entities therein; but it is conceived to be the height of true, clear, completely rational awareness of "things as they are," natural but super-normal in nature. Does it contain the actual thought-content of other minds? Though there are some suggestions that this is the case, certainly the Buddhist does not intend to suggest any mystical union of substances or merging of selves. The universally-aware self remains distinct from others, never more so, in all the fullness of this super-selfhood. It is rather the achievement of a state of complete emotional neutrality on the part of the saint, who extends to all beings an impartial, unattached, universal will-to-their-good; and because his consciousness is not walled in upon itself nor darkened by any taint of preference, emotion, self-attachment or even mine-thine distinction, it penetrates clearly and cleanly into the minds and hearts of others.

Is this supra-individual consciousness the same as that one which is able increasingly to gain a "vision" of Nibbana? Is that action of penetrating the thoughts of others and generalizing one's own awareness until the boundary between own-self's joy and welfare and other-self's joy and welfare is wiped out, the very same act as Nibbana realization? The answer is a qualified, No. The Buddha's moments of projecting his omniscient awareness throughout the universe in search of "souls" in need, and of his refreshing awareness of Nibbana, were separate in time. But that consciousness which is most capable of one is also most capable of the other; the level of consciousness, if not the act, *is* the same. And hence both are intrinsically good (though perhaps the nibbanic awareness is higher in the scale) because both possess that selfless quality that is the essence of Nibbana itself.

Thus are we led in the end to affirm the identity of result, and perhaps even of quality and process, of the "negative" (nosoul) and the "positive" (supra-personal consciousness) approaches to Nibbana. The first speaks of the unreality and destruction of the illusion of selfhood. The second hopes for the development and enlargement of the mind-powers of that self into a universalized consciousness. But the net result is the same. It is discovered that the barriers which defined and guarded the self also blinded it to larger realities. The dissolution of those barriers is the aim of both negative and positive methods. And the delivered or destroyed self—which really is it?—finds that with self-walls gone, a kind of universal awareness floods into consciousness.

d. *In the Good Life One Moves from Attachment of All Sorts to Unqualified Detachment*

It should be noted that in a Buddhist context "attachment" includes a wide range of elements, all of them evil in the final (nibbanic) analysis. It may be interpreted intellectually. The central activity of the ordinary intellect or active consciousness is distinction making: between subject and object, differences between sense-objects and experiences, logical contradictions, varieties of meaning, and the like. And the mind is attached to these, its own distinctions, as to life itself. So also it may be interpreted emotionally. Emotion clothes the entities distinguished by the intellect—and assumed by it to be genuine and solid realities—with its garments of beauty or ugliness, pleasantness or unpleasantness, ethical goodness or badness. Resultingly the total human being moves toward some items with desire, and away from others with repulsion, or is sometimes pulled in two ways at once. Thus every object of man's sense experience and intellectual creation is caught in the web of positively or negatively desirous attachment.

But attachment of whatever sort is the essence of man's predicament, for attachment brings suffering, indeed *is* suffering. The ups and downs of the fullfilment or frustration of desire, the presence or absence of logical order, and the awareness of ethical goodness and badness tear the human psyche apart. Yet, treacherously shrouded in the mists of ignorance, desire—in its basic form of the will-to-live, in order to know, feel, act—blindly drives each being ever forward through the perpetual rebirth and redeath of repeated existences. Hence in the end we must say that it makes no difference at all *what* the desire or attainment may be, be it to the pleasant or unpleasant, the ethically good or the ethically evil; so long as any attachment remains, it binds man to rebirth and separates him from Nibbana. Thus:

> All attachment, whether to vice or virtue, is a barrier to the taking of the final step leading to Nibbana. The one who has attained freedom is not contaminated by any of the contraries on which experience rests and between which ethical choices are made. He knows neither likes nor dislikes and is as little stained by virtue or vice as the lotus-leaf which is not wetted by the water it grows in and rests on.
>
> Therefore the criterion of moral judgment is whether a particular action would or would not obstruct oneself or others in the attempt to win release from Samsaric evil into Nibbana.[23]

The same author goes on to suggest in another article that desire must be so thoroughly rooted out, that even the kind of attainment represented by "motivation" must be destroyed:

> Actions will no longer be conditioned by intentions and motives, but will arise from the understanding of the necessity of action. A motivated action is an incomplete action, even if the motive is good and pure. But an action rising from the understanding of its need will be a perfect action, in which the will of self *(cetana)* has no place.[24]

The language here is ambiguous. Apparently "motivation" means "*e*motivation," the self-centered, distorting drive behind an action. However since the "necessity" of action is not an impersonal mathematical calculation done by the forces of nature, it always involves certain values, personally and emotionally perceived. (And who is more dangerous than the man who professes to have no emotional attachments or ambitions, but to move only from considerations of sheer logic?) For one man's need is another's luxury; or his "necessity" the destruction of his fellow's very existence. But the intention of the statement is clear:

---

[23] G. P. Malalasekara, "Buddhism," *Light of the Dhamma*, I, No. 2 (January, 1953), 58, 57 respectively.

[24] "Buddhism," *The Illustrated Weekly of India* (April 17, 1960), 18.

Emotional attachment to the results of any action, no matter how ethically "good" the results may be in the kammic sense, is a pollution of the purity of that action, viewed in the absolute context of nibbanic perfection.

Here again in moving toward the absolute good, even on lower levels, we progress away from attachment to causes, persons, ordinary ethical values of either personal or social quality, and from a close relationship to any individual or individualized entity, toward that shoreless, distinctionless, ineffable Goodness of man's true end. Whether this may be translated into the disinterested, i.e. non-attached, service of men and society in any significant way must be discussed later.

e. *Ultimate Goodness is Supra-Individual Rather than Social*

There is a considerable difficulty in stating the personal-social bearing of Nibbana on Buddhist ethic correctly. As observed above in dealing with the conception of Nibbana, there are both individualized and super-personalized elements to be found here.

Certainly in the narrow sense individuality is primarily characteristic of the kammic realm. There it is iron-clad and absolute, even though made up of a temporary combination of temporary elements (*khandhas*); for through countless ages in the past there has been no mingling of personal qualities or destinies. Each one of us inherits his own kammic nature and must make his own lonely way to Nibbana. Even into non-individual Nibbana there are only private entrances. But even in nibbanic terms and within the realm of nibbanic living there is also an affirmation of individuality. Indeed it may be said to be intensified here, rather than destroyed. For the purpose of the total meditative discipline is to produce the saint who is a completely autonomous individual, impervious to sense enticements and sometimes even completely unconscious of them, completely *self*-controlled, *self*-contained, *self*-aware, living "within" the *self*. Thus in the scripture:

> Just as a rock of one solid mass remains unshaken by the wind, so neither visible forms, nor sounds, nor odours, nor tastes, nor bodily impressions, neither the desired nor the undesired,

can cause such an one to waver. Steadfast is his mind, gained is his deliverance.[25]

Or let us take the full perfection of nibbanic character, to be found only in the Buddhas but theoretically open to all living creatures. The Buddha is the product of countless ages of *self*-development, and is *self*-perfected and *self*-enlightened even to the degree of omniscience. He is a self depending only on Self, built up consciously and deliberately out of millions of former selves, a Super-Integrated Self integrated about a center of nibbanic awareness. Though bodily still a kammic individual living in time and space, such a Super-Self, inwardly Self-centered, actually lives far above the whole kammic realm in his Transcendent Selfhood.

In this Transcendent Buddha-Self, or even that self of the arahat, an "individual"? And is the nibbanic quality of life, or the approximation thereto that is found in mature spiritual individuals, a sheerly intensified individualism? No doubt Western and Eastern interpretations will always diverge here, with the West tending to answer, yes, and the East, no. But what we must say is that though we *seem* to be traveling in a circle—with the denied and "obliterated" kammic self returning in intensified form in the nibbanic self—actually we have a *spiral* movement. The nibbanic selfhood of saints and Buddhas is not the same self as that of the ordinary (kammic) man. It has been transformed in the process of development into something different. In fact the nibbanic self feeds on the destruction of the kammic self. As one realizes the truth of the anatta (no-self) and cuts away at his attachments to that illusory self, the nibbanic self (though the Theravadin would insist on calling it a non-self) and its generalized, supra-individual consciousness, grow ever stronger. Thus nibbanic awareness, in which the lines between own-self consciousness and other-self consciousness fade away, destroys the old narrow and individualized self.

Is then the supra-individualism of nibbanic good *social* in nature? This of course depends upon one's definition of the social. There *is* some fellowship among Nibbana-seekers; the Sangha

---

[25] *Anguttara-Nikāya (Gradual Sayings)*, Nipata VI, Sutta 55. Quoted in *Buddhist Dictionary*, Mahathera Nyanatiloka, p. 99.

(order of monks) is ideally this. And those who have attained
something of the nibbanic quality of life can recognize it in others.[26] Likewise there *is* sometimes a contemporary example of
such interpretation:

> This Nirvana can be attained in this very life by the wise who
> follow the Path to its Realization. To live in the Light of Realiza-
> tion of the Truth about Life and the Deathless element, to under-
> stand one's own life and the life of others, to crave for nothing,
> to love all and pardon all, serve others without a desire for a re-
> ward or even appreciation, to live in peace and bliss as long as
> one's very life lasts, this is called the Nirvana attainable in this
> very life.[27]

But when all this has been duly noted, the question of the individualistic or social implication of Nibbana and the drive toward its
realization still remains. And perhaps it may finally be stated
thus: Nibbana and its ethical dynamic are indeed non-individual-
istic and non-personalistic, but not essentially social in nature.
Nibbana is not an ideal social commonwealth. The individual
loses his individuality when he reaches Nibbana but he does not
thereby gain sociality, nor does he join a heavenly communion
of the saints. As a personal existent he becomes "extinct" and
therefore his personal essence cannot contribute to any society
whatsoever. Nibbana is an undifferentiated and non-personal
continuum of peaceful serenity.

Even with regard to nibbanic societies on earth, there are
qualifications. The term *"nibbanic society"* may be used relatively
to indicate an ideal society in which each self works for a common good and loses its narrow self concern; and presumably it
would be a social order in which there would be a minimum of

---

[26] Thus, a well-known and revered monk who had meditated in seclusion for many years and reached a consciousness of nibbanic peace in
his meditation, was visited by a layman who had also been meditating
for many years, as he was able. As the latter sat silently before him, the
monk suddenly broke the silence: "When did you get it?" he asked. "It"
referred to Nibbanic peace experienced by both.

[27] Venerable C. Nyanasatta, "The Problems of Buddhism," *Light of
the Buddha,* II, No. 3 (March, 1957), 9. Dr. Richard A. Gard of Yale
University also reports some interest in defining a "nibbanic society"
among Japanese Buddhists.

greed, hatred and delusion. Yet this is a considerable dilution of nibbanic meaning. And even if it is granted legitimacy, one must say that it still lacks the qualities of mutuality and fellowship. For the generalized supra-personal consciousness of nibbanic living flows out, god-like, without expectation of result or response. It is of a rarity that lives far above those it "includes" in its "society." It seeks to achieve detachment from beings in their individuality—and individuality is of the essence of the social. In short, it seems impossible to achieve any genuine social content or practice from the sheer negation of individuality or its absorption into a supra-personal consciousness.

PART II

Content and Application—
Buddhist Ethics in Practice

TRANSITIONAL

The basic framework of psychological and metaphysical elements in which actual Buddhist ethical practice operates has now been outlined. The essential nature of the ethical life in its widest scope is that of the development of the self to a kind of supra-personal perfection of consciousness. It is also conceived to be an infinitely long spiritual pilgrimage through countless existences to an existence-transcending state or condition called Nibbana. This way to salvation is held to be one unitary path which leads ideally in an arrow-straight route through morality, concentration of mind, and attainment of insight, from the life of the ordinary man to that of the saint or Buddha.

But in the very heart of this structure, as we have seen, lies a basic tension—that between Nibbana and Kamma-Rebirth. This tension affects all ethical relations, values, and judgments. Kammic morality is by nature relativistic and hedonistic; nibbanic morality is by nature absolute and beyond all sensual delights or preferences. Kammic morality adds virtue to virtue, merit to merit, trying to reach more blessed and fortunate realms of being; Nibbana is above virtue and merit and scorns rebirth as both worldly and evil. The law of Kamma binds one evermore, whether by good or bad action, to the space-time order of existence *(saṃsāra);* Nibbana is an eternal order fully transcendent of samsara, readiness for which may be reached even in the twinkling of an eye when the essential discipline of mind and heart has been achieved.

This dichotomy affects all concrete ethical thought and practice. The kammic goods in general are those of ordinary con-

ventional virtue. Kammic virtue is the virtue of the good citizen
and of the loyal member of the social group to which one belongs,
particularly the family. It is that level of living on which the
humanistic qualities of love, compassion, mercy, helpfulness,
gentleness and the social practices of honesty, truth-telling, so-
briety, dependability, respect for those in authority, and regular-
ity in sexual relationships are looked upon as unadulteratedly
good. Community concern and public service may possibly be
grafted on to this structure, though the general effect of kammic
thought is to channel the doing of good rather narrowly into
one's own kammic destiny, or at best of those whose destiny is
closely related to his in the present existence.

Nibbanic goods, on the other hand, have a strange and unworldly quality about them. They do not pretend to conform
to conventional usages. To be sure, nibbanic good is not licen-
tious or antinomian, but it is rarified beyond all ordinary conception and practice. Social obligations are sloughed off, indeed very
deliberately avoided, that one may serve the Absolute Good and
only that Good. In this context the service of the community is
not that of outward or tangible action but the radiation of inward purity. The virtues of the citizen and family man are looked
upon as of the lowest order and poisoned with that attachment
to being and doing which, in the light of Nibbana, is of the essence of evil no matter how "good" socially. The questers and the
finders of Nibbana live as pilgrims and strangers in the society
of their day.

What then is the form which this dichotomy takes in practical
Buddhist ethical practice? How has it been manifested historically in Buddhist ethical teaching and practice, and in the formation
of Buddhist cultures and societies? What conflicting currents in
Buddhist thought and practice has it created? And what are the
directions, ethically speaking, in which contemporary Theravada
Buddhism is tending?

It is to these questions that the remaining chapters are devoted. We shall first deal with one type of very specific ethical
analysis, of a somewhat legalistic or at least moralistic quality:
that of the determination of the exact meaning of the minimal
Five Precepts and their application to concrete situations. Then
the basic pattern of Buddhist ethic on a personal level will be out-

lined. From personal ethic we shall proceed to the Buddhist social ethic. The Sangha, or Order of monks, will be considered as the historical embodiment of the Buddhist Ideal Society. But there is also the matter of the more secular and less ideal Buddhist society. It is in this area that much contemporary thinking and experimentation is taking place; we may say that Buddhism is now in search of a social ethic, or seeking to find ways to apply its traditional ethic in the modern world. To several expressions of this contemporary concern we shall give some attention.

Finally, assuming the privilege of the observer's detached viewpoint, we may ask Whither Buddhism?, ethically considered.

1. Introductory

As it was observed in the first chapter in the discussion of the place of ethics in Buddhism, ethical and psychological analyses are mingled in Buddhism in a highly confusing manner. One can never be certain whether those distinctions and values which seem to be ethical in the Western meaning of the term—those which have to do with definitions of the right and the good in a personal-social context—are what Buddhism is speaking about in the final analysis. It may rather be about whether a given action will produce a pleasant rebirth in a deva-world or is conducive to a certain state of higher semi-mystical consciousness that the Buddhist is speaking when he uses "ethical" terms.

This is even the case when we come to deal with such unambiguously ethical analysis as there is in the Buddhist context. (For there *is* such analysis as we shall see.) But the nature of that analysis needs to be carefully characterized and delimited. And to this end it may be helpful first to sketch in the factors that limit such purely ethical analysis to the narrow and lowly confines it occupies in Buddhism.

One such factor, that is perhaps more cultural and sociological than moralistic (but which yet has ethical bearing), and is especially noticeable in Burma, is what we may call the *personalistic* quality of its society. It may be stated thus: There is a strong preference for settling questions of equity and justice on a person-to-person basis rather than by a legalistic technique or by stated principles. The traditional mode of settling a dispute is that of face-to-face negotiation between the disputants, with a trusted and disinterested umpire presiding. This umpire may be a trusted acquaintance chosen on the basis of his personal character and experience, or the village headman, or sometimes a well-reputed monk. In any event the umpire is not a legal authority who knows the rules and principles involved and, after learnedly expounding the meaning of "justice" in such a case, will then render a learned decision. He is rather a catalytic personality whose function is to bring understanding and agreement out of a tangled and acrimonious situation. The desired result is not the definition and application of an absolute principle nor a juridical upholding of the majesty of the law. It is rather that the parties involved in the dispute come to a mutually satisfactory adjustment, whether "justice" in a mathematical sense has been done or not. There is here something of the "sense of the meeting" idea, or the Quaker technique of adjustment and readjustment of viewpoints until unanimity of opinion is reached.

In part this approach to ethico-legal decisions is simply the result of a relatively primitive organization in which social units are small and intimate, and in which the authority of any central or national government is looked upon with suspicion. But it also derives from a distrust of analytic principles as over against personal judgment, concept as against intuitive judgment, and the abstract principle as opposed to the concrete situation. Whatever other elements there may be here, the net result is understandable: such soil is unfavorable to that type of systematic intellectual analysis of the Greek, and to some extent of the Hindu, mind. And on the other hand this non-analytic atmosphere *is* consonant with much in the specifically Buddhist context as we shall presently observe.

But secondly and more basically we may observe a fundamental difference between Buddhist-Eastern and Greek-Western ethical traditions. Whereas in the latter, religion and ethics are often specifically and deliberately divided, in the former they have been maintained in organic union. This statement of the situation will no doubt be rejected by most of those interpreters of Buddhism, Western or Eastern, who incline to view it as primarily a moralism. But if the terms of the statement are made clear perhaps it will be less objectionable.

What is meant by calling Buddhist ethic a *religious* ethic is that no Buddhist ever considers it a "mere" ethic, or Buddhism as "mere morality," in the sense of being only or primarily a practicable useful code of human behaviour. There are indeed such elements within Buddhist ethic, and they are very important. And contemporary Buddhists are stressing them. But Buddhism as such is an ethic plus. It is an ethic plus the hope of salvation, either in the half-salvation of a better rebirth (as a result of being ethically 'good') or finally and ultimately in the rebirth-transcending realm of Nibbana. To see justice done in the earth, to get along with one's fellows, to create a benevolent social order—these are only incidental by-products of the ethical discipline, or instrumentally good for the achievement of nibbanic frames of mind and ultimate liberation from the world of time and space. In a word, the process of ethical development and the way to salvation—a salvation that is religious because it is ultimate and of metaphysical proportions—are one and the same.

This behind-the-scenes ubiquity of Nibbana in all Buddhist thinking, ethical or psychological; that ultimate reference and context which it provides for morality, we have already dealt with extensively in the previous chapter. Here our interest is momentarily to note, with some necessary re-emphasis, how the presence of Nibbana as the "religious" pole of the Buddhist structure affects basic Buddhist ethical analysis even on the lowest level of the Five Precepts. We may describe these effects—which find their natural sociological counterpart in the personal-relations factor just described—as three in number: (1) A fundamental aversion to conceptualizing any values, particularly the "higher" ones; (2) the consequent subordination of the definitely ethical to the ethico-psychological; (3) the consequent down-grading of morality to the lowest and most elementary level of the life of self-development. Concerning each of these a few words may be said.

It is always necessary for the Westerner to keep reminding himself anew in each different context of Buddhist thought of the basic presupposition of all such thinking: Conceptual truth is not the essential or ultimate truth. Intellectual definitions do not get to the heart of the matter in any effort to reach truth, reality, or goodness. Indeed they may obstruct such efforts because of

the inveterate tendency of the human mind to take mere terms
for realities, and abstract words for concrete experiences. Nowhere is this more the case than with regard to religious realities
where firsthand experience or piercing intuition is the only route
to true understanding. Obviously this is the direct result or
converse side of nibbanic doctrine. For Nibbana, the Supreme
Good and the Highest Reality, is in essence incommunicable,
i.e. ineffable. How, therefore, can one truly analyze or conceptu-
alize the "good" when its true essence is inexpressible?

With regard to the intermingling of the ethical and the psychological categories, this has already been sufficiently illustrated
for our present purpose. What may be pointed out here is the
specific bearing of the nibbanic doctrine and experience upon
the matter. If it be held, as it is, that the essential discipline of
the Buddhist life is that which prepares one for Nibbana and that
this discipline is essentially the training of the mind and development of its innate powers, this means that the emphasis will be
upon the inner psychological experience rather than the socio-
ethical milieu of individual lives. What is required to achieve
such experiences will be the *truly* good technique of living; and
those states or experiences themselves will be the supremely
valuable goals of "ethical" endeavor. Thus it is that the ethical
judgment is subsumed under, or converted into, a judgment of
psychological effectiveness and personal integration.

The third effect, or corollary feature, of the presence of the
nibbanic transcendence in the ethical context upon ethical statement and analysis, is the subordination of morality *(sīla)* in the
Buddhist value structure to the supra-moral values of the nibbanic quest. Reference has already been made to this in the first
chapter. But at this point we may consider it in a slightly different and more extended manner: What is the effect of this depres-
sion of the specifically ethical upon the whole process of ethical
analysis and theory in Buddhism? And it may be said in antici-
pation, that the position of Sila in the value structure defines
both the height and breadth of such analysis.

2. Subordination of Sila

Theravada Buddhism insists that when it calls Sila the first
of the three stages on the path to perfection that it does not mean

thereby to suggest inferiority but rather essentiality; or to change the figure, Sila is the prime foundation of all further progress toward enlightenment and Nibbana. And it is of course true that even the basic precepts, let alone the higher moralistic motives and attitudes, are capable of definition and practice at many levels. Yet it is also true that Sila *is* considered to be elementary (the merest "A B C" of the good life); and that for the Buddhist thinker the unavoidable connotation of the terms "moral" and "ethical" in their usual sense *is* that of the merely rudimentary spiritual process. They connote ordinarily the external ethic of the restraint of anti-social actions contained in the Five Precepts. And the whole situation signifies that the life of the layman, who must needs live in the context of such externalized relationships most of his waking hours, is a kind of very poor relation of the higher spiritual life and hence need be given only a minor species of attention.

Such is the general flavor of the Buddhist scriptures themselves, at least those of the Pali Canon, despite a contemporary effort to magnify the degree of attention given to laymen therein. The flavor of most of the Suttas that deal with lay life is somewhat casual, as befits dealing with the mundane world and its ways, rather than being indicative of a matter of first importance. They seem to say: "*If* you are no more developed than to desire to be a success in this world, then be thrifty, diligent, honest, and use your intelligence. If you *really* wish to be born in the deva-worlds in your next life, then be generous, particularly to members of the Order of monks, observe the Five Precepts of basic morality, and even the Eight Precepts as often as possible. (And to this, later Buddhism added the performance of the good works of worshipping before the Buddha images, propitiatory offerings to spirits, the use of beads, and the like.) But it is only the spiritually undeveloped, the ordinary worldling who really desires *such* goods. The truly wise man looks upon all worldly success, and even birth among the gods, as a delusion and snare."

Or when the mundane ethical duties *are* more generously recognized, the implication is that they are not very difficult of performance and offer no great complexity for analysis. It is the inner psychical discipline of the way to Nibbana, through mental concentration and purity, that is given the primary emphasis as the *essentially* Buddhist way.[1] And if this is true in the Sutta scriptures, how much more so in the Abhidhamma which spends practically no time at all in the consideration of moral-social problems but entirely concentrates on the analysis of mental states and their psychological-metaphysical significance.

The sphere then of the *specifically* moral in Buddhism, to which the ordinary type of ethical analysis has been applied, is both small and lowly. It has little to do with the *fundamental* questions of ethical valuation, such as the ultimate meaning or intention of such terms as "right," "wrong," "good," "bad" or the like. In such valuation as we do find here, it is assumed that the kammic-rebirth context gives a sufficiently distinct and useful meaning to these terms. That which conduces to a more fortunate rebirth is right and good; and that which plunges one down to the nether planes is wrong and bad. The higher nibbanic and transcendent values are only marginally or implicitly taken account of, if at all. The ethical judgment as exercised on this level is primarily a matter of the identification of certain actions as belonging to their respective categories, whose goodness or badness is already decided upon by other means. And such further analysis as takes place has as its goal the certification of the correctness of the aforesaid identification. Thus it is held that the taking of life, human or animal, is "wrong," i.e. leads to unfortunate rebirths. There is no questioning of this verdict. The basic question to be analyzed is: When is an action *really* a killing? It is in the determination of the correct answer to *this* question that the most considerable analysis and interpretation of the "constituent factors" of the ethical situation occur.

This then is the area to which we shall confine ourselves in this chapter, that of the basic Five Precepts which denounce

---

[1] The *Jātaka Tales* are often referred to today by Theravada Buddhists as containing extensive and definite social teachings. Their social-ethic content will be referred to in more detail later but here it may be observed that most of the material there is pre- or non-Buddhist in flavor. It gives a picture of Indian society and sets forth a general schema of socially esteemed virtues, but little that is distinctively Buddhist. What there is of the latter is more by adoption and adaptation than of its essence—though it does not thereby *conflict* with Buddhist lay ethic.

killing, lying, stealing, illicit sexual relations, and use of intoxicants. It is not, as I have endeavored to make clear, the sum total
of Buddhist ethical concern. It does not include the full range of
personal and social application of Buddhist principles, with
which we shall deal later, nor those transcendent values of the
nibbanic life. All these must be considered in any *final* analysis
of Buddhist ethics. But here in the present narrow context we
have a clear example of a systematic and analytic dealing with
practical ethical concerns more like Western ethical reasoning
than anything else in Buddhism. And though the field be narrow, and admittedly on the lowest level of the total ethical realm,
it is not uninteresting and has been of considerable practical
significance in the moral life of several Buddhist cultures.

Such are the limiting factors in the situation. But before we
turn to specific examples of this ethical analysis, we must take
note of one basic consideration that in actuality somewhat ex-
pands our field, or at least suggests that there *are* doors which
open out from its narrowness to the higher and wider regions
of the total spiritual life of Buddhism. This is the interpretation
which Buddhism gives to the concept of "action." An action is
not merely a physical deed, or even a volition with a physical result. Action includes in its completeness, thought, word, and
deed, because each of these activities produces important kammic
results. A "mere" thought that apparently has no tangible result,
not even the moving of a muscle, is nevertheless considered to be
an action with definite effects. Likewise an emotion, whether resulting in visible consequences or not, is a deed of sorts which
starts kammic ripples of influence. A *vocalized* thought, of
course, is well on the way to a full-scale action. Thus:

> A Buddhist should refrain from killing any living being, either
> by the use of physical force, and weapon, any trap, recitation of
> mantras, will-power or any agent.
> In discussing this first precept of nonkilling, we should not
> lose sight of the very important principle of Buddhist morality,
> that any good or evil action . . . caused, praised, or approved, is
> equal in effects or consequences to an action committed by one-
> self.[2]

---

[2] U Baw Kyaw, "The Buddhist Conception of Moral Purity," *Light
of the Buddha*, II, No. 10 (October, 1957), 21.

Whether the author is to be taken quite literally in this passage may be questioned. If the mere "praise" or "approval" of an evil action is as bad as the actual commission of the action itself, it raises some difficulties and does not seem always to agree with other statements of Buddhist ethical principle. This *might* mean that one can cynically decide that he may as well be (kammically) hung for a sheep as for a lamb, i.e. go ahead to actually kill the being, if the mere motion of a semi-approving thought has the same effect—though this interpretation is most unlikely. Nor does there seem to be much social concern over any possible effect upon other persons involved here. But we will note in some following paragraphs that, despite such possibly extreme statements, Buddhism tends to say that the full-bodied action of thought, word, and deed which is perceptible on the social and historical plane *is* of more importance than the mere thought itself.

Nevertheless the author does have an essential and important point, somewhat similar to one made by Jesus when he said most emphatically that the thought of lust and the hating disposition make a man an adulterer and a murderer, respectively, in the "eyes of God," that is in reality. Was Jesus thereby suggesting that the hater might just as well go ahead and commit the murder on the object of his hatred? Scarcely. Rather he was pointing to the inner and motivational aspect of the deed that always precedes and causes it; and he was placing the deed in the socially transcendent context of Divine judgment. Such is the principle involved here. Actual killing is no doubt worse socially, and perhaps even in its kammic effect upon the killer, than the mere thought or approving sentiment. Yet these latter too are wrong; perhaps they are more fundamentally wrong than the physical deed itself because that deed roots in them originally; it is actually their expression. And placed in the kammic context, which transcends the *present* social-personal situation, their effects may be more disastrous than that of the physical deed, springing as they do out of the essence of the man himself. At any rate we are forewarned that even in externalized, Five-Precept level Buddhist ethics, intention (or motivation) and attitude are of major importance in judging all actions whatsoever.

3. The Constituent Factors of Immoral Action

In any discussion of practical ethical distinctions we seem necessarily to deal in large part with "negative" distinctions, because ethical rules are usually put in prohibitory form. At least one reason for this is obvious. It is perhaps much vaguer and less meaningful, for example, to say of an honest man that he intended to be honest, made an effort to be honest, was indeed actually honest in fact, than to define the constituents of the dishonest action. Hence vice always has more legalistic definition than virtue. And Buddhism, of course, is no exception in its treatment of basic ethics. Both because of Buddhism's preference for negative statement and its conception of the good life as the controlled and restrained life rather than the self-expressive life, as well as its adoption of the usual pattern of negative moral precepts, basic Buddhist morality is put in the language of the avoidance of evil deeds and its analysis is therefore necessarily in terms of the elements of *im*morality rather than morality, as it were.

We may use as an example of such analysis the Buddhist method of dealing with its First Precept which prohibits the killing of any creature. Or to put it in more Buddhistic terms, it is not precisely the *prohibition* of killing, since there is no God to command it, but the counsel to avoid killing because of its unhappy kammic consequences for the killer. Now an act is held to be killing when it fulfills the following five conditions, called "constituent factors:"

> (1) It must be a living being [that is destroyed]; (2) it must be known [by the killer] that it is a living being; (3) there must be a desire or an intention *(cetanā)* to kill that living being; (4) an endeavor must be made to kill that living being; and (5) that living being must be killed through the efforts made [by the would-be killer]. A person who commits an act of killing, fulfilling all the above conditions, may be said to be guilty of killing.[3]

a. *The Role of Motive*

Because of the key role of motivation in all ethical considerations we shall turn first to the *third* factor, in which the term

---

[3] *Ibid.*

cetanā, translated as desire or intention, is used. We shall take it to mean the motivational aspect of the moral or immoral deed. The Pali Text Society's *Dictionary* defines *cetanā* as meaning "state of ceto in action, thinking as active thought, purpose, intention, will." Though the emphasis here is upon the active quality of the intention, and the reason or basis of the intention or purpose, this is clearly as near to motive as we can get in these terms. For a man's intention or purpose must certainly include the reason for his attempting or purposing some action. If he decides to kill because he wants another's money, dislikes his physical appearance, or is jealous of him, these are an integral part of the intention—even though in the usual Buddhist analysis only the reality of the intention, not its nature, is emphasized. That is, the statement here indicates that there was a genuine intention or the fullbodied will to kill, and that the act was deliberate, not merely a reflex action or only *half*-conscious defensive gesture.

Thus deliberate intention to do an immoral deed is an essential part of that deed, if it is to be judged as immoral. As Dr. Malalasekera puts it: "Buddhism considers as ethical only those deeds which are volitional."[4] But we may go a step further. A specific volitional action, while essential to the ethical quality of a deed, is rooted in basic attitudes or dispositions, that is, the deeper character of the actor himself. There are of course out-of-character actions now and then in most persons' lives—or at least they seem to be such. But most deliberate actions rather truly express the underlying moral disposition; this is the soil out of which the act grows, naturally and inevitably. (Perhaps even out-of-character actions—unless one is *forced* to do these, and then they are not volitional—indicate a hidden trait of character.) Therefore even more important than the specific volition is its nourishing attitude or emotional context.

One contemporary writer would carry this consideration to the extent of making it an absolute principle of Buddhist ethics. He states it thus:

> Superficial appearances to the contrary notwithstanding, Buddhist ethics is essentially an ethics of intention. Actions them-

---

[4] "Buddhism," *Light of the Dhamma,* I, No. 2 (January, 1953), 57.

selves are neither good nor bad: for the Buddhist even more than for Shakespeare, "thinking makes them so." *Kusala* and *akusala,* literally skill and unskill, the more precise Buddhist expressions for what is morally good and morally bad, are terms applicable only to karma-producing volitions and their associated mental phenomena. By the figure of speech according to which qualities belonging to the cause are attributed to the effect, an action is termed immoral when it springs from a mental state . . . domi- nated by the three unskillful or "unwholesome" roots of greed *(lobha),* hatred *(dosa)* and delusion *(moha),* and moral when it proceeds from mental states characterized by the opposites of these.[5]

This statement will need qualification later but here we may note its important and correct emphasis upon the central role of intention and mind-state, or character, in the Buddhist ethic. It is almost unqualifiedly correct to say that for Buddhism it is the *attitude* that is good or bad, not any given action. We may take as examples of the worst attitudes, greed, hatred, and delu- sion. These attitudes or dispositions are *always* bad under all circumstances and in every form, no matter how diluted. And it follows by implication at least that the opposite qualities of loving-kindness *(mettā)* compassion *(karuṇā),* sympathetic joy *(muditā)* and equanimity *(upekkhā)* are always morally *good.* Our emphasis here, however, must be upon the analysis of the evil attitudes, since they have been more extendedly analyzed in ethical terms than the morally good attitudes. And some inter- pretation will be required since the Evil Three are extended more widely than one would suspect from their literal statement.

We may first speak of the immoral disposition of greed. This includes materialistic covetousness; and perhaps on the minimal Five-Precept level of observance, that is its basic meaning. But this is by no means its total significance for Buddhism. It also includes almost any emotional, intellectual, or physical crav- ing of any sort: the intellectual's delight in making precise distinctions; the artist's or esthete's intense devotion to the de- lights of sound, form, and color; emotional delight in sense- experience or personal relationships—all these are as much ex-

---

[5] Bhikshu Sangharakshita, *A Survey of Buddhism* (Bangalore, India: Indian Institute of World Culture, 1959), pp. 142–3.

pressions of greed as love of money and coveting another's house and wife. They may be more subtle and eminently respectable in society, but they are forms of greed nonetheless and all the more dangerous because subtle. In the absolute sense, however, we are far beyond the realm of minimal Five-Precept living when we say: all attachment of emotion or thought to any thing, person, experience, or state of being is a form of greed.

The forms taken by ill-will or hatred are likewise both widespread and subtle. There are the outbroken forms of malice or even virulent hatred that result in everything from tale-bearing, slander, vituperation and verbal abuse to the doing of physical harm, torture, murder, and warfare. But there are also the unspoken, though emotionally felt, currents of ill-will within a person himself. Nor are they the less evil for being hidden. As with greed, the subtle forms of hatred are the more dangerous. Hatred in all its forms is sheerly evil, for as the often quoted passage from the *Dhamapada* has it: By enmity, enmity never ceases.

This raises an interesting question. Is there such a quality as *righteous* anger allowed in Buddhism? Is there room in its hall of virtues for prophetic denunciation? The answer must be somewhat conditioned by the level on which we approach it, as is almost everything in Buddhist ethics. Certainly on the practical level of ordinary social relationships the proper moral standards, i.e. the Five Precepts, should be enforced. The good Buddhist is quite aware of the necessity for laws providing for the punishment of theft, adultery, rape, perjury, drunkenness, violent assault, and murder. And he empowers his society to enforce such laws.

Yet in the final ethical analysis all anger of any sort is evil. Nyanamoli Bhikkhu in an article entitled "The Practice of Lovingkindness" states flatly: "There is no righteous anger in the Buddha's teaching."[6] And this seems in general to be correct. A Buddhist arahat would be quite incapable of the fierce "righteous" anger of an Amos or Hosea against the sins of his people. Prophetic reformist denunciation would be completely foreign to him; rather, with complete indifference

---

[6] *Light of the Dhamma*, VI, No. 3 (July, 1959), 29.

to his own outward weal or woe he would radiate detached
(i.e. unemotional) but benevolent goodwill toward the evil
doers. Outward social reformation would be left to other hands
in the conviction that at best it is superficial and in any case
can be achieved only when a majority of people are inwardly
reformed—which may not occur for ages to come, if ever.

Buddhist writers therefore are more deeply concerned with
the process of rooting out absolutely all traces of ill-will or
resentment in the individual than with social change. And
while again we are here rising from the level of basic ethics of
Precept grade to the higher levels of the super-moral saint, yet
this hope of complete purity from illwill is relevant to the lower
level too; for it remains the moral *ideal* of *all* Buddhist living.
Thus it is that Buddhaghosa in his *Path of Purification,* a
standard manual of the good life among Theravada Buddhists,
details at length various methods for killing resentment and
extending loving-kindness toward all beings—much in the manner
of a Catholic confessor.

Resentment is to be out-maneuvered and choked off by a
number of mental devices: By trying to carry the overflow of
good-will from friends on over to enemies; by reflection on the
fact that to wish evils upon another only brings them in the
end (by the law of Kamma) upon oneself; by remembrance
of the virtues, such as they are, of the person we tend to hate;
by recalling that our enemy may fall into one of the hells, and
our hatred contribute to such a fearful consequence; by con-
templating the Buddha's inexhaustible good will (as a Catholic
meditates on the merits of Christ and the saints); by the remembrance of the personal peace which non-hatred brings; by
meditating upon the disliked person as a mere combination of
mind-body components and asking whether a mere collection of
elements is worthy of hatred. Such a discipline is calculated to leave
no greater foothold for anger in oneself than "a mustard seed
finds on the point of an awl or a painting on the air."[7] And
finally, and rather anti-climatically, he recommends the giving
of a gift to the enemy if his resolution (intellectually, of course)

[7] Thera Nyanamoli (trans.), *Path of Purification* (Colombo: R. E.
Semage, 1956), p. 332.

into a mere collection of non-hateable elements proves to be impossible.

Or there is the reverse side of the method: destroying resentment by the active exercise of goodwill. This must be done in the proper order otherwise its attempt will prove abortive. First one must extend loving kindness to himself, wish himself well; for a self-hater cannot extend love to others. Having filled himself full of such loving-kindness first, he induces it to overflow to a respected one, such as a teacher or elder. Then he may extend it toward dear friends; and then to a neutral person, or unknown one, as though to a dear friend; then to a hostile person as though to a neutral person (who has meantime become as a dear friend): and finally he is to permeate all the universe with all its beings with loving kindness. This order is calculated to avoid trying the impossibility of loving one's enemy at once; and to escape the danger of a too-loving or lustful attachment to friends by beginning first with *them*. The goal is "unspecified pervasion," i.e. completely non-discriminating, non-individualized goodwill to all beings alike.

This condemnation of even the merest shadow of resentment is sometimes put into an extremely idealized form. (Buddhaghosa quotes many examples from the Pali Canon to make his point.) In the *Majjhima-Nikāya (Middle Length Sayings,* Text i, 129) there is the following passage, for instance, in which the Buddha is portrayed as saying to his disciples:

> Bhikkhus, even if bandits brutally severed limb from limb with a two-handled saw, he who entertained hate in his heart on that account would not be one who carried out my teaching.[8]

Likewise Buddhaghosa adduces many instances from the past existences of the Buddha in which he personified complete non-resentment in the most provoking situations. After escaping from a mass live-burial he harbored no hatred toward the one who had commanded the burial; when he was scourged with thorns, had hands and feet cut off, and was cruelly murdered by his then father, he had no thought or feeling of

---

[8] *Ibid,* p. 324.

malice; as an elephant he did not hate the trophy-hunter sent
out by the queen to shoot him with a poisoned arrow, but cut
off his own tusks to present them to the queen; as an ape he led
to safety the man who had gashed his head with a thrown stone,
by deliberately marking the right path with his own blood;
as a serpent, pierced in eight places by spears, with thorns
inserted into these wounds, and dragged along the road by
village boys with a rope through his nose, even though able
to turn his tormentors into ashes by a mere glance, he felt no
hatred, no disturbance of his calmness and equilibrium.[9]

The final goal is that super-personal consciousness to which
we have already referred, in which emotional discrimination
between individuals is to be totally destroyed. Perfect non-hatred
would seem to be that condition in which another's—any other's,
all others'—pains, joys, feelings, and maybe consciousness itself, are indistinguishable from one's own. Here we may note
the way in which such complete non-discrimination would work
in a practical situation. When a person who thus knows "no
barriers" of individualized consciousness (having rooted out all
preferences completely) finds himself in a company of four
persons, *one* of whose number is demanded by bandits as a
blood sacrifice, he could

> not see a single one among the four [including himself] who
> should be given to the bandits [rather than another]; he directs
> his mind impartially towards himself and towards those three
> people [because] he has broken down the barriers.[10]

In a word, the eradication of hatred and ill-will has as its ideal
limit in the saint, the complete eradication of any personalized
preference of any sort, either in thought or emotion.

The third great evil, that of delusion or muddle-headed-
ness, is more properly a generalized condition than a motivating
factor. Delusion, related at least to ignorance, or better, one of
its forms, is "immoral" or "evil" because of its effect upon the
total moral life. It tends to strengthen the forces of greed and
hatred because it obscures the true nature of things as they

---

[9] *Ibid*, p. 328.
[10] *Ibid*, p. 333.

are. Specifically, it consists at root of the delusory belief in the permanence and substantiality of physical "things" and psychic "selves." Believing thus the deluded individual clings to things and selves, including his own self, with greed; and he fends off with hatred those ideas, forces, and persons who seek to loosen his intellectual and emotional attachment to them. Thus delusion as the third of the evil trinity intensifies and multiplies the harm the other two do to human life.

And why, we may ask, are these forces or dispositions so evil? Partly because of their outbroken social effects. Certainly on the level of the practical keeping of the Five Precepts this is a most important consideration, since most social ills root in dispositions of deluded greed and hatred. Yet this is not the basic answer that Buddhism gives. That answer is implied in the above story of the Boddhisatta as a non-malevolent though wounded snake. *Nothing that the boys could do to him destroyed his own calm and equanimity.* Or to put it otherwise: Evil is evil, bad dispositions are bad, not primarily because of their social effects, but because they disturb and moil the perfect purity and peace of their subject's mind. And a muddied mind cannot achieve Nibbana.

But we must return from the nibbanic dimension of ethics—though it is always intruding itself—to the lower and less ideal levels of Five-Precept morality. We may now ask, in view of Buddhism's strong insistence upon absolute purity of disposition and motive, whether it is indeed true, as might seem to be suggested by Bhikshu Sangharakshita in the quoted passage, that motive is the *only* determinant of the goodness or badness of an action, even on the mundane level. This can hardly be the case logically because of other factors that are involved; and certainly it is not the case in actual Buddhist practice. Bhikshu Sangharakshita, himself, though writing from a Mahayana view-point, goes on to assert quite definitely that the mere subjective thinking of an action to be right or wrong does not indeed fully settle the matter. Buddhism does not really espouse the philosophy that the conventionally "evil" deed can be committed with a "pure" heart or from "'good" motives:

> It is not possible to commit murder with a good heart because the deliberate taking of life is simply the outward expression of

a state of mind dominated by hate. Deeds are condensations of thought just as water is a condensation of air. They are thoughts made manifest, and proclaim from the housetops of action only what has already been committed in the silent and secret chambers of the heart. One who commits an act of immorality thereby declares that he is not free from unwholesome states of mind.[11]

And he further recognizes that particularly in the Theravada tradition the morality of the Five Precepts is not mere human convention or relativistic standard but is "universally regarded as an integral part of that eternal and immutable order of the universe, simultaneously physical and mental . . . termed Dharma [Pali *Dhamma*]."[12]

The net result seems to be somewhat the same as in Christian ethics. On one level of consideration the motive is all important— in the eyes of God, or on the absolute ethical plane. And in this context Buddhism and Christianity would agree that no deed can truly be called either good or bad in a genuine ethical sense apart from the presence of some ethical motive, or volition to use the Buddhist term. And still further both would agree that no matter how good the result of an action may appear to be, no matter how fortunate or beneficial its physical-social effects, it is not perfectly, or perhaps even essentially, good unless it has been done with a pure motive. The reverse is also true; no matter how disastrous a "bad" deed is, it is made worse by an evil motivation.

We may note another similarity between Christian and Buddhist viewpoints. There is a direct linkage between character and deed. Intentions grow out of character and deeds grow out of intentions as their natural fruitage. When we see a certain kind of action, usually called bad, it implies an evil character behind it. In Jesus' words, an evil tree (person) can no more bring forth good fruit (deed) than a thistle can produce figs. Or as Bhikshu Sangharakshita suggests, in his adaptation of Jesus' words, "deeds proclaim from the housetops of action only what has already been committed in the silent and secret chambers of the heart."

---

[11] *Op. cit.*, p. 143.
[12] *Ibid*, p. 146.

It must be observed in passing, however, that sometimes the true lineage of a deed is hidden. There are many intermediate stages between character and deed; and some of these are subject to many types of insidious coercion (social, circumstantial, psychic and not merely physical) that limit the actor's freedom and responsibility for his action, so that a deed is not purely and simply the offspring of a man's character. And perhaps it is easier to say with the Buddhist that a conventionally bad deed is a more certain evidence of an evil disposition than a good deed is of a pure character—or is this only because evil is always easier to define than goodness? In any case the Buddhist must tolerantly allow that only future kammic consequences will manifest the true character of any deed in all its goodness or badness; and the Christian must humbly refuse to pass ultimate judgment on any man, leaving this to God.

But we must finally say with regard to motivation in the Buddhist ethical judgment, that though its inclusion is essential to a true judgment, its identification is not all-sufficient for a full moral verdict. As Buddhism is very keenly aware, this is a world of cause and effect. Some deeds, no matter what their motivation, have more serious results, physically, mentally and socially, than others. Hence, even though Kamma conceivably might deal only with motive and Nibbana be exclusively related to inner attitudes, the rest of the order of nature and human society must take into account other factors beside motivation in adjudging an action good or bad. And indeed Buddhist ethic does take such factors into account as the presence of other constituent factors in the definition of any misdeed indicates. To a consideration of these we now turn.

b.   *Remaining Constituent Factors*

Still continuing to use the First-Precept exhortation to avoid killing as our main example for an analysis of the process of ethical judgment, we may turn to the factor of *knowledge* or the *second* constituent factor. Before the destruction of life becomes killing in the ethical sense, the doer of the deed must know that the entity which he is destroying is indeed a living being. Thus if he strikes a bayonet into what he supposes to be a dead body or a straw-filled dummy, but it turns out that said object is a live body, then the deed is not killing in the sense of guilt attaching to it, though physically he has destroyed life. Of course if he were thrusting the bayonet into the body or dummy with violence and ill-will, that would entail unwholesome kammic consequences, but not those attendant on killing.

If we ask whether such an one, who becomes a *de facto* killer under a misapprehension of the true facts, is responsible for his ignorance that produced the evil result, the answer presumably would be in the affirmative. Such ignorance as he might reasonably have corrected in himself is culpable. Yet, kammically speaking, the killing done under a misapprehension is not killing in actuality even though that misapprehension is blameable also; for the state of one's knowledge, or the lack of it, has here an effect upon the motive itself. That person who does not know that the body he attacks is living, does not *intend* to *kill* it. Therefore a prime requisite for "killing," indeed the single most important factor, is missing and the deed cannot be defined as murder.

What of the reverse case in which an individual believes that a dead body is a *live* body and seeks to destroy life in it under the influence of false information or belief? Again one must say that such a state of mind from which the will-to-kill can spring is unwholesome (kammically bad) and puts a person in danger of committing other immoral deeds, as well as having bad kammic consequences in itself alone. That is, the thought and intention themselves are also defined by Buddhism as "actions," in this case evil in character. Yet the deed itself is not actually murder, either socially or kammically considered, and its total consequences are not so serious as they would have been had actual killing been added to murderous intent.

Turning now to the *first*-listed constituent factor we may define it as perceptible *fact* or *actuality*. Is the entity to whom violence is done an actual living being? We may well inquire at this point: But what is a living being? The general criterion is quite clear and is in general the common-sensical, rule-of-thumb definition—though some further elaboration might be necessary in view of the modern refinement of medical knowledge about the human body. A living being is a sentient being, capable of feeling, and presumably of a certain degree of consciousness, a being that is still possessed of what we roughly call life, or warmth, power of movement, pulse, breathing and the like. In the case of temporarily dormant life, or those raptures of the saint such as *Nirodha-Samāpatti* (Attainment of Extinction in this life) in which

> the bodily, verbal and mental functions have been suspended and come to a standstill, but life is not exhausted, the vital heat not extinguished, and the faculties not destroyed,[13]

life is still present; and such assault as would destroy the potentiality for becoming actively alive again, would be called killing. Presumably such would be the case also with regard to beings in states of coma or deep sleep: as long as life-process is present the being is living.

If we ask down to what level this quality of life descends the answer is less clear. Certainly it includes animals and insects of the lowest order—for they move and have being, hence live. (A passage that threatens a term in one of the hells for the killing of an insect has already been quoted.) It also includes the foetus of an animal—apparently from the very moment of conception, since Buddhist doctrine holds that the kammic force of a dying individual goes immediately (by split-second timing) into a female ovum at the moment of its fertilization by a male spermatazoon; ovum, speramatazoon, and kammic energy produce the living being.[14] Whether it includes microbes or not might be a point for further discussion. The monks of Buddha's time were provided with water-strainers to avoid drinking miniscule forms of life, the nearest approach possible at that time to the conception of germ-life. But on the whole Buddhists have been somewhat less extreme here than the Jains to whom even the life of plants is sentient existence and its destruction is killing, though as we have seen, the question of a kind of sentience in plants is raised occasionally even in Theravada Buddhist circles.

---

[13] Mahathera Nyanatiloka, *Buddhist Dictionary* (Colombo: Frewin and Co., 1956), p. 101.

[14] Abortion is considered killing, but there is no prohibition of, or blame attaching to, birth control.

There is the further consideration that some forms of life are more valuable than others. Of course in the absolute sense this might not seem to be so; for all life is one. The insect of today was man or even deva yesterday, i.e. at some time in the past; and he will almost certainly be a man or deva at some future time. Therefore killing is always a crime against kammic being and productive of grave consequences at whatever level. Yet it is generally held to be a greater crime to kill a being of more intelligence and fuller life-force than one of lesser attainments. To kill a human being is more sinful than to kill a snake. And to kill those worthy of reverence, such as parents or an arahat, or even to shed a drop of the blood of a Buddha, is a sin that condemns one to the hells for many an aeon.

The *fourth* constituent factor is that of the *effort* involved in the killing. The principle here is that some effort must be expended before a life-taking is actually a killing. And when effort is spoken of, the implication, of course, is one of deliberate effort; it is the maturity in action of the knowledgeable intention to kill a living creature. Usually this implies some physical effort, the making of some motion, the use of one's muscles, and perhaps the employment of a weapon of some sort. But the Buddhist definition of action as inclusive of thought, and the further Buddhist conviction of the efficacy for good or bad of mentalistic forces, should warn us not to confine the act of killing exclusively to the external physical process. This is the sense of the earlier quotation (p. 118) in which the reader is reminded that the use of mantras (magic verses) or of "will power" as killing agents, is killing just as truly as the use of physical means. Will power and mantra recitation are not merely expressions of the intention to kill; they may in themselves be killing forces.

This brings us to a distinction often made by Buddhists as to the amount of energy employed in killing and its bearing on the degree of guilt. Generally speaking the greater the amount of energy employed the greater the guilt. Thus a slight tap of the finger will serve to kill a small insect; but to kill a man or an elephant a considerably larger effort is usually required. And of course a greater effort implies fuller and more extensive preparation and a move of deliberate intention.

Yet it is not quite as simple as this in the final analysis. The degree of guilt resulting from killing cannot be equated simply with the amount of physical effort involved at the moment of the act itself. Were this the case the pressing of the button that dropped the first atom bomb on Hiroshima was no more culpable than the tapping of the finger on the small insect. To be sure the *immediate* guilt of a person involved may not be much greater; for a hand-to-hand struggle with an opponent for half an hour certainly arouses more emotional forces of anger and hatred than the mere placing of a drop of poison in a drink or the pressing of a button. Poisoning may be done in a semi-detached and impersonal manner without great passion or rage; and the presser of the button may only be "doing his duty," not expressing any personal hatred thereby.

Nonetheless in the total situation and including *all* those who are involved, the degree of guilt and kammic consequence of pressing the bomb-releasing or bullet-sending trigger is far greater than that of a man who knifes his fellow-man to death after a struggle. For the latter deed is often unpremeditated, or at most the plan of one man only. But the former is a total process of massive planning that has involved much scientific research, tremendous expenditures of money, and a very deliberate calculation of the result desired—the killing of thousands of people. The total amount of "effort" involved here is almost beyond calculation; and so also is its kammic penalty. Presumably this penalty will be apportioned justly according to the respective degree of responsibility found in each of the individuals taking part in the enterprise.[15]

The *fifth* and final factor is that of *result,* or perhaps better, the *actuality of result.* Is the living being actually done to death

---

[15] This still remains something of a presumption, however. For the main tendency in Buddhist thinking here is to relate all deeds and their respective degrees of kammic consequence to each other, not so much in terms of social as of subjective effects. The serene mind-state dispels or negates the social evil to some extent. But even a minor sin, in social terms, is very serious if it flows out of a disturbed and angry frame of mind. However, as we noted in the discussion on intention, the separation of mind-state and resultant action cannot be carried to extremes in Buddhism, even though their linkage is not always kept close and tight.

by the assault of the would-be killer? While this is the last-mentioned factor and in some sense the least important, it is by no means *un*important. Its presence among the factors gives the lie to those interpretations of Buddhist ethics that would insist that intention alone is enough and physical result imma-terial. Obviously the fact that a death actually results does make a difference. Of course this is true socially: If the victim of an assault does not die as a result, the offence is not adjudged as murder; and if he does, it is. But this is also apparently true in the kammic sense. No matter if there be present the full inten-tion to kill, the knowledge that it is a living being that is being attacked, the fact that it is indeed living, and the exertion of considerable effort to encompass the death of that being—if the being is not actually killed, the offence is not that of killing and hence not so serious. *All* of the factors must be present to make it such, in whatever context it may be considered.

c. *Summary*

The discussion has been confined thus far to an examination of the moral judgment as it is exercised in the context of the First Precept.[16] This makes the process of analysis simpler; and since the same constituent factors, with appropriate modifica-tions to suit the particular Precept, are used with respect to the other four Precepts, the above analysis of the First Precept is typical for all. The other four Precepts teach the avoidance of stealing, improper sexual conduct and sensuality in general, lying, and imbibing intoxicating liquors or drugs. But in each case of breaking the Precept, all the factors must be present.

There is the necessity of a *factual* situation: There must be some property of genuine value present; some definite sexual action between an actual man and woman,[17] or indulgence of an

---

[16] Some related questions of considerable contemporary interest, yet somewhat aside from our main interest here, will be discussed in Appendix A. In particular the controversial matter of meat eating will be considered.

[17] Actually homosexuality is forbidden too, especially among the monks, but because heterosexual offences are more common, it is chiefly these that are spoken of in connection with the Third Precept. And the

appetite; the possibility of real truth and falsity; and the presence of an actually intoxicating substance. There must also be the *intention*, or we may say, a *knowledgeable* intention, which truly knows that there are things to steal, disallowed women or men to have sexual relations with, lies to tell, and intoxicants to take, and fully intends to do so in a particular proposed action. There must be an *effort* made—the hand stretched out to take, the actual attempted assignation with the fellow-adulterer or fornicator, the false word, gesture, or action, and the swallowing or injection of the intoxicant—and an effort *voluntarily* made, of course, before the Precept in question is violated. Finally there must be the actual accomplished *result*. Whatever the intentions, efforts, and facts involved in the situation, unless there is property actually taken, a sexual act or indulgence of sensual appetite actually accomplished, persons who are genuinely deceived, and intoxicating substances having their effects, the fullness of evil has not been accomplished.

Needless to say there are many interesting points that might be discussed with considerable casuistry; and others that have been raised by new knowledge and circumstances. There are many forms of stealing in the modern complex world unknown to the ancient one in whose culture the Precepts were framed; propaganda and advertising may be highly skilled and complex forms of deceit; many new avenues are now open for the indulgence of human appetites. So also there are those fine points of definition: Is a "white" lie really a deceit? Does the consent of the woman in question to the proposed sexual act make it less evil, and what is the "age of consent"? How clearly can "intoxicating" be defined—as witness the American attempt at a 3.2 percent definition during prohibition days? But since these and other like problems are not near the heart of our concern here, we shall bypass them.

4. Conclusion

Two or three other matters of secondary interest may be mentioned in conclusion. One is the matter of balancing or

implication is usually that it is the man, as sexual aggressor, who must be prevented from illicit relations.

compensatory factors. Can an evil deed be compensated for in any manner whatsoever by either a "good" intention or "good" result? We have already discussed the fundamental aspects of this question in the consideration of the role of the intention or motive. And the general answer is a two-fold, "No"! For there cannot be a truly good intention producing an evil deed; and kammic consequences cannot be neglected. Every deed must bear its fruit! Yet in some cases of a borderline nature there may be a kind of compensation. Should I kill a venomous snake that seems to be in the act of striking a small child, for example, there might be some compensation here. The snake was killed, to be sure, and this is a sin with evil consequences; but the child's life was saved (presumedly) and that is a good. Or at least "good" intentions modify its evil to some extent. Both will register in the further account that Kamma adds up for me. However, a strict Buddhist may well say that killing the snake is most certainly a sin, while it is *not* so certain in fact that the child would have been killed or might not have been saved by other means. Hence my supposedly good deed is of dubious ethical worth.

A second question suggests itself: If it is the kammic destiny of an individual to meet death, for example the child *or* the snake of the above illustration, should I interfere in the impartial course of kammic "justice"? And if I do "interfere," am I not in any case simply the agent of Kamma and hence guiltless? While Kamma has often been an excuse for inaction, as we shall note in future chapters, most Buddhists today would say that man is given his free will for use; and that apart from wrong actions, vigorous doing of what the present situation seems to demand is the kammic *duty* of a person, the building up of his own good Kamma for the future. And with regard to being the passive agent of Kamma in whatever he does, this also approaches much too near to a fatalism to be acceptable. True, his actions are not causeless and will fit into the general kammic pattern; he may indeed be the actual agency that brings to the snake its appointed doom, i.e. the consequences of past bad

Kamma.[18] But nevertheless he is not guiltless; even though offences must needs come, "woe unto him by whom they come." For though Kamma may dispose a man toward evil, it does not compel him to it.

Such questions might be multiplied with regard to ethical distinctions on this level. Nor are they mere quibbles for the man who is concerned to judge his moral responsibilities exactly. Yet because they are endless and because there is much more in Buddhist ethic than mere logical distinctions, we must move on to wider considerations and a more comprehensive outline of the body of the ethic in practical application.

---

[18] A Buddhist friend commented that the contemporary (1959) Burmese army campaign to kill rats, crows and stray dogs would undoubtedly have its evil kammic effects but that the Buddhist consoled himself by thinking "destruction was the appropriate kammic destiny of each of the destroyed animals."

CHAPTER V

While almost every Buddhist scripture might be said to have some ethical significance, particularly if we think of ethics as that process of self-perfection which ends in the attainment of Nibbana, the field is much narrower for the practical purposes of concrete ethical specification. For the life of the householder in the beginning at least was the sub- or marginally-Buddhist life, and its concerns were completely of secondary religious importance. Therefore lay morality was charted out rather casually and in very small compass as befitted that which belongs to the merely mundane world. To be sure the commentarial literature, written after the layman had come into his own in the Buddhist community, recognizes his role more largely.

Nevertheless lay morality still remains somewhat the poor relation of monkish (and nibbanic) morality in the Theravada tradition. Its actual literature has necessarily been made much of by later tradition. From among the discourses of the Buddha three suttas in particular are today selected as especially important for their ethical content: The *Mangala Sutta,* the *Sigālovāda Sutta,* and the *Mettā Sutta.* These suttas are quoted or referred to in Buddhist circles somewhat as the Beatitudes, the Sermon on the Mount, or Paul's description of love in First Corinthians (chapter thirteen) are referred to in Christian circles. And there are besides these some miscellaneous socio-moralistic motifs scattered through the *Jātaka Tales;* and some of the *Tales* contain longish prescriptions for the guidance of rulers.

Besides these specific scriptures there are also some favorite themes or formulations of general ethical import that apply on the whole to the "'normal" style of ethical living for a layman on the kammic plane. Here one may speak of the lower levels of the Noble Eightfold Path, e.g. three Sila or moralistic items (Right Speech, Right Action, Right Livelihood) and of the Five, Eight, and Ten Precepts. Further one may speak of the Four Illimitables or Divine Abidings that represent moralistic *attitudes* somewhat in contrast to or in extension of the external moral deeds dealt with by the Precepts. To these attitudes, casual reference has already been made: Loving-kindness *(mettā),* compassion *(karuṇā),* sympathetic joy *(muditā),* and equanimity *(upekkhā).*

One might, of course, include the monk's Vinaya Rules as the prime example of Buddhist moral legislation. The *Vinaya* is one of the major divisions of the Tipitika or Three-Fold Pali Canon and regulates the life of the monk down to the last detail. There are some 227 major rules with many interpretations and specific applications added thereunto. But this is a study in itself and in actuality is largely irrelevant to our purpose here. For it has little or no bearing on the life of the layman. And the basic ethical quality of life even in the Sangha, as well as the Sangha's role as the Ideal Society, can be understood without a minute and exhaustive analysis of its rules.

1. The Practical Ethic of Kamma and Rebirth

While the Buddhist tradition does not neatly divide its formulations thus, we may for the purposes of discussion classify the morality of the Precepts, the morality of charity or liberality *(Dāna-Sīla),* and of the Blessed Dispositions (Four Illimitables) as belonging to the Kamma-rebirth realm. With the possible exception of the fourth Illimitable, equanimity, the other good deeds and virtues may all be said to be dedicated to the matter of "getting ahead" in the worlds of rebirth by accumulating merit—with Nibbana as only a kind of stratospheric possibility.

a. *The Precepts*

In the previous chapter we have considered practical ethical judgment at work on the Precept materials. But here we must consider the Precepts in the totality of their organized form. The Precepts, whether in their five-, eight-, or ten-fold version, represent the basic Buddhist moral law for personal life in the world. The term "law" is not quite appropriate in the Buddhist view, since it suggests a set of commandments spoken by a Law-Giver. But as Buddhism rejects the idea of God, it considers "commandments" the wrong term to apply to its Precepts even though it may regard them as rooted in principles universally valid in any world of existence. It prefers to say that the Precepts are counsel to the wise, based on the fact that their observance brings blessed (kammic) consequences both in this life and lives to come, and their non-observance produces grief, pain and misfortune. Thus one may take or leave the good advice for he is not *commanded* to accept it.

Actually the distinction between commandments and precepts is academic. Should one compare the Five-fold Precept formulation with that of the Hebraic Decalogue he would be struck with the great similarity of the two in content and form— with the exception, of course, of the first four "religious" commandments of the latter. Both deal with the same basic personal-social actions; both are negatively phrased, one counseling to "avoid," the other commanding, "Thou shalt not." And both provide the same fundamental basis for social law in their respective cultures. Said an officer of the Buddhist Democratic Party of Burma: "There could be no society without the observation of the Five Precepts as the basic law. Otherwise the jungle customs of lawlessness would be the result."

The minimal set of moral precepts, held to be binding in at least their external form upon all Buddhists alike whether lay or monk, are the following, known as the Five Precepts:

(1) Avoid taking life (animal or human);
(2) Avoid stealing (taking what is not offered);
(3) Avoid illicit sexual relations (and sensuality in general);
(4) Avoid lying;
(5) Avoid intoxicants (and drugs).

This list of moral precepts is repeated (in its Pali form) at almost every Buddhist religious gathering; for not only is it *minimal* morality, but *basic* morality capable of many degrees of fulfillment as we shall later note. Therefore the Buddhist seeks ever to remind himself of his fundamental principles.

These Precepts are largely self-explanatory so that we need not discuss them in detail, though as we have observed in the previous chapter considerable discussion as to the specific meaning and application of a Precept in a given situation is possible. We may therefore pass on to the other formulations, which are essentially the original Five with various others of more refinement or greater difficulty added. The Ten-fold formulation increases the Five-fold with the addition of the following items:

(6) Avoid eating at unseasonable intervals, i.e. after midday;

(7) Avoid worldly amusements such as plays, sports, gambling;

(8) Avoid the use of perfumes or ointments on oneself;

(9) Avoid sleeping on luxurious beds, i.e. high soft ones;

(10) Do not handle or possess gold or silver.

Obviously the full Ten Precepts can be kept only by a monk who lives in an isolated dwelling or at least in a monastery.

So far as laymen are concerned we have the possibility of an optional gradation in the keeping of the first Eight or Nine of the Precepts. Some few, who somewhat resemble Roman Catholic lay brothers, may elect to keep the Ten Precepts continually, and even observe the first Five more rigidly than the ordinary layman; non-killing will be interpreted to mean a vegetarian diet only, and the avoidance of sensuality to mean complete sexual continence.

In general, however, the observance of more than the Five Precepts is confined to special seasons, fast days, and sabbath days. Many laymen observe the first nine precepts every sabbath day, i.e. four times each lunar month, roughly on the 1st, 8th, 15th and 23rd days thereof. Buddhist "Lent" *(Wesak)*, which usually begins in July and roughly coincides with the rainy season in South Asian regions, may also be a period of additional Precept observance. Or a person may choose to thus observe eight or nine precepts for a stated period of time in fulfillment of a vow he has taken. Indeed, if he desires, he may enter a monastery for a day, a month, or a year, and observe all Ten Precepts as well as the more detailed monks' rules.

There is still another formulation of precepts, likewise ten in number and building on the basic Five, but somewhat different from the above. The additions are not so much observances of further self-denying ordinances, as rules of good character that penetrate beyond the external observances of the first Ten-fold formulation into the realm of motive and attitude. This formulation is often called *Dasa-Sīla*.

The five additions to the basic Five are these:

   (6) Avoid slander and reviling;

   (7) Avoid avarice and covetousness, i.e. one form of greed *(lobha);*

   (8) Avoid enmity and malevolence, i.e. hatred *(dosa);*

   (9) Avoid self-praise and idle talk;

(10) Avoid wrong (heretical) views and the deriding of the Buddha, his Teaching *(Dhamma),* and the Order of monks *(Sangha).*

This leads to a necessary observation with regard to all Buddhist morality which must be reiterated here. It is part and parcel of what we have earlier called the Buddhist doctrine of levels (Cf. pp. 76-8), that even basic moral precepts may be observed differently in many different contexts. There is the simple minimal observance of the Five Precepts that consists only in the physical avoidance of the wrong actions: murder, theft, adultery and fornication, lying, and drunkenness or drug addiction. And even though this be the basic level of observance, the Buddhist sees two advantages to it in terms of kammic and even nibbanic consequences. Firstly if a man avoids killing, for example, even though restrained from it by force of custom or law, he *is* prevented from carrying out the full-fledged action whose kammic consequences are serious. His evil Kamma will not be as evil as it might have been; and there is as well the incidental advantage of the good of others. And secondly, since one of the best ways to achieve mind-control is through body-control, even the body-control level of observance of the precepts may be a genuine step toward that mind-control which is the key to ultimate deliverance.

Yet there are obvious limits here. Such an observance of the Precepts may carry one a little forward, but not very far.

It is like shearing off the top leaves or twigs of a tree in the hope of killing it. But not until the trunk and the roots of the tree of evil desires and wrong dispositions are cut down, dug up, and destroyed, will the basic attitudes that result in the external violations of the precepts be overcome and the Five Precepts be observed in their fullness. That is to say, the Five Precepts may also be observed in fullness and depth, as the principles of non-hatred, non-greed, non-sensuality, absolute truthfulness and self-control.

For example: In one sense we may consider that suprapersonal consciousness which Buddhism seeks to achieve on the highest and nibbanic levels of living, as the ultimate extension of the principle of non-killing; it is that state of consciousness from which is rooted out even the *possibility* of the hateful thought that produces killing, and for which all beings, including oneself, have become of absolutely equal concern.[1]

But we are clearly above the ordinary and kammic level of preceptual observance when speaking in such terms. We must return to that level with a consideration of the "positive" morality of Buddhism.

b. *Positive Morality*

The term "positive" is used here in contrast to the negative form of the Precepts, which are all stated as avoidances. It is similar to the contrast sometimes made between the negative formulation of Jewish ethic found in the "shall nots" of the Decalogue and the "positive" form given them by Deuteronomy and Jesus in the two great commandments to love God supremely and others as one's self. Obviously such a contrast is rather inaccurate since even the negative commandment is but the prohibitory social formulation of a

---

[1] The partial parallelism to the Wesleyan doctrine of entire sanctification is unmistakable. In remarkedly similar though Christian language the rooting out of man's carnal nature, i.e., his inborn tendency to do evil, his wrong dispositions such as anger and pride, and the purification of the inner fount of his motivational being by a second work of grace, is continually called for. The general goal of a purified inwardness which produces good deeds naturally and spontaneously is the same in both traditions.

"positive" value, e.g. that lying is wrong because truth-telling is good. Especially is it inaccurate in a Buddhist context in which almost all value statement is in negative form and where the assumption is that if evil in human nature is done away (i.e. hatred rooted out) then goodness will appear (i.e. loving kindness come into action). But it has some validity even here as indicating those actions and attitudes which are more positively stated. And it is a distinction that even Theravada Buddhists themselves use, though perhaps in self-defense against Western criticism.

(1) Dāna-Sīla

Dāna means liberality or generosity with one's worldly goods and includes the majority of charitable activities in a Buddhist society. Anything that calls for the sharing of material substance, whether through personal or institutional channels, could be classed as an example of dāna. Its motivation is two-fold: The building up of one's own store of merit and (secondarily) any benefit which it may provide to others. It may be considered negatively as the limitation of the giver's temptations to greed by means of curtailing his resources for self-indulgence; but it seems more natural from a Western point of view to think of it as the "positive" morality of altruism.

When we turn to its concrete manifestations we must immediately take into account the Buddhist doctrine of the *field of merit* briefly alluded to in a previous chapter. Stated simply this doctrine means that the worthier the man to whom the good deed is done, the more merit it produces and hence the "better" the action. The reverse is also true, though not so much emphasized; the *un*worthy man, or more especially the definitely evil man, such as a heretical teacher, is not to be subsidized in his error. At least such a deed will not produce merit. But returning to the idea of positive worthiness we may say that one's "worth" is roughly equivalent to his nearness to Nibbana or even his devotion to the quest of Nibbana.

To be sure Buddhism does not precisely state it thus. And it is not the *only* factor involved—witness the rating of parents and teachers high on the scale of worth. But when one speaks specifically of worth in the sense of worthy-for-offerings then the nibbanic factor is definitely determinative. For it is the Buddha, his pagodas or images—which represent his contemporary "presence" in the world—and his Order of Monks, or the Sangha, that are the most worthy. A Buddha is one who has attained Nibbana and his monks are those who are supremely dedicated to its quest.[2]

This selection of superior fields of merit has been largely determinative of the form and direction of Buddhist dana-sila and provided it with its driving motivation. We may observe first of all the place of the Sangha as a chief recipient of dana-sila. One of the commonest sights of a morning (of every morning) throughout Burma is that of the yellow-robed monk on his begging rounds. Either carrying his large black bowl himself, or having it carried by a small-boy assistant, he goes to the houses of the neighborhood to which he has been assigned by his superiors. Nor does he often go away empty-handed. The good Buddhist layman will not eat his main morning meal until the monk has been given the topmost best of the dishes. For the monk does not come as a beggar in the Western sense, but as a most honored guest whose coming is eagerly awaited, even though he does not remain to eat with the family. He need only to appear, without speaking a word, and his bowl will be filled. Begging is often and perhaps usually done singly; and few monks, except the sick, very aged, or very eminent, are exempted from collecting their own food. But periodically a layman's association of a village or city quarter may cooperatively provide a meal for a large number of monks from monastery or school, putting the morning's food in each bowl as the long line of monks files by. Or now and then a whole monastery population is regularly fed at the monastery itself.

There are other ways of providing the Order with its necessities. A family frequently celebrates its anniversaries by presenting *soon*, or food, in the form of an early morning meal to a number of neighboring monks. An individual layman may feel moved—the monk is forbidden to solicit such provision directly—

---

[2] Those who undertake meditation are sometimes honored in a special way, whether monks or not, because of their attempt in this direction. The very attempt itself constitutes the attemptors a better field of merit.

to present to a monk to whose support he is pledged, various gifts on the occasion of his ordination, or re-ordination which may be celebrated an indefinite number of times. Sometimes a wealthy man, mindful of both shedding the light of his example abroad and acquiring abundance of merit, may stage a "private" dana celebration in a public place. I saw one such at the Shwe Dagon in which a sizeable area had been roped off for the donor, the donor's family and friends, his portable shrine, his pile of gifts, and his musicians, and space provided for all others who might wish to rejoice in his liberality to the Order. Sometimes there is a formal institutional presentation of gifts—a meal on the spot for the representative monks, and robes, fans, mats, writing supplies, and some small tinned food gifts for all the monks of the monasteries they represent. The favorite time for such occasions is at the end of Lent in October and November.

Still another device, though of the same general order, for providing for the Sangha, is a kind of open-air street festival. Large pandals, i.e. columned and corniced structures of gilt and painted cardboard, are set up along the street on either side by merchants and business men. In some of these sit spectators, musicians, and donors with boxes of combs, pencils and so forth. In others are collected "gift trees," i.e. small branches or plastic imitations of trees, on which are fastened paper money and various small articles. After a time comes a procession of monks, each monk with his attendant layman, to receive one of the gift trees and other miscellaneous items at the stalls. And a good time is had by all, even the small boys to whom small coins are tossed out by the lay organizers, who themselves march at the head of the procession.

There are indeed few Burmese Buddhists who would criticize any liberality shown to a monk or a monk's project of building a monastery or pagoda—though some criticsm may attach to the monk who seems to be providing himself with over-fine robes and good living quarters at the expense of some fond *dāyaka,* i.e. layman pledged to his support. For the Sangha *is* a notable field for producing merit; and who can begrudge another his increase of this commodity?

Another notable expression of *Dāna-Sīla,* particularly in Burma, is pagoda building. It rivals, perhaps even outclasses, benevolence to the Order as a meritorious form of liberality; for in a sense the building of a pagoda reverences the Buddha himself since the pagoda enshrines his image. And He, by all odds, is the *supremely* beneficial field of merit. Writing in 1885 Shway Yoe had this to say about the proliferation of pagodas in Burma:

> There is good reason for this multiplication of fanes. No work of merit is so richly paid as the building of a pagoda. The Payatagah (pagoda builder) is regarded as a saint on earth, and when he dies he obtains the last release; for him there are no more deaths.[3]

He goes on to note that the merit gained by pagoda building is greater than that from giving roadside water pots or monastery donations; and that new pagoda building is far and away more meritorious than contributions to or upkeep of old ones, save in the case of famous relic shrines.

There are contemporary Buddhists who would quarrel with some of Shway Yoe's statements. They would categorically deny that Buddhism has ever taught that one can gain Nibbana by building a pagoda. And they would further deny that the merit of repairing a pagoda accrues only or even primarily to the original builder. (As we have seen, in any case, merit can be shared.) They would say that the hundreds of pagodas mouldering away in Burma today are not the result of the alleged inferiority of pagoda-repairing merit, but of the lack of resources on the part of would-be repairers.

It may well be that Shway Yoe's version, though not orthodoxly Buddhist, was an influential popular one. Whatever the exact truth, there can be no doubt that pagoda building has been and remains an eminently desirable way in which to spend one's surplus income. It has been said that the natural thought of a Burmese Buddhist, when he comes into a bit of extra money, is to build a pagoda with it, even if a very small one. And though the colossal scale of pagoda building represented by the Pagan centuries (1100-1400 A. D.) may well be a thing of the past, pagodas of considerable splendor are still being built.

---

[3] *The Burman and His Notions* (Macmillan, 1885), I, 184.

Within the last 10 years a large and magnificent structure, decorated with 100,000 Buddha images, large and small, was erected near Monywa, northwest of Mandalay, at a considerable cost. Nor do the larger and grander pagodas often lack the resources to gild their domes anew when the gold leaf on them wears thin.

This reverence for the pagoda as a shrine containing the relics (if possible) of the Buddha and his disciples, or at least his images, carries over to worship at these pagodas. This is not the place to detail that worship at length but only to observe that pagoda worship flourishes with unabated strength in contemporary Theravada Buddhism. There have been some efforts to reform it in this respect, and there are numerous individuals who look upon its crassness with disdain; yet all such protests have produced more noise than effect and have now largely died out so far as any organized expression is concerned. The reason is obvious: For the vast majority of both monks and laity the pagoda is a holy place where it is easier to feel the "presence" of the Buddha, where devotional attachment may center, and lastly, but not least, where meritorious deeds are best performed. And in the offering of incense, flowers, and pious wishes before the Buddha-image, who knows what glorious results may spring from even a little seed sown in this best of all merit-fields?

There has been another and negative effect of the heavy concentration of dana-sila upon the Sangha and the Pagoda: other less "worthy" interests such as public charities have suffered. Who will sow a seed in a poor stony field (of merit) if a rich and fertile field (of merit) lies close at hand? None but a fool. And not many are willing to be fools for the sake of sheer idealism, in Buddhism or elsewhere. Likewise there is again to be noted the depressing effect of the doctrine of the complete determination and responsibility of each person for his own fate expressed in kammic law. Why, again, should anyone waste his precious merit-producing power upon another whose destiny he can so little affect, and who is really suffering misfortune only because of his own evil deeds in any case?

Of course, as noted in an earlier discussion of merit, human nature has overflowed logic here also in actual practice. To suggest that Buddhist cultures are deserts of compassionless disregard for the unfortunate is quite contrary to the facts. There is indeed something of an inclination to shun the especially unfortunate because of the aroma of bad kamma that they emanate. Movements to take up public responsibility for such persons have often waited for the outside stimulus; such individuals may hope for improvement in their condition in the next existence, if they use their present situation in this one in a teachable spirit. Yet even to these unfortunates many individual, if not institutional, deeds of kindness are done, for loving-kindness and compassion are standard Buddhist virtues. And in Theravada countries where family ties are strong, many are the sick, elderly, and unfortunate relatives who are taken into an enlarged family group and cared for, meagerly perhaps, but as adequately as possible.

Indeed the impression one often gains is rather that of the characteristic lack of resource to help all the unfortunates to be found in a primitive society instead of inhumanness or indifference. Further, the disinclination toward public and impersonal forms of charity comes partly through lack of "know-how" and partly because the sick and aged themselves prefer to be at home among friends in poverty rather than alone among strangers in a munificent public institution.

Nonetheless one must record that public concern for the unfortunate, indeed the whole concept of public welfare, is in its infancy in most Theravada Buddhist cultures. And though the Kamma-Merit doctrine is not the sole source of such a condition, it has diverted most organized charity into narrowly religious channels at the expense of human need. But today there are stirrings in other directions as the organization and industrialization of Eastern societies proceed apace, and even some criticism of the excessively pagoda- and Sangha-oriented charities of traditional Buddhism. To this more detailed consideration must be given later.

(2) The Blessed Dispositions

If we go beyond the area of externalized moral action into the realm of those motives and attitudes that are to be considered ethically good, four specific qualities or types of attitude stand out above the many that might be mentioned, particularly in contemporary importance. They are called either *Illimitables*, because of their possible and desirable universal extension, or *Divine Abidings,* because of their qualitative likeness to life in the Brahma Spheres or Heavens. These four, which we will examine each in turn, are as follows: *mettā,* loving-kindness; *karuṇā,* compassion; *muditā,* sympathetic joy; and *upekkhā,* equanimity.

(a) *Mettā or Loving Kindness*

This is by all odds the most emphasized of the positive Buddhist moral attitudes today, particularly as Buddhism is confronted increasingly by the activist and socially conscious culture of the West. We may best begin its discussion by quoting some classical descriptions and modern interpretations.

In the *Sutta-Nipāta* is found the famous *Mettā Sutta* that reads in part as follows:

Whatever living Beings there be—
Feeble or strong, tall, stout or medium,
Short, small or large, without exception,—

Seen or unseen,
Those dwelling far or near,
Those who are born, or who are to be born,
May all Beings be happy!

Let none deceive another
Nor despise any person whatsoever in any place,
Let him not wish any harm to another.
Out of anger or ill-will.

Just as a mother would protect her only child
At the risk of her own life
Even so let him cultivate a boundless heart
Towards all Beings.

Let his thoughts of boundless love
Pervade the whole world,
Above, below and across without any obstruction,
Without any hatred, without any enmity.

Whether he stands, walks, sits,
Lies down, as long as he is awake
He should develop this mindfulness.
This they say is the noblest living here.

Not falling into Error (self-illusion),
Being Virtuous and endowed with Insight,
By discarding attachment to sense desires
Never does he come again for conception in a womb.[4]

The same quality of a universally extended loving kindness
is given expression in one of the prose scriptures in the form of
a frequently repeated refrain:

> Herein [is wealth] that a brother abides letting his mind
> fraught with love pervade one quarter of the world, and so too
> the second quarter, and so the third quarter, and so the fourth
> quarter. And thus the whole wide world, above, below, around,
> and everywhere and altogether does he continue to pervade with
> love-burdened thought, abounding, sublime, beyond measure,
> free from hatred and ill-will.[5]

The general concept of metta is thus clear. It is a spirit of
benevolent harmlessness which is to be universalized in the end
—though one must begin on a lesser scale. As with other similar
wish-thoughts, one begins first with himself, then proceeds to the
respected, the loved, the neutral, the hostile, and finally to the
whole universe as the *Mettā Sutta* makes plain. Metta in its universalized exercise becomes a part of that generalized supra-
personal consciousness that *can*not distinguish between one's
own and another's welfare. In the perfect exercise of metta one
gives to another, indeed to all others, the same quality of loving
concern that a mother gives to her only child. This is loving
"one's neighbor as oneself" with a universal vengeance!

At the risk of multiplying quotations unduly we may turn
to a contemporary interpretation of metta as expressed by a
prominent Burmese monk:

> Metta is much higher than sentimental sensual love.
> It is this Metta that attempts to break away all barriers which
> separate beings from one another.
> The Pali word Metta means literally . . . friendliness . . .
> also love without a desire to possess but with a desire to help, to

---

[4] Sister Vajira (trans.), *The Sutta-Nipāta* (Sarnath, India: Maha
Bodhi Society, n.d.).
[5] *Dīgha-Nikāya (Dialogues of the Buddha)*, Sutta 28, PTS Edition,
IV, 76.

sacrifice self-interest for the welfare and well-being of human-ity. . . . It is a dynamic suffusing of every living being . . . with dynamic, creative thoughts of loving-kindness. If the thoughts are intense enough, right actions follow automatically.[6]

The last sentence in the above quotation raises an interesting and vital point. How is metta to be exercised? One might infer from the expression used that metta is simply the rather universal principle (and hope) that kindly thoughts should be so ener-gized that they will carry over into action.[7] But there are subtle differences in the Buddhist context and meaning. Basic to the total Buddhist approach to the exercise of good will is what Mrs. C. A. F. Rhys-Davids in a perceptive phrase has called "televoli-tion," that is, the direct, dynamic, efficacious exertion of will-force at a distance. This is to be considered as a real force that has a definite effect upon men and other sentient beings. Nor is this a modern innovation; it is both ancient and central to the main tradition. Sometimes definite physical efficacy is attributed to it. Thus when some monks (here translated wrongly "priests") are reporting on the death of a brother monk by snake-bite, the Buddha replies:

> For surely, O priests, if that priest had suffused the four royal families of the snakes with his friendliness, that priest, O priests, would not have been killed by the bite of a snake.[8]

In the same work (VII, 3, 11, 12) there is the story of the Buddha turning aside, by the sheer power of his loving good will, the rush of a mad elephant sent against him by the evil Devadat-ta, a rival monk. There are also some accounts of the tempta-tion of Gotama just before his enlightenment, that are given a rather physicalist interpretation and portray Mara, the Evil One, as attacking him with hosts of evil spirits, fierce animals, con-

---

[6] Venerable U Thittila, "Buddhist Metta," *Light of the Dhamma*, V, No. 1 (January, 1958), 49–51.

[7] The author of the quotation stressed to me in conversation that thoughts which did not carry over into action were like flowers that bore no fruit.

[8] From *Cūla-vagga* of the *Sutta-Nipāta*, H. C. Warren, *Buddhism in Translations* (Cambridge, Mass.: Harvard University Press, 1953), p. 302.

vulsions of nature, and sensual temptations—all of which the
Buddha-soon-to-be- turns harmlessly aside by his calm benevolence.[9] And in the *Jātaka Tales* the theme of the turning aside
of the fierceness of vengeful man and raging beast occurs over
and over again.

Now and then this theme becomes mingled with sheer magic.
In the following passage from the post-canonical *Questions of
King Milinda* such spiritual control of physical circumstances
is attributed to the recitation—in loving goodwill of course—of a
Pirit *(paritta)* or selected verse of scripture which is used as a
charm against danger:

> And when the Pirit has been said over a man, a snake ready
> to bite will not bite him, but close his jaws . . . the club which
> robbers hold aloft to strike him with will never strike, they will
> let it drop and treat him kindly. . . . The enraged elephant rush-
> ing at him will suddenly stop. . . . The burning fiery conflagration
> surging toward him will die out . . . The malignant poison he
> has eaten will become harmless and turn to food. . . . Assassins
> who have come to slay him will become as slaves who wait upon
> him. . . . And the trap into which he has trodden will hold him
> not.[10]

How completely this physicalist interpretation of metta is
accepted today in Theravada countries is difficult to ascertain.
Certainly in the somewhat bastardized magical form of the
recitation of parittas it still goes on in much the ancient fashion[11] in popular practice. But it is also true that many contem-

---

[9] Contemporary pagoda art in Burma often portrays the Temptation
in dramatic style. Buddha, with a shining halo about his person, sits calm-
ly in the center of a veritable rain of arrows, darts, rocks, spears, and
clubs halted in mid-air by the power of his presence; and he holds at a
distance by the same power, a raging torrent of fierce animals and hid-
eous demons. In one pagoda there is a large Buddha statue seated, with
a small-size elephant tamely resting under the pendant fingers—the once-
raging Devadatta-sent monster.

[10] Chapter IV, Section 2.

[11] Thus: "For in Sri Lanka, Ceylon, at any rate, there is no Buddhist,
high or low, educated or uneducated, who has not at one time or other
felt the almost miraculous effect of chanting the verse enumerating the
nine *gunas* or virtues of the Buddha in allaying fear or even warding off
wild animals. It is a widespread habit in this country to chant the verse

porary Buddhists find themselves in a postion much like Christians who would maintain that *if* one had faith enough, he might indeed command the mountain or tree to be removed and cast into the sea—yet no one really has that faith. So most Buddhists would hold to the *possibility* of such effects of good will and paritta chanting, provided one is of sufficient purity of heart. But, alas, few if any of such purity are to be found—certainly not the speakers!

The more orthodox interpretation and practice of televolitional power at present tend toward what the modern Buddhist terms the "radiation" of good will or loving kindness, i.e. metta. Radiation may be taken as today's equivalent of the "permeation" and "suffusing" found in the quoted scripture passages. But through it is thus conceived in a more generalized and spiritual form, the exercise of good-will-power is still most certainly considered to be tangibly efficacious. Love as a radiated force is believed to have a genuine potency—if practiced—in the social and political world. Indeed it is *the* Buddhist solution for the modern world's ills. Thus writes a well-known Singhalese monk:

> A man with a meditative mind lives at peace with himself, and with the world. No harm or violence will issue from him. The peace and purity he radiates, will have conquering power and be a blessing to the world. *He will be a positive factor in society, even if he lives in seclusion and silence.*[12]

---

when the temperature rises in a child . . . when flood water surges into a hut, or a dangerous animal is met face to face in a jungle track."

The writer goes on to tell the story of a man seized by an elephant and raised in the air preparatory to being dashed down to his death. Repetition of the above-mentioned verse caused the elephant to put him down safely.

"The explantion of the elephant's behaviour is a previous experience in human form, carried by him (the elephant) in his subconscious mind." Arthur de Silva, "Gaining the Light of the Buddha," *Light of the Buddha,* III, No. 4 (April, 1958), 107.

What is true in Ceylon is also largely true in Burma where *parittas* are still much used. And it is reported of some holy monks and profound meditators that they are immune to mosquito attacks, while meditating at least.

[12] Venerable Nyanaponika, "Right Protection," *Light of the Dhamma,* II, No. 1 (November, 1953), 17. Italics added.

The basic image here is clear: The holy man in his cell in the forest may radiate a positive, health-bringing influence out into society far and apart from his own physical presence or action.

Other writers are anxious to impress upon their readers that the radiation of good-will-power is the duty and privilege of *every* Buddhist, and not only of the holy man:

> Metta should be radiated by every Buddhist at least once a day. In the early hours of the morning after one's daily ablution, one should meditate on Metta and radiate it to all beings, animate or inanimate. The task will not be long and weary, and in a matter of about five minutes one can daily perform this meritorious deed. This will greatly benefit the person in this very life or an after life.

> One always wonders why a certain person is liked or disliked not only by human beings but also by animals and dumb creatures. It is all due to the Metta extended or not extended by the person.[13]

Two observations about the exercise of metta may be made at this point. Despite the earlier suggestion that if metta is intense enough it eventuates in deeds, the usual flavor of interpretation is that it is to a great extent something of a *substitute* for the physical action of good will—and a superior substitute at that. The holier a person is, the more he turns from physical-action goodwill toward those few persons he might thus affect, to radiated goodwill to all creatures in the universe. Indeed there is a deep distrust of physical-action good will and social service in Buddhism, because of the suspicion that they often spring from unworthy motives and are a subtle form of the will to dominate those to whom we are doing "good." To this we shall return in a moment.

The other observation, growing from the last quotation, is that metta exercise is consistently portrayed as good because of the good results upon the exerciser thereof, not the recipient. The radiator of good-will will make himself be greatly benefitted

---

[13] Venerable M. M. Mahaweera, "Metta," *The Buddhist Supplement* of *The Burman*, October 8, 1958. The practice of radiating metta is unmistakably like Christian intercessory prayer, except without the God-reference.

—he will be liked by both people and animals! Or more fairly, his gentleness and benevolence will be instinctively felt by all. In any case this too is a consistent Buddhist emphasis: Charity must begin at home; only from a pure and loving heart can love be radiated.

Because this principle of "self firstness" in virtue is so central to Buddhist ethic and so contrasted with the Christian approach to virtue, we must take care to try to understand it. Writes the Venerable U Thittila:

> Metta—Universal Love—is generally taken to exist in connection with other people but in reality love for self comes first. It is not a selfish love, but love for self . . . By having pure love, Metta . . . for self, selfish tendencies, hatred, anger will be diminished. Therefore unless we ourselves possess Metta within, we cannot share, we cannot radiate . . . Metta to others.
>
> To love the self means to be free from selfishness, hatred, anger, etc. Therefore to clear ourselves from these undesirable feelings we must love ourselves . . . for Buddhism is a method of dealing with ourselves.
>
> In true meditation first you fill yourselves with love mentally "May I be well and happy." After a while you extend it to all others saying mentally, "May all beings in the Universe be well and happy." Mean and feel it.[14]

According to Buddhism, therefore, one's first ethical *duty* is to properly love himself. Metta directed toward the self is held to be no mere self-love, but a benevolent willing of true spiritual character, worth, and salvation to himself. (For if one is himself not sufficiently convinced of the reality and goodness of such things, how can he will them for others?) Self-directed metta aims not at the selfish advantagement of one's own interests and desires, but at the destruction of the narrowly personal elements of selfhood and the eradication of greed and hatred.[15] Only when this is done is he able to radiate love to others.

---

[14] *Op. cit.,* p. 51–52.

[15] There is a valuable psychological insight here. The person who hates and despises himself or is at war within himself, is incapable of loving others; he will radiate his own frustrations and bitterness to others if he tries to "help" them when in this condition.

But, we may well ask, just when is a person ready to radiate metta to others? If he must wait till he is pure or perfect himself, that may take a thousand more existences at least. Is there not here a super-subtle selfishness that puts off involvement with others indefinitely? The Buddhist answer is two-fold: A person may and should begin to radiate metta (even for five minutes daily) just as soon as he is able, though he must avoid the danger of garbing unloving influence with the cloak of so-called love. The two kinds of metta, metta to self and metta to others, are one and the same and their exercise mutually strengthens each other. Metta-exercise toward others will purify the self; and metta-exercise toward the self will strengthen, and inevitably overflow into, metta towards others.

The other side of the answer is pragmatic and experiential: Only as a man does in truth free himself from self-love, greed, and hatred *can* he extend metta to others. His increasing ability to do this is both the stimulation of and witness to his "growth in grace." His perfection will be reached when he spontaneously, as naturally as breathing and without the slightest thought or effort, loves others as himself.

The contrast here with Christianity is most interesting. Christianity urges men to begin loving *others* as they begin to live the Christian life. Love of others is a means of leavening the lump of selfishness; by deliberate and loving involvement with others the Christian seeks to lessen or crowd out self-love. He interprets Jesus' commandment to love others as our selves, as the commandment to extend to others the same quality of personal concern that one feels for himself. Self-love is not a beginning point but a standard of guidance. Therefore he distrusts the Buddhist approach as one which has no guarantee of freeing one's self from self-concern. On the other hand the Buddhist appears to be less afraid that a man remain stuck on the sandbar of self-love, than that he will try to rush into frantic other-love before he is ready for it. He stresses the unloving nature of much social work —the projection of one's own moral impurities upon others under cover of doing them good; the personal domination expressed in much active "loving" concern; the spiritual coercion of others toward our own values. Learning to love by deliberate involvement of oneself in the lives of others is an exception that *some*times works properly, but not a reliable method of regular operation.[16]

In ultimate goal and even in actual practice the two patterns are perhaps not as far apart as they seem. For the thoughtful Christian is also aware that the right kind of *doing* good can come only from the right kind of *being*, or personal quality. And the Buddhist does not actually wait for full self-perfection before he begins to exercise metta; indeed, as has been suggested, he practices metta as a means for achieving perfection. Yet a difference does remain. The Christian pattern tends as the rule toward the active involvement of one person with another in its version of love; and the Buddhist pattern tends toward the detached radiation of metta—though at present a new activist emphasis and reinterpretation of metta are observable.

(b) *Karuṇā or Compassion*

Karuṇā has the general flavor of New Testament compassion: pity and helpful sympathy for those in distressful circumstances, either material or spiritual. In the Buddhist context it is designated as fellow-feeling for all other suffering beings. It is the pitying sympathy of one, who himself is caught in the round of rebirth-suffering-death, for others who are likewise prisoners of the same process. And here again the goal is that of the spontaneous exercise of a compassion that cannot, or does not, distinguish between one's own suffering and another's; false distinctions between one "self" and another "self" are to be wiped out.

But there is a special Buddhist emphasis and flavor which must not be neglected in the interpretation of karuna. Compassion of the truly good sort does not mean emotionalized identification with the other's suffering; and the agonized vicarious bearing of the world's sin and suffering in one's own self is quite different from karuna. Thus to "lose" oneself in concern for another, says the Buddhist, is mere sentimentality or emotional

---

[16] So stated the Venerable U Thittila in conversation, when the author suggested that parents sometimes became truly unselfish somewhat by force of circumstances, i.e., through responsibility for their children's welfare; and urged that this was a universally valid type of the practice of love—especially when the involvement is voluntary. Why it is an *unreliable* method was never clear to me.

orgy; it is a manifestation of weakness and not strength. Nor does it help the recipient in the slightest. To use an analogy: Emotional identification with another's suffering after the Christian manner or trying to "share" his pain, is like a non-swimmer's casting himself into the water beside a drowning man in order to drown along with him.[17]

The *ideal* compassionator, as exemplified by the Buddha, is like a skillful physician rather than a fellow mourner. He fully appreciates the suffering of the patient, in this case every sentient being, but does not, dare not, give way to emotional sympathy for that patient. Instead, cool-headedly and emotionally self-controlled, he analyzes the diseased condition and prescribes for it (or performs the operation) in a detached impersonal manner. To become emotionally involved would be to undermine his own poise and thereby ultimately to harm the patient more than help him. So it is also with the spiritual healer, or even anyone who hopes to do another *any* lasting benefit. Only as he himself is calm and pure, perceptive but not emotionally attached—in other words embodying the essence of spiritual health—can he help another. His compassion must be clear and knowledgeable, not distorted by emotion nor attached by involvement.

In this connection we may note that compassion is to some extent within the range of anyone—though when we say so we seem to be moving back toward the more usual pity-sympathy context of meaning in which one shows compassion to those less fortunate than he. It is held that any human being is in some respects in worse situation than another. The rich man may be both old and sick while his servant may be young and healthy. Thus there may be mutual showing of compassion, the master for the slave's poverty, the latter for the first's age and illness. Only the Buddha as their superior could show compassion to *all*

---

[17] With regard to literal drowning, orthodox theory is that *if* one can remain perfectly neutral in feeling toward the drowning man, neither rejoicing nor sorrowing in the slightest over that man's death agonies, there is nothing *kammically* evil in letting him drown. That is, no evil rebirth will result from refusing to save his life. Humanly speaking, however, to remain emotionally neutral under such circumstances is almost impossible. But would it not be "good," kammically and nibbanically speaking, to do so?

other beings; yet even he, as one still in bodily distress at times, might in turn be compassionated. Therefore as with metta, karuna may well be exercised by any one, even though at first in very imperfect forms.

This restrained exercise of compassion contains a valuable antidote to that maudlin emotionalism which helps no one at all and is so often substituted for intelligent action and attitude. And so far as personal relations on a one-to-one basis are concerned, it is quite true, we may repeat, that emotional disturbance in another is more often healed by emotional poise and calm in the healer than by counter-disturbance. Whether it furnishes a dynamic or adequate social motivation is perhaps quite another matter; for here in de-emotionalized compassion one senses the cooling influence of nibbanic eternalism, that eternalism of refuge from, not changing of, the painful conditions of time-space existence.

(c) Muditā or Sympathetic Joy

Though currently less emphasized than either metta or karuna in Buddhist circles—possibly because it does not offer such an easily concretized expression as they—muditā has a very special quality of its own whose successful exercise indicates great ethical maturity. It is the capacity for sympathetic joy in another's joy or success, forgetful of one's own success or failure, distress or happiness, and totally without any envious or jealous feeling. It is the analogue on the happy side, to compassion on the unhappy side of human life.

Now such sympathetic joy is undoubtedly a difficult attainment except on those rare occasions in which another's good fortune is our own, either in phsyical fact or by social linkage. Ordinarily the good fortune of another does not actually include us. As often as not the good fortune of another only reminds us of our own failure or misfortune. Or even more poignantly: In the usually competitive situations of life, another's *good* fortune is actually our *mis*fortune; for both of us have been striving for the same prize, but only one of us can gain it. The perfection of mudita in this situation would be a real joy, indeed a completely joyful joying, in the other's success as though it were our own.

Must one wait until he has become a saint (arahat), who no longer competes with anyone for anything and whose consciousness has been totally purified of any distinction between ownself and other-self, before he can exercise mudita? Again the anser is, No! One may and ought to begin doing so even now, on whatever level of attainment he may be. For the saint's perfection is built only out of countless previous and imperfect efforts to exercise mudita under all circumstances.

(d) Upekkhā or Equanimity

Upekkhā will be listed in this section only for the sake of completing the quota of the Illimitables. For though it is indeed one of them it respresents their upper limit, as it were, and the upper limit of what we have termed kammic and rebirth morality. Even with the higher development or universalization of metta-karuna-mudita one can see the trend toward the "nibbanazation" of the ethical, and scarcely knows in which realm he now is. But with upekkha, or equanimity, considered to be the crown and fruition of the other aspects, one moves definitely into the realm of nibbanic ethic, or the ethic of equanimity.

2. The Transcendent Ethic of Nibbana: Equanimity

In one sense we can scarcely say that there is a nibbanic ethic. There is a nibbanic quality of life, and a nibbanic experience, and the hope of final attainment of full Nibbana. But just because of its transcendent position and quality it can scarcely be put in ethical terms. The most that can be done in this direction has been attempted in the discussion of Chapter III. To seek to give it specific form in the nature of a given code of action, precise definitions of what is right or wrong, or even what attitudes one "should" have, is most difficult. Nibbana as the ineffably transcendent Ultimate Value exercises a most potent influence in the Buddhist ethical structure—but likewise an influence almost ineffable in nature. We may call it the Power of Ethical Dislocation, so to speak, or the Pole of Ethical Transvaluation, and go on to observe the disturbances which are created in the ethical sphere by the pursuit of Nibbana.

We may begin by a consideration of the fourth and highest of the Blessed Dispositions or Divine Abidings, upekkha or equanimity. We should not, of course, think of the other three Abidings as leading up to this fourth like stair steps, each one of which is left behind in turn. They work together as a "team," each strengthening and complementing the other. Yet Equanimity is nearer to Nibbana in quality than such "activist" attitudes as loving-kindness and compassion, particularly in their lower-level manifestations. Or to reverse the statement: As metta-karuna-mudita are generalized in their expression, they become more and more like upekkha. Thus on the Kammaward "side" of Nibbana, equanimity is that quality which still retains some direct semblance of the ethical and yet in a considerable measure transcends it in the Nibbana-ward direction. It is the last-listed and perhaps highest of the seven Factors of Enlightenment.

Upekkha has been variously translated as "indifference," "neutrality," and "equanimity." (One is tempted to add "balanced serenity," not on linguistic but experiential grounds; though perhaps this is too emotionally connotative a term for Buddhist taste.) Many Buddhists today object to the first two translations as suggestive of total insensitivity to values and persons, and prefer "equanimity." Whatever term we adopt, something of its quality is evident: controlled balance of mind, emotional non-attachment or neutrality, and "beyondness" with regard to ordinary ethical uncertainties and struggles. It is seemingly a calm detachment of eternity-mindedness that has little interest longer in the ordinary affairs of men; for societies may come and societies may go, political ideologies rise and fall in favor, cultures appear, flower, and pass away, but equanimity and the quest for Nibbana go on forever. Or rather, the possessor of equanimity goes on, completely unshaken emotionally or mentally by the world's mental, moral, or social disturbances.

This leads us to consider another corollary facet of the "ethic" of Equanimity (or Nibbana). We have already observed that the quest of the *ultimately* (nibbanic) good inclines toward inward states of realization and away from outward action. In our present context this provides us with a definition of the *perfect deed*. Now the "perfect" deed, a creation of Nibbana, is not the same as the "good" deed, which is the product of Kamma. As we have already seen, kammic goodness refers only to the tendency of a deed to produce a fortunate rebirth—no more, no less. And to this category belong the deeds of ordinary virtue: keeping the Five (or more) Precepts, fulfilling one's duties and obligations to society, practising dana-sila to the extent of one's ability, and cherishing the blessed dispositions of lovingkindness, compassion, and sympathetic joy. But the perfect deed is far different. It is the product of equanimity rather than compassion and it rises far above merely ethical goodness. To be sure it is not ethically evil—it could not be a deed of murder or theft—but neither is it concerned to save life or relieve hunger and sickness. It belongs to the realm of emotional immutability, without any *feeling* of pity, concern, or distress for earthly condition.

We may put it differently, and perhaps better. A deed is perfect because there is no emotional attachment of any sort involved in it; one does it in the spirit of *complete* disinterest. And since there is no emotional clinging to the deed or its results, no kammic consequence, either good or bad, results. Hence the perfection of the perfect deed is not its outward, objective nature, but the inward attitude of its doer. Within the limits of kammic morality, the "same" deed—i.e. outwardly the same—may be either a deed entailing rebirth, and perhaps a "good" rebirth, or a perfect deed completely free of all kammic consequence. It is the inward attitude of detachment that makes the difference.

There is one more facet of the Ethic of Equanimity to be considered here, one that epitomizes the "opposition" between Nibbana and Kamma and their respective ethics in the sharpest possible way: the process of negating or "burning up" past evil Kamma. It is clear that some such process is necessary if final liberation is ever to occur. For even if by the continued performance of "perfect," i.e. non-kammic deeds, one keeps from *adding* kammic consequences to his account, it is already filled to overflowing with past deeds of evil consequences, as Ledi Sayadaw says:

> There exists in the heart blood of each and every one of the beings, untold old and accumulated unwholesome kammical volitions that are on the "waiting list," and untold evil kammical

volitions for the purpose of breeding future Ignorance and evils in future existences.[18]

Now this destruction of kammic results is precisely what the highest range of meditational discipline is constructed to achieve. And to put it in perspective we may note again briefly the structure of the meditational discipline. Its indispensable basis is Sila or morality. Then comes the first stage of meditation in which one hopes to achieve *samādhi* or one-pointedness of mental concentration. Various subjects and techniques are used to accomplish this—concentration on breathing, on *kasiṇas* or colored disks, or on a variety of themes ranging from the foulness of the body to the Divine Abidings—each suited by the meditation director to the meditator's personal need. This level of attainment reaches its peak in the jhanic trances or absorptions of increasing abstraction and formlessness, nine in number. In these trances one almost completely transcends the space-time world; he lives in a timeless atmosphere in which he develops super-normal psychic powers and has access to the higher planes of supra-mundane existence where the devas and Brahma-spirits dwell. And once having developed such powers, he will be reborn into the corresponding plane upon his death.

But fascinating as these states are, they are not of the essence of salvation. They do not accomplish the burning up of past bad Kamma—only the temporary cessation from deeds of kammic consequences. And they may be bypassed in their more intensive forms by that man who is urgent for salvation. Once he has achieved a necessary minimum of samadhi, he turns to *vipassanā* meditation. Now the goal of vipassana is the attainment of *paññā* or insight-wisdom whose perfection results in Nibbana. Here there is no longer any playing with the prospect of rebirth into even the highest Brahma-lokas or the Immaterial Spheres, but a pressing on to Nibbana itself. And here it is also that past bad Kamma may be burned up.

The "burning up" of bad past Kamma requires a word of explanation. It is maintained that in the higher reaches of vipassana meditation one is able to penetrate into his past lives and

---

[18] "Manual of Spheres of Action," *Buddhist Supplement* to *The Burman*, March 2, 1959.

become aware of that evil Kamma not yet come to fruition, but which contains a future threat, since all Kamma must come to fruition at some time in the normal course of affairs. But in meditation one becomes increasingly the master, even of inexorable Kamma itself. As detached meditator he sits beside the stream of his own consciousness as it flows by and spots his past evil deed come floating along on its surface, as it were. This identified source of evil he can induce to produce its effects then and there, though in modified form. Even these modified forms will be painful, producing strong emotional stirrings and physically painful sensations of piercing sharpness or intense heat. Yet they are only momentary and they are on the whole under his control. And certainly it is better to burn here than hereafter. The result in any case is that the vipassana meditator is thus enabled to overcome all his kammic past, piece by piece, eliminating it once and forever. It is the conquest of Kamma and all its works, good or bad, by Nibbana.[19] What must be done, is done; and the perfection of the deed is the saint who is totally freed from his past—because it has been meditationally burned up. And by the same process he has been purified completely in his inner motivations from all greed, hatred, delusion, and the desire to come to rebirth again. Such is the ultimate fruition of the Ethic of Equanimity.

3. Antithesis Stated: The Ethic of Kamma-Rebirth vs. the Ethic of Equanimity

We have now delineated the two types of ethical valuation and practice found in Buddhism, that of the Kamma-Rebirth realm and that of Nibbana. They are not the same. For the polar attrac-

---

[19] The psychological and experiential parallel to Christian sanctification is here again noteworthy. There it is the "carnal nature" which is destroyed by the purging fire of the Holy Spirit; here it is past Kamma, the bad potential of the kammic self which may flare into wrong action unless purified. In Buddhism there should also be the destruction of one's *good* Kamma, logically speaking, though it is never mentioned. This is perhaps not quite natural, however, since kammic goodness, though transcended, does lead toward nibbanic goodness in the end. The Christian equivalent here would be the renunciation of the hope of salvation by the "good" works of the law, but not renunciation of their continued performance.

tion of Nibbana, the Supreme Good, exerts a disturbing and distracting force throughout the kammic ethical structure. What is good in terms of the Ethic of Equanimity is largely unknown to the moral striver in the realm of Kamma; even the *prospect* of Nibbana threatens his kammic values and disturbs his sense of right and wrong. He cannot, in this new perspective, be sure that his usual "goods" and "evils" are absolutes, or whether he should pursue his kammic right and good with whole-hearted devotion. Eternity dwarfs all that concerns him in time and space into insignificance.

For the purpose of pointing up this basic tension between Rebirth Ethic and the nibbanic Ethic of Equanimity even more sharply, we shall here draw forth the implications of the immediately preceding discussion in terms of differences in technique, goal, and intrinsic quality.

With regard to *technique* the contrast is obvious. Rebirth Ethic works through Sila in the doing of conventional good deeds and the cultivation of the moral dispositions proper to life at that level. It seeks to produce that solid body of virtuous habits and dispositions in the individual which are usually termed character. This it does by means of making ethical distinctions between goodness and evil (on the kammic plane) and by shoring up these distinctions with the doctrine of Kamma, a force that rewards and punishes virtue and vice without fail.

The technique of the ethic of equanimity is, of course, meditation. Here attention is turned entirely to the internal aspect of deeds; the technique is calculated to produce a certain state of consciousness within the individual, not a given set of actions. Its chief virtue is detached serenity, or serenity through detachment from that very world of active dispositions and citizenly deeds in which Sila operates. Its technique renders its practitioner utterly passive to outward appearances—the more inwardly concentrated and outwardly passive the more successful. For the meditator in his moment of meditation lives in a realm where sense-life neither disturbs nor corrupts.

When we turn to the ostensible *goals* of each ethic, the antithesis seems so violent as almost to represent a mutual cancellation of effort. Or we might say, that though the *ultimate* goal of both ethics is reputedly the same, their respective routes to it are radically different. The logical goal of any rebirth is a better rebirth, one that is more pleasant or at least no worse than one's present situation. Above the human world stretch the planes of the devas and Brahmas, super-mundane in nature. Indeed they are "super" in every respect—so pleasant that suffering is almost forgotten, so enduring that they are almost eternal, so magnificent that life there beggars description. It is true that after millions of years here one may descend to a human plane. Yet if our expositors are to be trusted (pp. 23-4 above) an ex-deva is better off in his succeeding human existence than an ex-animal. He will be healthy, handsome, wealthy, famous, beloved, and die a quiet death, which in turn will enable him to achieve another fortunate rebirth, perhaps in the deva world again. Conceivably this pattern—which is "good", or even the best, in kammic terms —might go on endlessly to no one's very great distress.

Indeed there seems to be here a kind of built-in Nibbana-retarding quality. One may succeed too well; *kammic* success means *nibbanic* failure. What is called the first mile on the road to Nibbana seems actually to be the first mile along the Great Detour through the heavenly worlds. The life of the deva-worlds might seem to whet the appetite for further existence on such levels. And since almost every human being is ignorant of all his past lives, i.e. he has no personal recollection of any previous existence, he therefore never becomes jaded with life by virtue of its repetitiousness. Hence he may yearn over and over again for a more fortunate rebirth, deva-worlds preferred, wherein all things will be new again, and where he will reap the reward of his present-life virtue. Indeed he may even hope to be reunited with those whom he has loved here in this life, and continue the pleasant companionship throughout the ages. Thus may the kammically "good" man by the very force of his goodness embark on a never-ending Cosmic Merry-go-Round through the higher planes.

Nibbana as a goal is quite other. The way to it leads in what seems to be a sheerly opposite direction. Or if an "opposite" direction have no meaning on a Merry-go-Round, then we may say that the road to Nibbana takes off on a tangent into a totally different dimension. At any rate it is hard to conclude that the two ways are one and the same way, despite Buddhist insistence that they are indeed identical. For the essence of seeking Nibbana is the burning out of the feverish thirst for life, even in its kammically good forms; and the fire that burns it out is the triple-flamed torch of the truths of *anicca-dukkha-anattā,* the impermanance, the suffering, and the emptiness of all individualized existence. The Merry-go-Round of rebirth is a nightmare, and its rider a shadow-self. Why not end it by the vision of the Absolute Truth?

As to the intrinsic *quality* of the two ways almost enough has been said. The essence of the rebirth ethic is good deeds done in the world of time and space with a view to achieving a better personal status in that same world in the future. It is an active involvement in the concerns, a vigorous fighting of the battles of right and wrong in each separate life and in each age. But the quality of Nibbana-ethic is completely different. It is the turning of the self in upon itself; the achievement of blessed states of consciousness that are good and satisfying in themselves; it is withdrawal from the active life of historical involvement into a life of intense contemplation; it is the search for an experience of the timeless and ultimate; and it is utter detachment from good and evil, right and wrong, and from the very distinctions of the intellect itself.

It is obvious that we have here the description of two entirely different modes of life which, in their visible form, have come to be embodied in the way of the layman and of the monk. The way of Rebirth Ethic is the layman's way. His liveliest, and perhaps traditionally his *only*, hope is for rebirth in a better world. He can scarcely hope for Nibbana, and has not the appetite for it in any case. He must be content with the lesser conventional goods within his capacity and orbit of life. But the nibbanic Ethic is enshrined in the way of the monk. No doubt most monks actually have no immediate hope of arahatship and subsequent Nibbana; yet a monk is technically a Nibbana-farer, having so pledged himself upon entrance into the Sangha. Giving up all domestic, social, economic, and political concerns, he turns to seek the greatest of all goods. And the Order of which he becomes a member, is geared precisely and deliberately to that quest, and to that quest alone. The Sangha is the institutionalization of the Ethic of Equanimity.

4. Antithesis Qualified

Such is a *possible* portrait of the polarity between nibbanic and kammic influences in the Buddhist ethical structure. That this polarity is genuine there can be no doubt. And very probably also it represents an original sharp division between the authentic Buddhist way of the monk (Nibbana-seeking) and the way of the layman (better-rebirth-seeking) that was added thereunto. Now and then this situation is still recognized in Buddhist circles, as the following indicates:

> He the Buddha preached equally to monks and house-holders but he made it perfectly clear that the religious life can only be lived fully by a monk . . .
>
> For the house-holders . . . he did not speak about the idea of Nibbana but he spoke about charity, morality, heavenly life, harmfulness of sensual pleasures and the advantages of freedom from desire. . . .
>
> The doctrine of heaven and hell is especially the layman's religion . . . Householders who live in the enjoyment of worldly good but who are religious and attentive to teachings . . . may secure many births in heavens. . . . The husband and wife who have lived together here in equal faith, conduct, renunciation and knowledge, may hope to be together in the next world. . . .
>
> Although Buddha taught both monks and householders, he always wanted the latter to leave the world in order to fully observe his teaching which leads to the goal of Nibbana.[20]

But with the growth of lay Buddhism through the years and the smaller number of those who believe themselves to be arahats among the monks, the sharpness of the contrast between Nibbana-seeking and Heaven-seeking has been dulled. The two ways have been adjusted to each other to such an extent that it is stoutly maintained as an article of faith by Theravada Buddhism that the two ways are one, and the layman's way of heaven-seeking leads on directly to Nibbana—even though it is only the first stage on the road. Our viewpoint here will be that the contrast is still there, with the seam of the attempted joining still showing and with resultant tensions remaining; but that the traditional

---

[20] Shwe-man Tin Hla, "Buddhism as a Religion of House-Holders," *Light of the Buddha*, I, No. 3 (June, 1956), 8, 9, 11.

fusion of the paths has so moderated the contrast in various ways as to produce a working-harmony of values. Hence the title of this section, "Antithesis Qualified," in which we shall examine some four of these adjustments.

We may first note a *general* feature of the situation. It is that practical and experiential unity are often achieved in the midst of doctrinal diversity and illogic. The political, philosophical, and religious cultures of the world are full of marvelous instances of a kind of spiritual sleight-of-hand by which intellectual contradictions have been made to lie down together like the lion and the lamb of Isaiah's vision. The strictest predestinarianism finds room for, and even stimulates, the most vigorous action; and supposedly dynamic doctrines may result in a loose-jointed apathy. The theoretical contradictions intrinsic to doctrinal structure often serve as creatively related poles producing a dynamic situation by virtue of their very theoretical opposition.

So it is in Buddhism to some extent at least with Kamma and Nibbana. Kamma represents the world of outward, personal-social action fully and strenuously dedicated to the production of a better individual rebirth—if not so much to a better space-time world. Nibbana represents the inaction of the contemplative life whose energies are turned toward a goal that is transcendent even of the "ideal" rebirth. Yet if Nibbana is to be reached, this space-time world must be revalued, not in its own terms, but in the calm clear light of nibbanic insight. (Thus U Nu called for a socialist state to enable men the more easily to achieve Nibbana. (See below p. 266.) Nibbana is the calm, mature, disinterested appraisal of oneself and his own situation in the light of eternal and absolute values; but kammic action remains necessary in the space-time world as the ladder by whose rungs even laymen may approach the far-off Goal. Hence their relation is one of complementation, not contradiction.

Secondly, and following directly from the above, we must note again the doctrine of *levels*. In the Buddhist religious structure are many mansions, one for each level of capability and kammic past. Even the harlot who sells her favors to only one man at a time; or the thief-murderer-liar-adulterer but non-drinker; or the veriest (actual) sinner who has "taken refuge" in the Buddha, Dhamma, and Sangha, i.e. acknowledged his faith in them as man's true refuge, even if he is not able to observe the Precepts—all these have made some small beginning on the way of goodness. Indeed those who can attain to the Supreme Morality of Nibbana absolutely, are very few; they are the saints or arahats. And their way in its absoluteness is *not* for the many. The remainder of mankind, somewhere in between the two extremes, must try to keep the absolutes as absolutely as possible— which means as they are kammically able to do so. The result is a pattern in which the absolute and the relative, the nibbanic and the kammic, are almost inseparably mingled. Thus again we have, not a contradiction, but only the necessary and life-giving disparity between the high and the low. And if there is a seeming unconcern about hastening a man on toward Nibbana, an apparently slothful contentment with the lesser goods of rebirth, this is the expression of what Buddhists regard as both good and necessary—full-scale tolerance for human infirmity.

We may emphasize thirdly a point that has been made before, but one that is of particular importance among Theravadins: Sila or morality is not placed lowest in the scale of values because it is inferior to other values, but because it is fundamental and foundational to them. This is an emphasis often expressed by the Venerable U Thittila. He points out that moral decency and discipline are always considered the absolutely indispensable precondition of the practice of the "higher" virtues of samadhi and pañña. Only on a solid basis of good moral character and genuinely ethical living can one achieve mental concentration and insight. Nor does one leave Sila behind him as he climbs the ladder toward Nibbana; it must go with him, in practice and attitude, all the way there. It only becomes more "inwardized," being transformed from the mere keeping of preceptual morality in outward action into the attainment of complete purity of motive and emotion and the eradication of greed and hatred. Indeed these latter in their subtle forms are among the very last of all the fetters to be rooted out in the arahat. Ethical discipline must go on till the very end.

We may finally note as the essence of the above, and a kind of summary of the total situation of the cross-fertilization of kammic and nibbanic ethical values, what we might call the synthesis of the ethic of rebirth with the ethic of equanimity in a working harmony of values. This takes two forms: One is a fusing of techniques, and the other a qualitative modification.

On the surface it seems that the life of action according to the Precepts, dana-sila, and metta-karuna-mudita, is absolutely different from that of the meditational seeking of Nibbana. And indeed there is here a difference that we must never forget, no matter how the contrasts are de-emphasized. But they may be, and presently are being, joined in some sort of unity. Practically speaking the layman now seeks to meditate as well as live in the house-holder's world. It may be difficult but not impossible to combine the two modes of life. Mechanically speaking, periods of meditation (like seasons of prayer) may be interspersed regularly in the active life. *Experientially speaking the very materials of one's daily Sila-life may become the materials of meditational contemplation.* Moral action becomes meditative theme and meditative theme becomes action.[21] This is a very important point, especially for our later discussion of the new layman's Buddhism. For it makes possible the traveling of two roads at once: the route to the higher heavens and the Path to Nibbana. It is the perfect example of the mingling of the monk's and layman's life and the fusion of kammic and nibbanic ethical values. One may *aim* for Nibbana even as a layman, but *hope* at the very least to achieve a better rebirth. In other words: *Meditation becomes a good kammic work, conducive to better rebirths.* Thus it appears that the lines have been blurred and the world-transcending nibbanic technique has descended in part to kammic practicality.

With regard to *qualitative* modification we may notice the way in which contemporary Theravadins interpret equanimity, and the relation of equanimity to the other more "active" illimitables. With regard to equanimity itself one reads that it may be "radiated" to others:

> The main requirement in the process of transmitting vibrations of equanimity with good effect, is to try to secure a mental picture of the objective as if it were seen by your own eyes . . . a neutral person first and then a loving friend and finally your enemy. . . . Being firmly fixed in self-peace or tranquillity, the

---

[21] I am indebted to Professor U Aung Than, University of Rangoon, for pointing out this synthesis to me.

mission of diffusion should be practiced for the attainment of happiness in this life as well as for noble rebirth after death in the high spiritual realm, that is, the Brahma World.[22]

It may seem odd to a Westerner to speak of "vibrations" of equanimity that are to be sent out to others—with the ultimate goal of securing world peace. But such is the Buddhist view; good-will, compassion, even equanimity may be radiated with fully effective force—as waves of calmness, not agitation. For equanimity, the modern Buddhist repeats insistently, is not mere neutrality, but a kind of love without attachment and without expectation of reward. Indeed it works hand-in-glove with the other blessed dispositions as the following quotation makes clear:

> Love imparts to Equanimity its selflessness, its boundless nature, and even its fervour. . . . Compassion guards Equanimity from falling into cold indifference, and keeps it from indolent or selfish isolation. Until Equanimity has reached perfection, Compassion urges it to enter again and again into the battlefield of the world. . . . .
> Sympathetic Joy gives to Equanimity the mild serenity that softens its stern appearance. It is the divine smile on the face of the Enlightened One.

And in turn

> Equanimity rooted in Insight, is to the other three Sublime States their guiding and restraining power, pointing out to them the direction they have to take and seeing to it that this direction be followed.[23]

5. Concluding Summary and Transition

What then is the situation which we have here? Has it been more a matter of kammic values that have been "nibbanized" or nibbanic values that have been "kammatized"? Probably it is

---

[22] Venerable Anesakan Sayadaw, "How to Attain World Peace," *Light of the Buddha*, II, No. 4 (April, 1957), 98. The "kammatization" of the nibbanic is clearly visible here; its radiation produces a better rebirth.

[23] Venerable Nyanaponika, "The Four Sublime States," *Light of the Dhamma*, VI, No. 2 (April, 1959), 34.

impossible for anyone to say to another's satisfaction, particularly as between Buddhists and non-Buddhists. For the answer
given depends much upon one's own set of moral-religious
values and upon his consequent evaluation of Buddhist history
and ethical goods. Therefore when the following opinions are
expressed they will no doubt be fully pleasing only to the
author.

Roughly speaking it would seem that the tendency in Buddhism has been toward the "kammatization" of nibbanic values
and the smoothing over of the contrasts between the two value-
realms in favor of the layman. This has many roots, historically
and doctrinally, which cannot be discussed here. But that it *has*
occurred seems clear. What then is the net result in terms of
ethical emphasis? And here we come to a paradoxical situation; for *both* poles of the Kamma-Nibbana tension are today
being activated simultaneously.

Let the matter be put in this way: The contemporary world
political and cultural climate is pushing Buddhist cultures toward the Kamma pole, at least in one form. They are being
subjected to the tremendous pressures of scientific technique
and economic expansion characteristic of the world today.
These pressures call forth answering forces of growing popular
desire in Buddhist cultures for a higher standard of living, here
and now. Neither the promise of future rewards guaranteed by
inexorable Kamma in the next life, nor the pursuit of the transcendent peace of Nibbana, millions of existences hence, quite
satisfies this demand. Thus do Buddhists become more and
more aware of the demands of this space-time world, and concerned to build a good society on this earth.

On the other hand there is a strong new emphasis—though
not always among the same persons—upon the availability of
nibbanic peace here and now, and the accessibility of Nibbana
itself, perhaps even to the layman. Partly this is the result of a
brand-new emphasis within the last fifty years—which is "brand-
new" for Buddhism—upon a more direct meditational technique
for achieving equanimity and inner peace, which has nothing to
do with technical progress at all. And partly it is the Buddhist
answer to such progress; it is the assertion that Nibbana and
its ethic also have value for this present world, and may even

facilitate progress toward the optimum of happy living here and now in space-time.

Thus have Kamma and Nibbana joined forces for the good of the world. Love, Compassion, and Sympathetic Joy continue to emanate from the mind and act upon the world; but being guarded by Equanimity, they "cling nowhere, and unweakened and unsullied they return"[24]—to the saint who radiates them. But in this new union there still remain many cross-currents and contrasting tendencies. And, quite understandably, there is a considerable degree of uncertainty as to the truly good response to the contemporary situation. How central is it to the Buddhist concern to build a good society in time and space, when *both* the law of Kamma and the nature of Nibbana show it to be illusory and impermanent? What would be the ideal Buddhist society, and the role of layman and monk within it? What should Buddhism do to counteract the urgent materialism of the will-to-physical-abundance and the desire for political power abroad in Asia today? Is the quest of Nibbana relevant to the urgent problems of the new nations, or only an expensive luxury for the few, that must be foregone by the unselfish servants of the people? Can even a combination of Equanimity with Love, Compassion and Sympathetic Joy, though radiated with full benevolence to all beings, meet the needs of the day?

These are the pressing questions that today face the highly individualistic Buddhist ethic. Nearly all of them relate to *social* situations; and to social ethic Buddhists on the whole have given little direct or analytic thought. Therefore one cannot find in Buddhist thinking any clear or unanimous answer to such questions. Yet Buddhism has created a social pattern according to its own convictions of goodness and rightness; and in this pattern there is a certain social philosophy. This philosophy Buddhism is now seeking to articulate, implement and relate to the present situation. To the consideration of that philosophy and its implementation we shall turn in the concluding chapters.

---

[24] *Ibid*, p. 35.

CHAPTER VI

THE GOOD SOCIETY
AND ITS BETTERMENT

1. Lack of Social Theory

One of the features of the study of Buddhism most frustrating to the Western mind is the effort necessary to discover a social philosophy within it. The question suggests itself: *Is* there any? For the West has been theorizing and experimenting in socio-political matters, both in a secular and religious way, ever since the days of Plato. There is a vast abundance of statement and historical example to be found in relation to all aspects of the subject. Currently the West is more deeply concerned with the socio-political interpretation of world events and prospects than with almost anything else; and it sets up its political schemes, panaceas, and gospels for the cure of modern ills in rapid succession. It may also be noted that from the West have come the two most explosive and dynamic forces to be found in the contemporary world: nationalism and Marxism. In a word, the Western mind is socially, politically, and his-torically conscious in its every fibre.

Therefore when one who has been nurtured in this culture confronts Buddhist Asia and searches for a social ethic or philosophy, he finds himself aimlessly groping. Where is any theory of the state, any systematic philosophy of political power and its proper use, any interpretation of the meaning of human history? Has anyone ever protrayed the ideal state, the Good Society, or Nibbana-on-Earth? Is there any formal statement of what a Buddhist society should be? One can lay his hand on almost nothing in the classical scripture or ancient tradition that deals with such matters at all, let alone in any systematic way.

Some of the reasons for this are not far to seek. They have been dealt with previously in other connections. We may specify and focus them here in summary fashion in terms of their social bearing, and at the same time provide something of a qualitative characterization of the Buddhist approach to social ethic. We may note to begin with that the general cultural context out of which Buddhism developed was religio-philosophical rather than socio-political in its genius and outlook. And though Buddhism had important social repercussions, it was not basically or consciously a social reform movement aiming at the production of a certain type of society—save perhaps a society of believers, i.e. monks, who were called upon to forsake the historical-political world and its concerns. That is to say, Buddhism was (and largely is) a-historical in viewpoint. It deals not with man in society or among his fellows, but with the individual man facing his eternal destiny. And it turns man supremely toward seeking a Good (Nibbana) above all time and space orders.

To tell the truth the Buddha had little, either of concern for society as such or of firm conviction of its possible improvability. To be sure there was an existent society and it was not to be destroyed. And there would always be a society as long as there were human beings in some sort of universe. But its fluctuations, the rise and fall of its empires and social orders, its improvement and decay, its forms and names, represented for the Buddha only the stage on which each man plays his essentially solitary drama. Social conditions might help or hinder that man in his progress toward Nibbana to some extent, but they could never be *fundamentally* bettered. Social orders would revolve perpetually in meaningless cycles, all within the conditioned realm of Kamma-rebirth *(saṃsāra),* but arrive nowhere in particular. Certain it was that there was no real *salvation* to be found in the socio-historical context or in the improvement of its forms.

This means that Buddhism on the whole has surveyed political forms with supreme indifference. Or perhaps it might be stated better thus: Buddhism took the monarchical form of secular society that it found in India for granted and was not concerned enough to worry about changing it. There are of course some passages dealing with the duties of kings. (And we will note later the exemplary Buddhist sovereign, Aśoka.) But significantly most of these are found in the *Jātaka Stories,* not in the classic Suttas. And the *Jātaka Stories,* we may recall, are more properly non-Buddhist materials adapted by Buddhism than Buddhist creations per se.

But even though this be the case we may give an example or two of such "political philosophy" as is found therein. In *Jātaka* No. 534 *(Mahāhaṃsa Jātaka)* for example, a golden goose or swan (in reality the Bodhisatta or future Buddha) tells the king who captured him that he should marry a wife of equal birth, have true counsellors, avoid oppression, punish the bad, reward the good. His kingly virtues should be: alms-giving, justice, penitence, meekness, mildness, peaceableness, mercy, patience, charity, and moral purity. In a note to *Jātaka* 532 *(Sona-Nanda)* a king's four duties are listed as the giving of gifts, affability, beneficent rule, and impartiality. And the *Sumangala Jātaka* (420) portrays the good king thus:

> Self nor others will he vex
> Clearly parting right from wrong;
> Though his yoke is on men's necks,
> Virtue holds him high and strong.
>
> Princes reckless in their deed,
> Ply the rod remorselessly,
> Ill repute is here their meed,
> Hell awaits them when they die. . . .
>
> King am I, my people's lord;
> Anger shall not check my bent:
> When to vice I take the sword,
> Pity prompts the punishment. . .
>
> Mild and bland, but firm in worth
> I rule the world with righteousness. . .[1]

There has been one interesting development here, namely the idea of the Universal Monarch, which is of Indian origin with

---

[1] All references to PTS Edition of *Jātaka Stories.* This quotation from Vol. III.

some later Buddhist elaborations, particularly in Burma. The traditional accounts of the birth of the Buddha, at least in some versions, picture the wise men looking at the infant and in the light of his physical characteristics (thirty-two marks of the great man) predicting that he will either be a great (universal) monarch or a great sage. His capabilities, i.e. kammic potential, as shown in his physical form, fit him for either role. Of course, as we know, Gotama became the Supreme Sage rather than the Universal Monarch.

But the idea of the Universal Monarch lived on in the Buddhist tradition to bear its grandiose and sometimes tragic fruit. Many a Burmese monarch cherished the secret hope that it was written in the stars, or his kammic destiny, to become such. Sometimes indeed the hope was not secret. Maurice Collis, in his *The Land of the Great Image,* tells of one Arakanese king who embarked on various tragic and cruel enterprises to realise this dream for himself. And it may be that King Bodawpaya (1782-1819) was likewise inspired by some such ambitions. At any rate he captured the great Buddha image from Arakan, mounted warlike expeditions against Siam where the white elephants that belonged of right to the Universal Monarch were to be found, and talked largely of conquering India, China, and England as well, but actually succeeded only in subduing Arakan.[2]

And at least once a Burmese monarch developed the other side of the Great Man theory, the religious one. This same King Bodawpaya at one period of his life cherished, and indeed proclaimed, the idea that he was the coming Buddha Maitreya incarnate. Perhaps something of such high hopes might be found in germ in the religious aura that surrounded the kingly office; to be born a sovereign in Buddhist Burma could only result from an immense store of past merit, which a wild im-

---

[2] See G. E. Harvey, *Outline of Burmese History* (New York: Longmans, Green, Indian Edition, 1947), pp. 146–59. In Tibetan Buddhism the Dalai Lama is held to be the "Living Buddha"—and is both secular and religious ruler. In Thailand it is *assumed* that one whose past Kamma has fitted him to be a King is without doubt to become a Buddha in the next (or near next) rebirth. In Burma there has seldom been such an assumption. Perhaps too many adventurers achieved the throne.

agination such as Bodapaya's might stretch beyond limits. But
the Sangha of his day, to its credit, discounted his pretensions
completely and such claims were never repeated. Whatever the
pretensions of a Burmese king, however, he was in fact the
supreme patron of the Buddhist religion in Burma and Master
Builder of Pagodas. Once established in kingly power by whatever process of violence or intrigue, the sovereign considered
himself, and was considered by others, to be the Supreme Defender of the Faith. Some defended it more than others, now and
then seeking to impose some of their pet ideas upon the Sangha
or to advance favorite monks—usually unsuccessfully, since the
Sangha vigorously maintained its independence of thought and
action. But in any case the sovereign *did* represent royal patron-
age and there are still those Burmese today who think of this
as the *ideal* Buddhist society.

Obviously with this background and history (somewhat
paralleled in other Theravada countries) little analytic thought
was given to political or social matters. All of the intellectual
energy was given to philosophical and psychological analysis;
and all the practical energy was turned to building pagodas,
learning scriptures, and improving one's own kammic status.
Indeed there was nothing in historical or political circumstances
to force Theravada Buddhism to think at all in socio-political
terms save of the most elementary sort; largely undisturbed for
centuries in its near-primitive social, political, and economic
context it has scarcely moved consciously toward social or political definition until very recently.[3]

---

[3] On a purely practical level it is maintained by one eminent Burmese lawyer that not only has Buddhism no interest in ordinary worldly
affairs, but that it has had little or no effect upon the customary law and
legal structure of his own country. Thus:

"Though much of the material for the book [an early lawbook
fundamental to much later Burmese law] is drawn from the Buddhist
scriptures, that fact is no indication that the customary laws had
come under religious influence. It was . . . only natural for the jurists
to borrow the authority of the Buddha."

"Buddhism contributed largely to make the struggle [against the
then prevailing Hindu law] successful, but it sought not to assert its
own influences in the development of laws. Preaching the inexorable
law of *Karma* Buddhism stands detached from the earthly affairs of

There are other elements in the Buddhist tradition that have intensified, or at least not countered, its non-social cast of thought and practice. Its whole negative, reverse-order approach to ethical virtue has aided and abetted non-social conceptions. When one thinks of virtue, as Buddhism does fundamentally, almost completely in terms of the destruction of weaknesses within himself, this scarcely leads to the *social* definition of such virtue. To be specific: How does one become loving, generous and wise according to Buddhism? By the destruction of his own hatred (dosa), greed (lobha) and delusion (moha). If he achieves non-hatred, non-greed, and non-delusion the positive virtues will appear, like gold whose tarnish has been rubbed off. To be sure this *might* be interpreted à la Rousseau as the need to make society pure in order to allow the native goodness of man to develop. But historically it has not been so interpreted in Buddhism. The process there has been to achieve such purity by means of an internal self-discipline of meditational quality,[4] whose social expression is either passive or missing.

2. The Basic Axiom of Social Progress

Now this brings us very near to a fundamental Buddhist doctrine, usually taken for granted, but now rather specifically emphasized. It serves as the basic social axiom of Buddhism and may be stated as follows:

"*The individual progress is, after all, the social progress.*"[5]

In other words the goodness of society is but the sum of the goodness of its component individuals. Good personal

---

man. It promises nothing and offers nothing to man who must fight for his own emancipation; on man's material life, therefore, Buddhism seeks not to assert any influence. In his marriage and family affairs, acquisition of property, contracts and business relationships Buddhism is uninterested." Dr. Maung Maung, *Burma in the Family of Nations,* (Djambatan, Ltd., Amsterdam, 1956), p. 15.

[4] Perhaps in the case of greed, the dana-sila giving of alms may be considered a partial exception to the sheerly internal, self-first discipline. But this is only a partial exception.

[5] Thera Mirisse Gunasiri, "Buddhism and World Peace," *Light of the Buddha,* II, No. 2 (February, 1957), 41. Italics added.

character will result in good community character; which will in turn result in good national character; which will in turn produce good international relations. Or to apply the same philosophy to a specific problem: If every individual gains peace within his own heart, then world-peace will come. Ergo, the method of working for world-peace is primarily to cleanse one's own heart of greed, hatred, and delusion. And since these latter are nourished by the illusion of the reality of the self, one should really begin to work for world peace by purifying himself of the error of self-illusion through meditation.

In passing we may observe that few Buddhist moralists have yet faced the basic questions raised by Reinhold Niebuhr in his *Moral Man and Immoral Society:* Does personal virtue carry directly over into social virtue? Are the two actually the same, in fact? Does individual "progress" mean the same as social "progress"? The following passage is an example of one type of this failure of analysis:

> No religious teacher other than the Buddha evokes in man such determination and desire to strive for the conquest of all obstacles to progress and for achievement of one's ideal of perfection. . .
>
> It is the teaching that rouses up our energy, gives us self reliance, and thus induces us to strive to the utmost in leading such a life as will make for our economic, social, intellectual, moral and spiritual progress. . . .[6]

Obviously that "rousing up of energy" spoken of here has to do with the energy of interior mind-development and the strenuous pursuit of the higher levels of consciousness. Does this mean the same sort of energy that produces economic development, social reform, and political democracy? And does the man who is going on to that perfection of Nibbana, *automatically* become a good citizen and wise statesman? But more of this later.

3. Social Method and Guiding Image

Given such a basic philosophy of social progress, how does Buddhism propose to achieve that progress?—if we can use such

---

[6] Venerabale Nyanasatta, "Practical Buddhism," *Light of the Dhamma,* I, No. 3 (April, 1953), 35.

a deliberately conscious term for its social intentions. Now it may well be that though there has been a minimum of *overt* social philosophy in Buddhism it has not been completely without a socially formative dynamism and sense of direction. Such sense of social direction as Buddhism has had grows directly out of one of its basic notions which we have discussed before: televolition, or the radiation of good will. It may be put this way: *The "method" of social change proper to Buddhism is that of the individualized radiation of virtue and health out into society by holy persons.* Virtue here of course refers not to specific character traits so much as moral worth and power; and health is used in the figurative sense of mental-moral integrity or good character.

For just as social improvement is held to be the sum of the individual self-improvement of the members of a society, so the Buddhist view is that society must, or may, improve by individuals in a strictly individual way—by the radiation of their personal virtue or holiness. This general point, of course, is common to many moral and religious philosophies: The power of the example of a good man is great and may do more to change the character of a society than all manner of political schemes and policy statements. (Witness Gandhi's influence on Indian politics and society in the three decades before Indian independence.) There is a kind of contagion of good will. And also the same principle is often reversed: How can good policies be carried out by morally evil men? For the character of a man affects all that he does. There are no *impersonal* deeds.

But we must remember that there is a special Buddhist dimension to be taken into account here that goes well beyond the merely general principle of good influence and its example. It is that peculiar intensification of the generally acknowledged power of personal example by the above-mentioned belief in the power of televolition or the sending out of vibrations which, *independently* of sensory perceptions and *apart* from all tangible means, may work in an effective way upon others even at a distance and unkown to them. We may repeat here part of an earlier quotation:

> A man with a meditative mind lives at peace with himself and with the world. . . The peace and purity he radiates will have con-

quering power and will be a blessing to the world. He will be a positive factor in society, even if he lives in seclusion and silence. (Ch. V, p. 154.)

This might be called the ideal Buddhist method of social change: not the mechanics of laws, reform programs, and political maneuvers, but the reform of the inward character of members of the community spreading out from a central source of holiness. Thereby a given society may be healed of its divisions, strifes, illnesses, and find wisdom and strength to solve its problems.[7]

And this indeed accords with the manner of the actual historical progress of Buddhism through the countries of Asia and its "method" of influencing the societies and cultures into which it came. We cannot say on the whole that Buddhism has ever had a "reform program"; or that it usually thinks of its relation to society in such terms—certainly not if one means by this a blue-print of the Buddhist social ideal applied to a given social situation after the manner of Marxism, or even in terms of a New Deal or Five-Year Plan. Its approach to a society can be called rather *penetrative* and *infiltrative*. It seeks to convert individuals to its faith; and of course the more important they are, the better, for Buddhism values and needs state support like all other religions. (A converted monarch may swing the whole nation Buddha-ward.) But usually it has not sought to impose reforms upon the populace from above and to make men good by law.[8]

---

[7] It must also be assumed that there would be the auxiliary assistance of the devas, and in Burma, the nats, who generally favor the devout Buddhist and recognize in the holy man their natural superior whom they must assist. They would provide the material benefits accompanying the radiated virtue and support its exercise.

[8] It may be questioned, of course, whether a Buddhist monarch who is in some sense the "head" of the church, and regards Buddhism as the official religion, acts much differently from other religious rulers. For while it is true that Buddhism has not yet been rent by religious wars and has not made its converts at the point of the sword, Buddhist laws and wars are not unknown. King Anawrahta of Burma mounted a sizable military expedition to take the Pali scriptures from another king of lower Burma, when the latter refused to give them up. King Bodawpaya

Yet one must say that however passively Buddhism has entered the cultures that have come to be "Buddhist" in some sense or other, it has importantly modified them. Art and literature have been transformed into the Buddhist image as thoroughly as Christianity modified European culture up to the medieval period. Buddha's image and Buddhist themes in an endless variety of forms are to be found in painting, sculpture, architecture, social customs, and literature. So also despite some defections from the Buddhist way of peace (see note above) and a deplorable division of power from ethical principles by which cynical, ruthless monarchs have many times ruled over a passive people tamed by Buddhism, one can point to a gentling effect upon Buddhist cultures in general, and especially with regard to the taking of human and animal life.

If penetration is the Buddhist social "method," now we may define, or better, describe the central and guiding image of Buddhism in its process of social change. It is better to call it a guiding image than a concept or a goal; for it is seldom articulated and represents rather a semi-instinctive moving toward ill-defined goals and the formation of vague social patterns, than a clearly defined social philosophy or blue-print of the Good Society. This image is in conformity with the penetrative and permeative method of social change; and it grows out of the basic conception of the power of individually radiated moral virtue. The result is what we may call an image of the Good Buddhist Society, toward which Buddhist thought and practice gravitate and which has been approximated in many actual Buddhist cultures. The Good Society is a society in which *the Buddhist holy man or saint living in the midst of a holy community radiates virtue and social health into the surrounding society of lay-believers.*

The holy man may be multiplied, of course; the more arahats in a Buddhist country the better. And they are not

---

conquered Arakan in part to possess himself of the great Buddha image there, now in Mandalay.

What one *can* say is that, on the whole, rulers in Buddhist countries have been, in keeping with Buddhist principles, remarkably tolerant of other beliefs. The creation of Buddhism as the State Religion by U Nu's government offered interesting possibilities for speculation. See below.

necessarily, perhaps not often, officials within the holy community. They may be recluses who live in the forest or in cells
apart; but in any case their social value is to be found in their
spiritual attainment, not in any ecclesiastical office they may
hold. Yet, if not literally "in the midst" of the holy community—
which is the Sangha or Order of monks, of course—they are
products of it and their influence is reinforced by it. For the
Sangha too, in its entirety, is dedicated to the attainment of
Nibbana; and though few in this community may be arahats,
there should be a strong radiation of good influence emanating
from it throughout the environing society of laymen who themselves have not the will or capacity to enter the holy life. Here
is a kind of holiness in depth at the center of society, of circle
within circle of radiated spiritual power: the "invisible,"
i.e. humanly unknown, "church" of arahats in the center; the
visible church of the Sangha about *them;* and the environing
secular community, serving and guided by the sacred community, at the perimeter.

Such then is the seldom-stated but central and life-giving
image of the Buddhist Good Society. Within it the Sangha represents in its quality and organization the Buddhist ideal community. Like the monastic communities of Christendom, the
Sangha is conceived to be the nearest possible approximation
to the ideal social order possible in time and space, which *all*
men ought to approximate as nearly as possible in their social
relationships to each other. Thus we turn first to a description of
the Sangha as the Ideal Community (within the Good Society) as
it has been actualized in historical cultures.

4. The Holy Community

a. *Regulations*

The *ideal* role of the Sangha in a Buddhist society is now
reasonably clear in its essentials. It is the locus of dynamic holiness and virtue within the Buddhist society. To it the layman
looks for that power to sustain him in even the lesser virtues of
the lay life; it is his indespensable link with the higher life and
the hope of Nibbana. It is the life-giving center of all his mundane life and the guarantor of spiritual health in his secular

society. It will be his own spiritual home in some future incarnation when he is able to take its vows upon himself and seek
Nibbana single-mindedly. In it he sees the high and heavenly
model upon which he tries to mold his own social relationships.
And very practically it is for him the avenue through which
comes knowledge of the scriptures and the Buddhist way of life,
as well as the source of much practical moral support and
guidance.

So precious is this way of life—though originally it was no
doubt the *only* recognized Buddhist way of life—and so important its purity, that it is hedged round with multitudinous
regulations. We have already referred to the 227 major rules
of the *Vinaya* that every practising monk must learn. These
rules, and their extensive elaborations and applications, fill the
several volumes of the *Vinaya Piṭaka*. By them the monk's conduct and manner of life are regulated down to the smallest
detail. His requisites of robes (traditionally three in number),
water strainer, needle, fan, and mat are carefully detailed. The
robe itself must be worn in a specific and prescribed manner.[9] He
may not touch silver or gold; and so literally is this construed
that often the gilded palm-leaf scriptures have a broad red or
black painted band around them that the monk's hands may
not be defiled even by the touch of gold leaf paint on holy
scripture. He must not eat food after midday and must keep
his head shaven. So also, the times and places of his collection,
preparation, and eating of food; the manner of his association
with lower, equal, and superior monk, or with layman and laywoman, or with relatives or supporters; the routines of sleeping,
rising, personal hygiene, resting, meditating, and conversing;
the method of admonishing, censuring, disciplining and expelling
a brother monk—all these and much besides are found in the
Vinaya.

It may seem somewhat anomalous to find such legalistic

---

[9] The author has been present on two or three occasions when formal
pictures of a group of monks were taken. Not the least of the photogra-
pher's responsibilities was the careful arrangement of each monk's robe,
fold by fold, in the traditional manner.

There are variations of usage, also. Some strict sects forbid the wearing
of sandals, bright yellow robes, smoking, etc.

elaboration of apparent minutiae in generally non-legalistic Buddhism. The traditional explanation is that though the Buddha, when dying, told his disciple and attendant Ananda that his monks need observe only the *major* rules that he had given them, and use their discretion about how strictly to keep the others, Ananda forgot to ask him which *were* the major rules. Hence the community ever since has felt duty-bound to keep them all with rigorous exactitude. This appears to be a somewhat transparent device by which later elaborators justified their elaborations; yet so long have they been a part of the tradition that it would be impossible to separate the "later" from the "earlier" rules. Mostly they seem to be elaborations of the fundamental pattern to the *n*th logical degree.

The Theravada Sangha has always taken the Vinaya with all seriousness and has so literally attempted to follow it that one can truthfully say the present-day monk lives in a manner almost identical with his long-ago predecessors. To be sure there have been many minor variations in keeping with the changing world. A modern begging bowl has a set of four handy metal containers within it to keep differing foods separate; the bowl itself is carried sometimes on a cloth sling; the building materials of the monasteries and the materials from which clothing and sandals are made, vary somewhat from ancient days; so also a contemporary monk wears eyeglasses, rides on bus, train, ship and aeroplane on occasion, though there *are* those groups that consider some of these innovations to be evil. But to a surprising degree Sangha life is now the same as it was a thousand or two thousand years ago.

b. *Democratic Government*

Rigid as these rules are one would gain a totally wrong impression of life in the Sangha if he conceived it to be a strict pharisaical legalism in which the smallest infraction or the slightest variation is looked upon as a major sin. In general it may be said that if one has really made up his mind to live within the framework marked out by the *Vinaya* rules and has accustomed himself to them, they are no galling harness but provide both support and meaning for his life and allow him considerable liberty. The prescribed life of the Order provides an individual pattern of life in which a certain proportionate time is given each monk for fulfilling bodily needs, for study, meditation, rest, exercise, and some assigned duties. So too the monk is relieved of the pressing, decision-making activities of the layman who must provide for himself and his family. Worldly duties, ambitions, and anxieties are all far from him. And within this Order the general atmosphere is voluntary, non-coercive, kindly, and equalitarian. One is allowed to follow his own insights, seek to fulfill his own spiritual needs somewhat in his own way or at his own pace—subject to the general nature of the Buddhist way and under the advice of his spiritual counsellor.

With regard to the enforcement of rules within the Order: even in the *Vinaya* itself there is, despite Ananda's oversight, some graduation of offence. The offences that lead to expulsion are few and serious—major social crimes, for example, or out-broken and deliberate sexual relations with women. Others call for censure after a hearing by the local chapter of monks; others for only a mild admonition. There is indeed a stated procedure of confession in which a monk regularly confesses to another monk, or monks, his sins of thought, word, and deed. If there is no hiding of the offence, an apparent regret for it, and a hope of amendment in the future, or at least a genuine awareness that such thoughts or deeds *are* wrong—this is the end of the matter. There is no morbidity of a continuingly bad conscience, no further sacramental ritual of repentance, no fear of an unpardonable sin. For after all, if one does not "come clean," he himself will reap the kammic consequences and no one else.

It may be noted here that the causing of a schism in the Order is viewed most seriously. It is one of the four or five great sins which almost surely send a man to one of the hells—along with killing parents and shedding the blood of arahats and Buddhas. So the activities of a monk who goes about stirring up trouble of any sort between his brothers even on a personal basis, or who misreports another's statements, or is contentious about matters of doctrine with his superiors, are heavily censured, particularly if he persists in defending himself. Schism, however, usually occurs in the full sense only over major matters of doctrine. And while there have been and are still some sectarian divisions within the Theravada Sangha, they are largely minor, representing different degrees of the strictness of in-interpretation of the *Vinaya* rules or allowable minor differences of doctrinal opinion.[10]

Even in the matter of expulsion the rule is generally noncoercive. To be sure if it is a civil crime of consequence the civil authorities may step in and remove the offender who is thereby automatically expelled. But ordinarily, for lesser offences, there is no actual machinery for expelling the reluctant expellee. He will not be physically compelled to leave, even though he may be sent to a mild sort of Coventry. But if he can endure the disapproving silence of his fellow monks and still find those laymen to support him with food and clothing, he may go on actually living in a monastery.

This raises an interesting question, only to be touched upon, about possible ways in which the Sangha can protect itself against heresy and insubordination. And it must be answered that the protection is more in the uniformity of the tradition and the common devout adherence to the scriptures and their orthodox interpretation in the commentaries, than by disciplinary device. As the rule the junior monk has great reverence for his *gurus* and his superiors under whom he chooses to serve. Indeed this is true largely *because* a monk may, within reasonable limits, seek the monastery and teacher under whom he wishes to study and work. But this implies, as is indeed the case, that a monk may set up his own establishment and, if supported by his *dāyakas* or lay-followers, he is largely independent of the discipline of others. There is no machinery to enforce rigid uniformity of view and practice, though popular outcry and al-

---

[10] A seemingly trivial matter which divided the Burmese Sangha for a good many years: whether the right shoulder might be worn bare of the robe among the monks themselves, i.e., when not out in public or begging food. (The bare shoulder faction won.) But a principle was involved: The dissidents had introduced some of their own writings, passing them off as scriptures.

most uniform Sangha condemnation may place a "revisionist" socially beyond the pale.[11]

To be sure this "no machinery" statement needs some qualification. Many Theravada countries have an ecclesiastical Primate who is the official head of the Sangha. In Burma there have been such since the end of the 13th century, variously called Chief of the Sangha, King's Preceptor, and the Protector of the Country. During the monarchy such a one was the king's appointee, often the king's favorite advisor or chaplain. His responsibility was to keep the Sangha in order, and for this task he had somewhat of the royal power at his disposal. Nevertheless there was here no highly organized or heavy-handed autocracy. The king could not force the Sangha to do his will, nor could the Sangha head impose uniformity upon those under him. He worked rather through mutual counsel and persuasion than by force or ecclesiastical authority.

In this connection the Buddhist conception of true authority within the holy community is worthy of note. The basic authority, as already implied, is the authority of character and spiritual attainment, *not* of ecclesiastical power, political appointment, or inheritance. And this is also the pattern that the Sangha has sought to follow in the choice of the leader of each smaller community within the total community, i.e. the individual monasteries, which are the real religious units of the Sangha. The monastery head is presumably chosen on the basis of age, scholarship, and spiritual attainment. He "rules" by force of

---

[11] There have been one or two interesting illustrations of this situation recently in Burma. One man who claimed to be a living Buddha (and had four wives and drove a nice car) was put in jail because he offended public sensibilities. And a monk of rather extreme views was put in "protective custody" and his latest book confiscated by civil authorities because it had stirred up so much heated discussion in the Sangha. He had affirmed that rebirth occurred only into human form, not animal or purgatorial; but he may also have been considered unreliable politically.

Occasionally there has been a "defrocking" of a heretical monk. If such a one feels that his retaining the robe will occasion a scandal in Buddhism or his lay support fails, then he may withdraw from the monkhood, but otherwise cannot be forced to.

personal quality, just as does a village headman, not by the power of his office.

Nor is this mere theory. It has been practiced in actuality throughout much of the Buddhist world for centuries. Thus writes Walpola Rahula in his *History of Buddhism in Ceylon:*

> First, there is no leader or head of the Sangha. But the members of the community would always respect and follow any member who is virtuous, wise and learned. Secondly there is no centralization of authority and power. They maintained their unity and discipline as groups in different areas. . . .
>
> But these groups had no identity of their own. Wherever they lived, they followed the same constitution and rules [i.e. the *Vinaya* rules] that were common to all. . . . If two or more groups from different areas got together, they all formed automatically one assembly under one president for the occasion. There was no compulsion and everything was voluntary.[12]

As the Buddhist puts it: The presence of the Buddha's Teaching or Law is the presence of the Buddha himself.

That such a loose-jointed system would work at all seems a miracle of sorts. And apparently there were those who had practical questions about the Sangha's viability even in the early days. Later in the same passage just quoted the author points out that in one of the Suttas *(Gopaka-Moggalāna)* of the *Majjhima-Nikāya,* or *Middle Length Sayings,* Ananda is questioned on this very point by the chief minister Vassakara. The latter asks about how the monks get along with each other under so little authority, and whether there is in actuality any one monk in a monastery whom the others "respect, honour, revere and esteem" and upon whom they depend. Ananda replies in the affirmative. They know him by his manifestation of virtue, learning, contentment, possession of the four *jhānas* or psychic absorptions, miraculous powers, clairaudience, clairvoyance, power to remember his own and others' past births, and freedom from all fetters.

This last phrase, of course, is actually the description of an arahat, a saint who is ready for Nibbana. Presumably there

---

[12] Walpola Rahula, *History of Buddhism in Ceylon* (Colombo: M. D. Gunesena, 1956), pp. 171–3.

were enough of them to go around in Ananda's day to head all the monastic communities—though obviously it has scarcely ever been the case since. But even though the ideal specifications for the community head cannot always be met, the basic principle is clear: authority in the Sangha rests primarily upon spiritual and moral capacity, not ecclesiastical influence, political appointment, social position or wealth. It is part and parcel of what Shway Yoe calls a "republican tendency" in the Sangha, which, he says, ensures the love and support of the layman:

> It is this republican tendency of Buddhism that gives it such a wonderful hold on the people. Rank does not confer on the mendicant greater honour, or release him from any of his obligations. The most learned and famous Sadaw must go forth every morning to beg his daily food . . .
> His dress is the same as that of the most recently admitted koyin, and in the eyes of the world he holds honour, not because he controls the assembly, but because he is close to the verge of Neh'ban (Nibbana).[13]

Possibly senior sayadaws do not now go forth to beg quite as much as in Shway Yoe's day, yet this basic republican (or democratic) quality still characterizes the Sangha; and it *is* one of the reasons for the high esteem in which the laity hold the Sangha.

Thus we have in the Sangha the archetype of the "heavenly" social order of Nibbana, as it were, or as near as one may come to it in samsara. Almost certainly it represents the normal and typical Buddhist pattern of the original days; but with the growth of lay Buddhism it has become the exceptional way of perfection, the community of saints, or at least of would-be saints. As such it holds up to the Buddhist a high social ideal: A non-coercive, non-authoritarian, democratic society where leadership comes only from good moral character and spiritual insight; where everyone confesses his sins to his brother; where all goods are held in common possession and every one, high or low, eats and dresses alike. It is an order of society which has no political ambitions within the nation, and in whose ranks there is no striv-

---

[13] *The Burman and His Notions*, II, 132.

ing for leadership. It is dedicated to the attainment of salvation for oneself, the nourishment of fellowship and brotherhood with one's fellow-seeker, and the welfare of all beings. It seeks to persuade men to follow its way, by example and exhortation, but does not attempt to force any man into faith. If a lay brother wishes to enter the Order for meditation and study for only a few days, months, or years, or to spend his life-time there, he is equally welcome; and if he finds after a time that the life of the monk is too high for his capacities or secular duties call him back into the world, he may leave without disgrace.[14] Certainly in this gentle democracy of the spiritual quest for life's ultimate good, one finds the Buddhist ideal of the Good Society clearly and convincingly manifested. Here is the practice of the Ethic of Equanimity, the Nibbanic Society in actual historical existence!

c. *Teacher of the Dhamma*

But not all men, in fact only a small minority, are able to take up this supreme quest for Nibbana and practice its Higher Ethic. Hence there will always be a laity to which the Sangha must minister if its alms are to be deserved and its merit to nourish the people. And indeed this obligation to teach the laity has been recognized from the beginning. The Buddha himself divided his time between his own spiritual nourishment and the instruction of others, and taught his monks to do likewise. The detachment of the monk, except possibly for some few holy recluses who are earnestly pushing on to nibbanic realization in the immediate future, or for some stated periods in the life of every monk, is not to be so extreme that he has nothing of time or energy for the laity who support him. In the *Sigālovāda Sutta* of the *Dīgha-Nikāya (Dialogues of the Buddha)* we find the basic duties of monks set forth thus:

> . . recluses and brahmins show their love for the clansman in six ways:—they restrain him from evil, they exhort him to good, they love him with kindly thoughts, they teach him what he has

---

[14] This is true in Burma. In Ceylon, and perhaps other Theravada countries, one is a monk for life.

not heard, they correct and purify what he has heard, they reveal to him the way to heaven.[15]

This seems quite un-Buddhistic in its language of brahmins and heaven; and the route by which it made its way into the Canon may have been devious. Perhaps it is further evidence of the Buddha's primary concern to bring his monks out of the world and his secondary concern with the lay community that remained; so that herein we may have a left-over bit of attention that expresses itself only in terms of the traditional Indian pattern, or even perhaps a later insertion from a time when Buddhists had become more concerned with lay welfare. It is also interesting that contemporary Buddhism must turn to such fragments as major documents for charting lay-monk relationships.

Whatever the reasons for this situation, however, teaching laymen has long been the accepted responsibility of the monk.[16] Now when we speak of Sangha teaching we must have two kinds in mind: preaching-teaching and teaching-teaching. Preaching-teaching is evangelistic—if the term is not too violent to characterise the usual Buddhist monk's discourse. Its purpose is to make converts to the monkish way of life—originally its only meaning. Of later years it has included also the "conversion" of non-Buddhist laity to take the three-fold refuge in Buddha, Dhamma, and Sangha, i.e. make a profession of Buddhist faith. And we might also include here that ordinary and regular preaching-teaching to the laity on the sabbaths and holy-days at the pagodas or in the monasteries.

---

[15] Pamphlet edition of the *Sutta* (PTS Text) by Burma Buddhist World-Mission, Rangoon, no date, p. 11.

[16] There is a nice point involved here. Who is fit to teach whom what, in the Buddhist pattern? The Enlightened One could teach all men, of course, even the gods. But that is part of being a Buddha. What can lesser men do? Even though the arahat is fitted for Nibbana, and though some of the original disciples were encouraged by the Buddha to expound His doctrine, an arahat does not become a teacher by virtue of being an arahat. The essential task of the monk is therefore simply the repetition of the Buddha's word, and the exposition of it when his study has progressed sufficiently; and possibly the direct tutelage of the layman in meditation, by one whose gifts so fit him—that is, by one from whom pupils receive spiritual profit.

An often-forgotten but very important fact must be kept in mind here: The Theravada Buddhist layman does not read his own scriptures—with rare exceptions. The reasons are these: Not only are the scriptures voluminous, unindexed, and so costly as to be beyond the resources of most lay people (or so rare as to be confined to the palm-leaf manuscripts of monasteries), but for the most part they are in an essentially foreign language that the layman can neither read nor understand. Even though the Pali of the scriptures is written in the characters of his own tongue and he can pronounce its sounds, he does not know its meaning. Even those traditional passages which he has learned by heart in the monastery school (see below) are mostly holy sounds without sense.[17] Whatever knowledge or understanding of the Buddhist teaching itself may come through to the laity depends then entirely upon the efforts of the Sangha.

But the Sangha has not relied upon preaching-teaching alone to accomplish its teaching mission. It has also turned to teaching-teaching as well. As it became an institutionalized Order in the midst of a lay community it took up the task of education as such, that is, education of the young. So it is that in Theravada countries the Sangha has been the prime educative agency for the children of the faithful from time immemorial. The monastery school (phongyi kyaung) in which every girl up to the age of ten and every boy into his teens was educated, was once a standard part of every Burmese community. And the nature and spirit of the educative process was similar to that of Colonial New England Puritan education: The child was to learn his letters and his religion by the self-same process. In the phongyi kyaung, under the tutelage of the monks, the children learned to chant and to read the sacred verses, and write the letters of the alphabet on their slates. The village neighbors catechized them on the way home, and parents and

---

[17] This situation is now changing to some extent. The Pali Canon is now in printed book form—but still expensive, still in Pali, still unindexed. And some translations are being made into the vernacular, at least of selected portions. Whether the Sangha will ever allow free translations or paraphrases of its age-long sacred Pali terms in a popular version of the scriptures, and what would be the probable effects of such a translation, remain unknown.

monks reinforced the learning process with a firm, judicious application of the rod.

Thus, though some other subjects were also taught—whatever of history, geography, literature, mathematics and practical medicine was deemed necessary—the main subject was Buddhism. Even though much of the scriptures would remain forever unknown to them, those who came through the monastery schools learned at least the rudiments of Buddhist teaching and morality, and numbers of the favorite scripture passages by heart—whose meaning as well as whose sound they might *sometime* learn. Thus taught, the layman and laywoman were ready to take their places in a Buddhist society.[18]

One exception to the generally inhibitive effect of the language barrier may be found in the *Jātaka Tales,* especially in Burma. These were not only favorite homiletical themes for the preacher-teacher monks at the pagoda or monastery, but also filled a large place in the children's education in the *phongyi-kyaung.* The reason for their popularity both for preaching and for children's education is evident. The *Tales,* ostensibly accounts of the past incarnations of the Buddha as man, beast, and god, are full of the colorful and fascinating folklore of the ages. They are much like Aesop's Fables; a fitting tale to illustrate almost any moral situation can be found among them. And besides, what fun along the way, seeing animals, ogres, spirits, and men and women scheming, plotting, adventuring, and trying their wits against each other! And through them all moves the figure of the future Buddha as the best, the mightiest, the wisest, the most unselfish being, and the finally triumphant conqueror in each situation. Even beyond the monk's sermon illustration and child's school-lesson material, the *Tales* moved on to the fireside and became the core of the older Burmese Buddhist family culture.

---

[18] The Sangha has always been very zealous, of course, in teaching its own members. They have traditionally learned long passages of the scriptures—some holy men supposedly knowing the entire *Tipiṭaka,* eleven times the Bible's length, by heart. As with the layman, memorization comes first, meaning afterward. But the monk, with his Pali instruction and ample time at his disposal, could be presumed to arrive at a kind of understanding of his scriptures denied to the layman.

The situation now, at least in Burma, is far different. Foreign occupation, missionary and secular government schools, and the invasion of the outside world, have together discredited and emptied the monastery schools. Many Burmese see in the current situation a basic threat to the whole moral and religious character of the nation. And under the 1961-62 government, which promised to make Buddhism the State Religion, some attempt was made to reinstitute the monastery school at least on the kindergarten level. Of this more will be said later.

d. *As Moral Counsellor*

One other social function of the Sangha must be mentioned before we turn to the lay Buddhist society. But because it is ill-defined and not institutionalized it is difficult to give it a name. For want of a better term we may call it a moral counselling service; or designate the Sangha as a kind of Moral-Influence Bureau. The form which this has taken has depended much upon local contexts. At various periods in Ceylon's Buddhist era the rulers trusted much to some of the leading monks for diplomatic and political advice. One monk so impressed his sovereign that the latter publicly proclaimed that all of the monk's orders or decisions should be as authoritative as his own. And we have already referred to the custom of appointing an official Sangha head in Burma, who acted as the monarch's chaplain and ecclesiastical advisor. Many of these men were men of genuine religious and moral conviction who used their office to restrain the king in his excesses, temper his violence, rebuke his wickedness, and turn him to mercy and justice.

And they had some official power to extend their religious influence even down to the village level. Under them certain monks were appointed in the villages or districts, whose powers may be described as follows:

> The monks who were appointed as officers of the Primate were empowered to bring to the notice of the king through the Primate any case of mis-government or abuse of power by the local authorities concerned, to set the matter right by verbal warning and if the miscreant official persisted, they were authorized to report the matter to the king. For this purpose these monks were supplied with palm-leaves stamped with the royal seal to send

their report in. Thus the monks had a certain say in the local affairs.[19]

But such official relationships do not represent the characteristically Buddhist manner in which the Sangha exercised its moral leadership. The typical manner was unofficial and personal and of that indirect quality which the Buddhist loves best. The monks, particularly the elder and revered ones, set the moral tone of the whole village, though they did not always make their influence felt by direct pronouncement. There is the story, for example, of certain individuals who thought to come into a village on the occasion of a large pagoda festival to sell their liquid wares, i.e. country liquor, at a fancy price. But the word was quietly passed down along the grapevine by the headman that such doings would be highly displeasing to the learned and holy *sayadaw* who was head of the local monastery. Consequently any who desired to imbibe had to take a trip of considerable length to do so; for the liquor sellers, unideal Buddhists though they might be, would not venture to go against the wishes of the *sayadaw* in his own village.

On other occasions the monks were invited to act as arbiters of disputes, not so much because of their detailed knowledge of the factors involved, as their knowledge of the *persons* involved and perhaps even more, because of their reputation for impartiality and good character. In such an atmosphere, that is to say, in such a presence, all disputes could presumably be settled in a righteous, or at least mutually satisfactory manner. And this is still the orthodox mode of the Sangha's social and political influence: not a direct mingling in such matters, a taking sides on political issues, or a propounding of policies and statements for the public consumption of guidance of rulers; it is rather the indirect pressure of holy living and moral influence—in a Buddhist framework of ethical values, of course— upon persons and policies.[20]

---

[19] From a paper "A Brief Survey of the Burmese Buddhist Sangha and its Relationship with the State and the Laity," by Professor U Aung Than, University of Rangoon.

[20] In passing it may be noted that even today, when there is a sporadic tendency for the Sangha to enter into politics, most Buddhists are reluc-

It may be in place here also to notice, in conclusion, that the monastery has had a tradition of generous hospitality, both for its own members and for the laity or stranger. This does not mean that laity could come and stay for indefinite periods as guests of the monks; for it was the laity who supported the monks, not vice versa. And most laymen would feel unworthy to stay in such precincts for long. Yet the layman did feel at home with the monks in a wider sense, welcome to come for advice or even a friendly visit. Many a weary traveler was refreshed in the mon-estery, and even kept over night. And in a recent emergency, the World War II period, the traditional isolation of the monas-tery was broken and it became a haven for the refugee:

> During that period of horror, the Burmese Buddhist monks, disregarding their personal convenience and the minimum com-forts they happened to enjoy, gave accomodation to the people who sought refuge with them; they protected them from all kinds of outward dangers and difficulties even at the risk of their own lives and looked after them with care and concern which in nor-mal circumstances is to be expected in households alone.[21]

Thus is the Sangha a most important and central entity in a Buddhist society. It may be questioned whether there could be such a society without it. Not only is it the Ideal Community which serves always as both inspiration and rebuke to the secular order; it is also the teacher of youth, the avenue of culture, the purveyor of the Dhamma, and the laity's link with the Buddha and his Nibbana. As Walpola Rahula well sums it up for Singhalese Buddhism:

---

tant to see their "clergy" become socially active. Their strong protest against the incursions of communist philosophy into Burmese Buddhism seems to be allowable; however, political participation much beyond such a point is frowned upon. And this poses a problem for future lead-ership in Buddhism, as we shall note later.

This has not prevented some monks from considerable political activity, of course. U Wisara, whose statue adorns a traffic circle at the head of a street named after him in Rangoon, was a martyr to the cause of Burmese independence. In the first part of the twentieth century some politicians actively used monks to support their campaigns; and as late as 1959 some politicians warned monks to keep out of politics. But this represents "bad" Buddhism.

[21] Professor U Aung Than's paper. See above.

The most obvious and outstanding feature of the religion of the laity was their tremendous devotion to the Sangha. This was due to two reasons: first, the monk was the most trusted teacher and guide and friend of the people. He intervened at all critical moments and settled disputes—even in state affairs. In all matters great and small, people went to him for advice, guidance, and consolation with greatest trustfulness. Secondly, the monk was even more helpful to them in the next world. . . . It was the monk, and no one else, who could help them here. . . .

"Merit" was the investment that ensured security in the next world. The sangha is called *punnak-khetta,* "merit-field," where one could sow seeds of merit and reap a good harvest in the next world. If the field was not fertile, the crop would be poor . . . If the Sangha was impure, the charity bestowed on them would bring poor results.

The vast majority . . . had neither the earnestness or peace of mind necessary for practising the higher teachings of the Buddha . . . So they expected the monks . . . here and hereafter, to practice the religion for them.[22]

5. The Buddhist Lay Society

We have now sketched the outlines of that image of the ideal society which is the touchstone of social goodness so far as the Buddhist is concerned, and described the actual historical embodiment of that image in the institution of the Sangha. But what is to be said with regard to the context in which the Sangha is set, the surrounding lay society? Is there any guidance in the Buddhist tradition for this society per se—aside from its implied duty to cherish the Sangha and provide for its necessities, and the observance of that personal code of ethics already described in the previous chapter? What would be the hallmark of a Buddhist *lay* society that by definition can never be expected to reach the moral heights of the Sangha?

We must repeat again here with special reference to the lay society, what was said at the beginning of this chapter about social-political thought in general in Buddhism: It is a meager afterthought to the *main* interest of the scriptures—which is Nibbana-seeking. Society per se is not genuinely prescribed

---

[22] *Op. cit.,* pp. 259–60.

for. And the only counsels which we find for statecraft are the *Jātaka Tale* exhortations to piety and charity. Nevertheless there are *some* materials, even in the classical tradition, which are made much of today in Theravada circles, that point in that direction. There are two scriptures in particular, the *Sigālovāda Sutta*, (already quoted in part) and the *Mangala Sutta*, and one notable historical example, namely the famous Indian monarch, King Aśoka, that we shall use as instances of such prescription.

The *Sigālovāda Sutta* is one in which the Buddha is portrayed as finally yielding to lay entreaty and laying down specific rules for their guidance. The importance with which it is treated in some Theravada circles today is evident in the following quotation from the introduction to the pamphlet edition of the *Sutta* by the Burma Buddhist World-Mission:

> The Sigalovada *Sutta* . . . forms a comprehensive summary of what constitutes good living for laymen. As a guide to a wholesome and happy life it is unequalled, being universal in its significance and applicability
>
> His [the Buddha's] language is simple, clear and direct; his thought embraces every aspect of the ordinary man's daily experience. All the problems of humanity would dissolve and vanish if this Sutta were to be universally studied and put into practice. Social problems, economic problems, as well as the problems of personal conduct, each of them has its solution here. The Sigalovada Sutta stands unique in the world's religious literature. . .

The *Sutta,* though quite short, cannot be repeated here. But its pattern is simple. It begins with the Five Precepts as basic rules for each layman. To these it adds that the virtuous layman should avoid unseemly, i.e. late, hours on the public streets, fairs or places of worldly amusement, gambling, idleness, and association with evil companions. The motivation that is stressed in the *Sutta* for such avoidances is that indulgence in the above habits leads to ill health, social disharmony, and waste of resources. Secondly, there is a description of a good versus a false or bad friend. The good friend, for example, is one who is always helpful, gives wise counsel, is sympathetic and is constant in good or bad fortune. The bad friend is the reverse, of course.

Finally, in a manner somewhat reminiscent of Confucius' Five Great Relationships, the *Sutta* divides human relationships into six basic types and prescribes their respective duties. In respect to the first three—child-parent, pupil-teacher, wife-husband—it is counseled that child, pupil, and wife should give respect, loyalty, and faithful service to parent, teacher, and husband, respectively. The latter in turn should provide guidance, loving concern, and material necessities as appropriate. The fourth relation—clansman to clansman, or we might say, equal to equal—calls for man-to-man equity of treatment. In the fifth the servant gives zealous, contented service to his master; and the master, with paternal solicitude such as a king is to show to his subjects, suits the servant's work to his strength and capacity, and cares for him in sickness and in trouble.

The sixth relationship, between monk and layman, we have already described so far as the monk's responsibility is concerned—benevolent regard, instruction, and religious counsel. The layman is to respond by "affection in act and speech and mind; by keeping open house to them, by supplying their temporal needs"—"them" referring to monks of course.

The *Mangala Sutta,* often quoted and also known as *The Thirty-Eight Blessings for World Peace,* is often used as a paritta, i.e. a recitation which will ward off evil. (See p. 153 above.) Francis Story in his "Foreword" to the World-Mission's edition of this *Sutta* calls it "unrivalled" as a teaching for the daily conduct of a man's life. As with the *Sigālovāda Sutta,* it is too long for repetition here but covers much the same ground as that Sutta, though in a more general way. The *Blessings* are Buddhist Beatitudes that praise certain types of actions because they are presumed to bring happiness and prosperity. Their substance may be summed up as follows: one should not associate with fools; he should honor the honorable, refrain from evil, speak pleasantly, cherish wife and children, discuss the Dhamma at proper times, pursue a right livelihood or occupation, and avoid intoxicants. Reverence, humility, gratitude, contentment, obedience, visiting holy persons, and—curiously—having good *past* Kamma, are all pronounced blessed.

What is notable about both of these statements is that they

are couched in the functional-personal terms of the social *status quo* of the time of their writing. So far as the social situation itself is concerned, there is no prescription for a good society or the ideal structuring of human relationship. There is here no possible doctrine of social revolution or change of any sort. All that is called for is that each man do his duty with faithfulness and gentleness in the place or relationship where his destiny has put him. Consequently the values that are mentioned here are the purely individualistic ones of personal attitude and habit, that one be a "good" man in the conventional sense. There is indeed little that is characteristically or peculiarly *Buddhist* in these prescriptions; such exhortations to wives to be obedient to husbands and husbands to be protective toward wives, the obedience of children and loving discipline of parents, service from servants and consideration from masters—all this can be found in many another code of ethics.

The other observable matter of interest is the great attention given by contemporary Theravada Buddhists to those two suttas. On such meagre and non-Buddhistic materials they would seek to erect a total social philosophy. This witnesses to that meagerness of social-ethic materials in the Buddhist scriptures and tradition already referred to. Or perhaps it would be fairer to say that it demonstrates the meager development which has been given to such materials of this nature as there are in the Buddhist tradition; and to the twin fact that at present Theravada Buddhism, under compulsion of new conditions, is most eagerly seeking in every way to socially orient the basic Buddhist way of life and to find a warrant for such orientation in the scriptures. Some of this is bound to be naive—like the Christian's statement that if only everyone would follow the Golden Rule, all the world's problems would be solved. But it is representative of a new and important trend in Theravada Buddhism toward a social philosophy, some of whose more specific contemporary expressions we shall describe in the next chapter.

6. King Aśoka: The Ideal Buddhist Ruler

But if scriptural social-ethical materials are few, or still un-

discovered, there is one notable example of a monarch whom
modern Buddhists regard as the ideal Buddhist ruler, providing
a superlative example of Buddhist social philosophy in action.
There is some question as to how fully or uniquely "Buddhist"
Aśoka was, a question to be discussed later. But for the moment
we may go ahead to briefly describe his reign and reforms.

Aśoka was one of the later Mauryan kings, reigning from
265 to 234 B.C. in northwest and central India. His first years
were spent in peaceful administration, but in 261 he launched
a war against the Kalingas who controlled the territory on the
east coast between modern Calcutta and Madras. He was successful in the prosecution of the war, extending his domain as
far south as today's Madras and Kerala provinces in east and
west respectively. But the wholesale carnage and suffering that
accompanied his conquest sickened him. He became a convert
to Buddhism. And though the most powerful monarch in South
Asia, he forebore to extend his empire further, as he might well
have done. To be sure he did not give up any of the territory
which he had acquired by conquest; but during the twenty-five
or more years of his reign that remained he sought to rule as
a "Buddhist"' monarch.

Therefore we have here a specific and deliberate attempt,
it would seem, to apply a Buddhist political philosophy and
method to an actual situation on a large scale. And fortunately
Aśoka has left a considerable record of his social ideals and
achievements in his edicts, carved upon pillars and rocks throughout north and central India. In two of his Edicts he sets forth
his philosophy of ethical goodness.

> There is indeed no better work than the welfare of all the
> people. And whatever efforts I am making are in order that I may
> discharge (my) debts to (all) beings, that I may make them hap-
> py here (in this life) and that they may attain heaven in the next
> (life).

This is in Rock Edict Six. And the following in Rock Edict
Thirteen:

> That conquest which has been won everywhere by this the
> practice of the Dharma generates the feeling of satisfaction.
> (And) that satisfaction is obtained in conquest by the

Dharma. But (of) small (consequence) indeed, is that satisfaction. It is (matters) of the next world alone that the Beloved of the gods [Aśoka's name for himself] considers to be of great consequence.[23]

The Dharma (Pali *Dhamma*) means for Aśoka the central teaching and way of the Buddha. He defines the essence of it in another edict as "little sin, many good deeds, mercifulness, charity, truthfulness, (and) purity."[24] And as sovereign he sought to put the Dharma as he interpreted it, into immediate and practical effect. He sought to inspire certain (Buddhistic?) virtues among all his subjects, especially those who served him as officials. Following is Amulyachandra Sen's summary:

> mercifulness toward all living being; charities and gifts to the Brahmans, ascetics, friends, relatives and acquaintances; truthfulness, purity of thought, honesty, gentleness, gratitude, self-restraint, steadfastness, non-injury to animal life, and fear of sin; moderation in spending and in ownership; respectfulness toward parents, elders and teachers; proper behaviour towards Brahmans, ascetics, relatives, servants and slaves; avoidance of ferocity, cruelty, anger, pride and envy; exertion in good works; relieving the sufferings of the aged, the indigent and the sick; toleration of and respectfulness towards others' faiths; avoidance of meaningless rituals; avoidance of sectarian bigotry, etc.[25]

Nor were these mere ideals that Aśoka grandiosely but emptily proclaimed. He went ahead by wide-scale practical measures to effect them throughout his large empire, as far as humanly possible. Thus again in Sen's summary of the statements found in the Edicts:

> In order to inculcate such virtues Aśoka led the way by prohibiting animal sacrifices and drastically reduced the meat eaten in the royal household; he forswore further conquest, though he did not disband the army; he gave many charities to the Buddhists—a rather minor religious sect at the time—and encouraged the propagation of their teaching; yet he also constructed temples

---

[23] Amulyachandra Sen, *Asoka's Edicts* (Calcutta: Indian Publicity Society, Institute of Indology Series, No. 7, n.d.), pp. 78, 102.

[24] *Ibid*, p. 146.

[25] *Ibid*, p. 33.

and gave gifts to other non-Buddhist religious sects; he dug wells, planted gardens, constructed hospitals, sought to improve the situation of women and the aboriginal tribes; he sent religious and medical missionaries abroad; he sought to secure a moral and efficient government administration throughout his own realm, and so administer it that all people would regard the king as their father.[26]

No one should attempt to detract from the height and nobility of Asoka's social ideals. What government anywhere in the world, before or since, has done better in this respect? Nor can there be any doubt about the practical earnestness with which he sought to implement his ideals. Here is a large-spirited, far-sighted, humanitarian statesmanship of the first order. No, Aśoka did not free the slaves or relinquish his territories; but to do so in the world of his time would have been to invite social and political chaos of the first order. Such "failures" cannot be urged against him. It is sad indeed to relate that after such splendid accomplishments he seems to have been somewhat disillusioned with their effectiveness. Or perhaps he is only stating his basic spiritual philosophy rather than any overcoming world-weariness with reform when he writes that all that he has done is "of little avail indeed," but "it is by persuasion indeed that men's progress in the Dharma has been promoted to a much greater extent in respect of non-injury to living beings."[27]

When we come to a consideration of the specifically Buddhist quality of these reforms some qualifying comments are in order. Interestingly enough, and apparently not just through excessive modesty, Aśoka disclaims any particular *originality* in his measures. After listing what he has done by way of practical measures he goes on to say that with these same "various comforts indeed were the people made happy by former kings as also by me."[28] Aśoka himself evidently does not regard his pattern of government as being specifically Buddhistic, but within the bounds of the general Indian pattern of social morality. Perhaps his eminence in this respect is the practical energy with which he carried

---

26 *Ibid*, pp. 166, 168.
27 *Ibid*, pp. 166, 168.
28 *Ibid*, p. 162, Pillar Edict Seven.

out hitherto latent ideals, rather than any newness of ideal. Of course it is certainly true that his practices are not in *dis*cord with Buddhist principles; but neither are they with Hindu-Indian principles, with the possible exception of his strong emphasis upon non-injury to living beings. This apparently is a specifically Buddhist emphasis which Aśoka took very seriously.[29]

It is noteworthy also that certain basic Buddhist themes are missing from Aśoka's description of the Dharma, almost all of them indeed except non-injury to living beings. In fact doctrinal emphasis of almost any sort is absent, whether Indian or Buddhist. Thus to quote Sen again:

> Liberation, meditation, asceticism and renunciation that occupy the Indian religious thought so much, are never referred to by him, whereas the goal of religious aspiration that he frequently stresses is the attainment of heaven. . .
>
> Nirvana, *dhyana,* the doctrines of sorrow, impermanence, non-soul, the Chain of Causation—are never mentioned by him.[30]

In summary then we may say that Aśoka's Buddhism as portrayed in his Edicts at least was very much the religion of the layman whatever else may be said about it. Whether Aśoka himself was moved by the hope of Nibbana we do not know; certainly his edicts never once mention it with regard to his or any one else's practice of the Dharma. The heavens of blessed rebirth are held up as the exclusive and absolutely good goals of ulti-

---

[29] Prof. K. M. Panikkar in his *Survey of Indian History,* p. 31, says with regard to Asoka's Buddhism:

"Aśoka is spoken of as a Buddhist Emperor and his reign as a kind of Buddhist period in Indian history. But the distinction between Hinduism and Buddhism in India was purely sectarian and never more than the differences between Saivism and Vishnaivism . . . Asoka was a Buddhist in the same way as Harsha was a Buddhist . . . but in the view of the people of the day he was a Hindu monarch following one of the recognized sects. . . .

His own name of adoption is Devanan Priya, the beloved of the gods. Which gods? Surely the gods of the Aryan religion. Buddhism had no gods of its own. The idea that Asoka was a kind of Buddhist Constantine declaring himself against paganism is a complete misreading of Indian conditions. . . ."

It may be added that Harsha, though "Buddhist," prayed to Siva.

[30] *Op. cit.,* pp. 34, 35.

mate human endeavor. Does this mean that he was not genuinely Buddhist? Not necessarily so, though perhaps not so narrowly or exclusively Buddhist as later interpreters would have us believe. His limited expression of Buddhist doctrine very probably indicates the original situation in Buddhism itself: Only the monk was encouraged to hope for, or even think much about, Nibbana. The layman's religion still looked upon the gods in friendly fashion and aspired no higher than rebirth among them. As a layman Aśoka remained entirely in the layman's sphere of values and action: Kamma-rebirth morality without any awareness at all of the nibbanic transvaluation of all lesser values. And this is precisely why his practical morality is almost indistinguishable from that of contemporary Indian varieties.

7. Transition

Such is the portrait of the traditional basis for the Buddhist social ethic in terms of its central imagery, its scriptural pronouncements, and some historical instances of its implementation. The questions that now confront us are these two: What is it that we actually have as a basis in the tradition? And how can this tradition be adapted to modern conditions?

With regard to the first question: There is in the Buddhist tradition the basic imagery of the holy man within a holy community that permeates the society about it and him with healing, health-giving power, useful in this world even though the saint's mind is set on Nibbana. To a considerable degree Buddhist societies have conformed to this pattern even though indirectly and to some extent unconsciously. But this is an ethic of transcendent personalism, the radiation of spiritual strength and moral vitality, rather than specific social techniques or practical plans. This is essentially the ethic of the monk that may stimulate the layman to be better, more confident, and more resourceful, i.e. bring him to a peak of personal competence, but which provides no direct guidance for society itself.

Yet in contemporary Theravada Buddhism, particularly in Burma, it is *this* aspect of Buddhism that is being rejuvenated in the new emphasis upon meditation. In terms of our earlier analysis, the nibbanic absolutes are being brought into touch with the kammic and practical realm, and a living synthesis is being attempted between the two in the person and the practice of the new man in Buddhism—the meditating layman. What will be its results? Will the cross-fertilization of the two streams of (a modified) monkish discipline and the householder's life really succeed? (Such a thing could not have happened in Aśoka's day.) And what will be the resources within the Buddhist tradition for such a synthesis?

This latter question is of course one which Buddhism is today asking itself. As we have observed already, Theravadins are diligently searching their tradition for new answers (or even good old ones) for new situations. In Western eyes those materials seem to be primarily of the intra-personal sort—the inward discipline of the individual—or largely of a personal-ethical nature, which do not directly apply to current social problems and situations facing Buddhist cultures. And some of the basic doctrines of Buddhism—detachment from this world, individualized kammic destiny, the goal of transcendent Nibbana—seem eminently unfitted for the production of a vital and viable modern society.

But it should be remembered that a tradition actually *is* what one finds within it. And one of the most fascinating aspects of the contemporary ethical situation in Theravada Buddhism is what *is* being found in the ancient tradition to fit the current need. It is somewhat similar to what occurred in Christianity when, as an other-wordly millennial gospel, it was adjusting itself to the task of creating a "Christian civilization." But the present situation in Buddhism is more pressing and the adjustment must be more quickly made, in a matter of a generation or two rather than in a century or two. It is to a description of some of the attempts to fill old words with new meanings, to reinterpret the Buddhist tradition in contemporary terms, and to some of the first efforts to deliberately create a Buddhist social philosophy, that we turn in the succeeding chapters.

Our portrayal of Buddhist social morality up to this point has
related to the past, in the sense that it has been mainly a description of the patterns of thinking and practice that have been traditional in Theravada Buddhism for many centuries. It is a morality of personal relationships rather than a social philosophy or
even an articulate conception of the Good Society. Its basic approach to any social situation that needs change is the simple
statement that society can be made perfect by perfecting the individuals who compose that society. Such personal goodness in
the leaders of the world, as well as in their followers, will solve
all the complicated problems of international finance, economics,
and politics; and peace within the individual will bring peace to
the nations. But within this simple-sounding solution of personal
goodness applied to society within the framework of conventional
moral standards, there is a tension that produces a serious ambiguity in the actual social response which Buddhism makes to
contemporary situations. It is that same fundamental cleavage
which we have observed between the "high" Buddhism of the
Path to Nibbana, embodied originally in the monastic way of life,
and the "low" Buddhism of the ordinary layman who aspires at
most to the material rewards attending the accumulation of good
Kamma. Which is to be the morality of Buddhism? Does Buddhism have one, or two, moralities? These questions are particularly crucial as Buddhism faces the new day which is now dawn-
ing in Buddhist cultures.

1. The New Situation and Its Challenges

The traditional pattern of Buddhism, particularly in the Theravada nations of Southeast Asia, was one fitted to the simple agrarian society of small and stable social units, cut off from the rest of the world, and contentedly sufficient to itself. But a new day has come to all these countries, for which Burma may serve as an example. The political atmosphere is today revolutionary, not static. To be sure, Burma's political course has been one of considerable turbulence through *all* her known history. Her frontiers have ebbed and flowed ceaselessly from generation to generation as the many ethnic groups within her territory have contended for mastery; and her external relations with neighboring China, Siam, and Arakan have varied. But these were mainly petty quarrels between small sovereignties. With the coming of the British, Burma became marginally involved with a world of whose vastness she had only the faintest idea. And then with the advent of World War II and independence in 1948, she was thrown bodily into the maelstrom of world politics and power blocs and herself deeply infected with the two most dynamic forces in modern politics: nationalism and Marxism.

Both nationalism and Marxism are powerful forces in Burmese political life. Sometimes they have been combined with each other, sometimes opposed, especially in the latter years. Many of the leaders of Burma's anti-British independence movement were schooled in Marxism and used its philosophy of revolution to oust the British, and its concepts of state socialism as guide in the formation of independent Burma's constitution and political-economic life. However, Communism has since become suspect because it is the chosen philosophy of some of the insurgent forces that continue to threaten Burma's peaceful development and political unity, because it motivated the attack on Buddhist Tibet, and now and again mounts ideological attacks upon Buddhism itself. But nationalism remains a most potent force and is at the present time a kind of twin-force with Buddhism in Burma. To be a first-water Burmese is to be Buddhist—though there is no persecution of other religious minorities; and there was considerable sentiment for the policy of making Buddhism the state religion. (See below) Culturally Burma is awaking to her past and is slowly seeking to identify, preserve, and fortify her own traditions—and these of course are strongly Buddhist in flavor. For the time being at least, nationalism is strengthening the force of Buddhist traditions, though in a number of various and perhaps inconsistent ways as we shall note at a later point.

World involvement has also brought an invasion by foreign religions. This might not have been significant under ordinary circumstances, for Buddhism has lived side by side with Hindu and Moslem cultures for centuries and on the whole held its own, particularly in Theravada countries. But with Christianity there was a difference, at least so far as Burmese Buddhism was concerned; for Christianity was the religion of the conqueror. And while British rule did not specifically "impose" Christianity upon Burma, and though much of the missionary work done there was by Americans, yet new systems of missionary and government education were allowed, and imposed in the case of the latter. These new schools, both by virtue of a new faith taught in some of them and the new educational methods used in all of them, sapped the life of the *phongyi-kyaung* and today's Burmese children are educated largely either in the secular government schools, taken over from the British by the Burmese, or in the private missionary schools. Many a good Buddhist sends his children to the latter because he prefers the quality of education there. Thus, as earlier noted, the *phongyi-kyaung* or monastery school is very weak as a contemporary educational force, and many a "Buddhist" child learns of Buddhism only what the force of his parents' devotion to and understanding of Buddhist values can give him.

No less important are the scientific and economic pressures of this new day upon the Buddhist social orientation. With science as an intellectual force we have no primary interest here, though its effect is considerable, and though Buddhism is strenuously seeking to adjust to it. But in terms of the industrial revolution and continued technical progress that science is producing, we are here indirectly involved. For economic and technical changes are working a revolution in Burmese social life and presenting new challenges to the Buddhist pattern of society. No longer is Burma a self-sufficient rice economy in which everyone from peasant to potentate can count on enough to eat and wear every year because of nature's bounty, and has no great concern to pile up a fortune. Industrialization is coming to Burma though slowly, and even the remote villages are being affected by it. Both because of the insurgent threat and technical advance, people in recent years have been on the move. Going are the old days of country-life isolation and generations of mutual family associations and intermarriage. The bus, the radio, the newspaper, the politician, now penetrate everywhere, even to the furthest village. Sizeable industrial communities will continue to grow, and the old simple agrarian pattern will be changed fundamentally even if slowly.

The strain which the new economic situation brings upon the Buddhist ethical structure is obvious. While Buddhism has made no pronouncements upon how much wealth a man might have, has indeed looked upon presently-possessed wealth as the mark of past moral virtue, and future wealth as a reward for present virtue, nevertheless the basic emphasis of the classic Buddhist teaching is upon the *restraint* of one's desires and simplicity of living-style. Contentment is one of the major virtues and greed a major vice at almost any level in the Buddhist scale of values. Thus though there is no particular tradition of the "righteous poor," or the "righteous because poor," in Buddhism, perhaps the subconscious ideal is that of the man who limits his desires deliberately, even though able to fulfill them, and is not unduly concerned about that which he does not possess. But the new situation is different. Technical progress has come with its dazzling visions of what life in this world *might* be like: motor-car, radio or television, refrigerator and pukka (brick-masonry) house, in place of ox-cart, neighborhood gossip, day to day food-buying in the bazaar, and a one-room wooden hut. And Marxism has loudly proclaimed to all who will hear—and many do—that all these things can be had tomorrow, if only the right people are put in control and each man is given his just deserts. What then happens to a way of life which teaches that the body and all its desires are a "wound"; that the good way of life is to limit desire, to achieve detachment, and fix one's eyes on desireless Nibbana? Does not such a gospel seem, in the words of the Marxist, an "opiate" for the people?

The strain is all the more pronounced because of its sudden-
ness. Whereas in the West the industrial revolution and technical
out-thrust have been taking place for two centuries or more—and
still leave the West rather breathlessly behind in its thinking and
socio-political adjustment—in a Southeast Asian country like
Burma all this has come within less than a score of years. Under
British domination Burma was "shielded" from industrialization
for her own good—and the purely incidental economic profit of
British commercial interests; but with the coming of independence industrialization has become a concern of first importance
whose wise accomplishment is a matter of immediate necessity
for the national health and stability. So it is that new questions
and new crises, all having to do with this mundane world but
deeply affecting even Nibbana-bent Buddhism, descend upon
the Theravada nations with the speed of a bolt from the blue.
The responses which are today being made by Buddhist writers
and thinkers, political leaders, laymen and monks are extremely
varied and interesting. We cannot deal with all of them here in
their detail. But there are some common features and some significant new attempts toward achieving an articulate Buddhist
political and economic philosophy that will illustrate something
of the variety of that response which contemporary Theravada
Buddhism is making.

2. The Conservative Response

Probably no change of any sort ever occurred at any time
or place in human history that there was not someone present
who was opposed to it and desired to go back to the "good old
days." In so staunchly a traditional context as Theravada Buddhism, that prides itself on being the inheritor, guardian, and
perpetuator of the pristinely pure and original teaching of the
Buddha, much of this is to be expected and can indeed be found.
It takes various forms of widely divergent nature. It may be an
unfriendliness to tourism because of the pernicious foreign and
worldly influence of free-spending foreign visitors upon Burmese
customs and morality. It may be an antagonism to foreign im-
ports, which enlarge the scope of sensual desires and deepen their
hold upon Buddhists—as well as draining away much-needed for-

eign exchange and undermining home industries. This attitude casts a suspicious eye upon all foreign financial aid, free advice of visiting experts, and proffered opportunities for Burmese nationals to study abroad. It may also be expressed in a defensiveness of attitude with regard to national customs and ways of life, many of them not really of Buddhist significance but belonging to the ancient pattern of life that is now being threatened. Now and then it takes the form of vocal opposition to all foreign missionaries—though on the whole Buddhist tolerance has been quite genuine here. Not many years ago the matter of the foreigner's wearing shoes in the pagodas was made an anti-British political issue. Conservatism has expressed itself most recently in the persistent demand to make Buddhism the State Religion of Burma.

Some of these attitudes are as much nationalistic and political in their bias, as religious. Yet Buddhist conservatism has strengthened and supported most of them. And in the forefront of this conservative leadership we must place the Sangha. Much of the Sangha's reaction is, of course, sheer defensiveness. For the Sangha feels threatened today in several respects. It feels threatened economically. There have been many, of socialist and Marxist learnings, who have openly suggested that the 100,000 or more monks were a non-productive segment of considerable size in Burma's struggling economy. (One defender of the Sangha pointed out in return that Sangha celibacy kept down the Burmese birth-rate and helped thus to maintain a proper food balance). And equally openly they have suggested that monks be put to more constructive work than meditation.

Likewise the Sangha feels threatened in its traditional leadership of the community. This has come about for several reasons. The British invasion disrupted the ecclesiatical system of control, such as it was, in Burma. In the opinion of G. E. Harvey (*British Rule in Burma*) this factor alone has contributed significantly to the contemporary indiscipline within the Sangha ranks.[1] This in-

---

[1] Items suggesting such indiscipline appear all too frequently in the newspapers. Sometimes it is a monk refusing to pay a bus fare; or getting into a fight with a layman; carrying on an affair with a woman; or even of a hand-to-hand fight between monastery groups of monks which the police have to quell. These are by no means characteristic, but frequent enough to cause some scandal. Now and then a notorious insurgent lead-

discipline has resulted in the loss of public esteem for the Sangha. Also, of course, the British control of government meant that the Sangha was shouldered aside from its historical role of spiritual advisor to the rulers—and has sometimes come down to the role of satellite to ambitious politicians in this day of freedom. But perhaps most importantly the Sangha has been bypassed in the educational advance. Most Sangha members receive only the narrow traditional education of the monastic system. As noted before, this is heavy on the side of recitation of the scriptures, traditional exposition of Buddhist doctrine, and Pali studies. In the other areas of modern education there has been almost nothing for the monk. (So that should he teach the children of the nation again it *might* be still in terms of pre-Copernican cosmology and pre-scientific everything else.) Even those who desire further education were excluded from the University system in Burma by parliamentary edict in the early 1950's—though not in Ceylon and Thailand—because it is not fitting, according to the rules of the *Vinaya,* that a monk should thus mingle shoulder to shoulder on an equality with laymen, or still worse, take instruction from a woman.

What are the Sangha's own ideas concerning the remedy for this situation? A minority, though possibly an important minority, favor the enlargement of the scope of the monk's education, somewhat after the pattern of the Buddhist universities of Ceylon and Thailand, where a liberal arts B.A. is open to monks as well as laymen.[2] Others (as well as many laymen) distrust this urge for the higher learning and would revert to the ancient pattern. But nearly all the Sangha *did* unite on the desirability of two measures to restore the falling fortunes of the Order. First was the

---

er has disguised himself in the monk's robe. This does not suggest political connivance with insurgency on the part of the Sangha, but rather its lack of systematic membership rolls and the prevailing easy entrance and exit from the Burmese Order.

[2] There is in Burma the Sangha University, begun in 1955, which seeks to move in this direction. Taking applicants from those monks who have passed their traditional Pali College examinations with credit, it has enrolled about 100 annually since its inception and hopes to achieve ultimately a 7-year course, leading through a high school and B.A. equivalent.

establishment of Buddhism as the State Religion in Burma; and second, and somewhat corollary, the compulsory education of all Buddhist children in Buddhism. The former, though slow in coming to definition would, in the Sayadaws' (senior monks') minds somehow have revived Buddhism as a whole; and the second measure would insure their role again as the dominant educators of the nation's youth. Thus reads a newspaper report of the Third Annual Convention of the All-Burma Presiding Sayadaws' Association in the winter of 1959:

> A resolution calling upon the Government to declare Buddhism the State religion, was proposed by the Sinyin Sayadaw of Sagaing. . . . He said that if democratic principles were observed, it was only right that Buddhism be declared the State religion as 90 percent of the populace were Buddhists. . . .
>
> This resolution was seconded by U Pyinnawintha who stated that the declaration of Buddhism as the State religion would not affect the status of other religions in the country. . . .
>
> It was also said that some minority religions in the country were making attempts to dislodge Buddhism and adherents of these minority faiths were seeking to interfere in some matters. . . . For that reason it was not possible to declare the Buddhist Sabbath Day as a Government Holiday. Minority religions were pushing forward their proselytizing campaigns through "secret funds" which were being used to "buy orphans" who were then converted to their own forms of religion. . .[3]

The same convention went on to condemn the laxity of monks' behaviour in certain respects: their carrying of money on their persons, mingling with crowds at *pwes* (dance-dramas) and the cinemas, carrying cigarettes openly, and sending their lay disciples to the bazaars to beg meat and other delicacies. Another group of monks, met in convocation at about the same time, turned their attention to the educational problem per se. A resolution was passed calling for the reinstitution of primary education in monastery schools:

---

[3] *The Nation*, February 18, 1959. The Burmese government always observed half-Saturday and Sunday as holidays, not the Buddhist Sabbaths which follow the lunar month, until U Nu added the latter in 1961.

Monasteries have been the centers of rudimentary education for boys from time immemorial, but with the advance of modern educational methods and the increase of State schools, the number of *phongyi-kyaung* students has declined. Religious leaders, disturbed by this trend, maintain that the future of the monasteries and religion itself depends on the boys who come to the *phongyi-kyaungs* for their secular and religious instructions. They reason that there can be no monasteries without monks and no monks without *phongyi-kyaung* boys, many of whom receive the robes after schooling at the hands of the monks,—i.e. become monks themselves.[4]

This group too passed other resolutions, all looking toward strengthening the Buddhist character of Burma: compulsory teaching of Buddhism even in State schools; establishment of new schools under the control of monks; the banning of all alcoholic drinks in keeping with the Fifth Precept; the using of Burmese dates on official documents. (They did *not* favor going back to the ecclesiastical courts of yesteryear, however, fearing the favoritism of the decisions of such courts.) And that these resolutions did not fall on deaf ears is evidenced by the Government appointment of a commission during that same year to discuss the rejuvenation of Buddhist education on a nation-wide scale.

There has also been some *political* activity on the part of the Sangha in recent years. At the time of the flight of the Dalai Lama from Tibet, many mass meetings of the Sangha were held throughout Burma for the sole purpose of denouncing Communism as an enemy of Buddhism and calling upon all and sundry to defend themselves against its insidious wiles. These protest meetings were also accompanied by the simultaneous publication by the Government of the notebook of a Burmese Communist propagandist among the insurgents who was inveighing against Buddhism as an opiate of the people and Nibbana as a stultifying and delusive hope. Still more: there was the formation of a Sangha Party which also favored the establishment of Buddhism as a state religion, and went further into political specifics by agitating for economic and social measures advocated by one or other of the political parties.

---

[4] *Ibid.*

It must be said that in general neither the Sangha nor its supporting laity favor such outright and specific participation in politics on the part of the Sangha members, however. The prevailing viewpoint is still that organized religion and politics should be kept apart, and that the monk's main business is meditation, study of the scriptures, living a holy life according to the *Vinaya* pattern, and instructing the laity in the Dhamma.

3. The Progressive Response

The term "progressive" is here used only in a relative sense for purposes of contrast. For most of those who espouse the following views or express such attitudes consider themselves to be the most orthodox of Buddhists. After the manner of religious reformers in all ages, they conceive themselves to be going back to the original sources of their faith and purifying the present situation of its non-Buddhist and post-original additions. Nor does this adjective represent either a distinct group or well-defined tendency of uniform quality. It is various in its expression as well as in the nature of the persons who give expression to such views. What we have here is the response of an old tradition in terms of new situations, a searching for resources within itself to meet the serious contemporary challenges to its faith and way of life, a determination to prove itself adequate to those challenges. And though it is thus varied and unorganized in nature, one must say, in the one major qualification of its variety, that the "progressive" response is more largely found among the Buddhist laity among than the Sangha. Of this rather general feature of the new Buddhist response to the contemporary world we may speak first.

a. *The New Buddhist Lay Activity*[5]

One might almost speak of the New Buddhist Layman—except that he is not aware, as the rule, that he is a novelty. He does not propose any doctrinal innovations, nor does he lack in reverence for the Ideal Sangha—though he may have some impatience with the tradition-bound incapacity of the actual Sangha to

---

[5] Some materials in this and the following chapter have been partially used in another form in an article by the author in the *Antioch Review*, Summer 1961.

act, and with its current indiscipline. Nor does he usually think of himself as a leader, in the sense of seeking to displace the Sangha in *its* leadership. Rather he finds himself distressed at what is, or is not, occurring in contemporary Buddhism and wanting to do something about it.

The reasons for the rise of the laity in Buddhism above its former humble role of being merely the material provider for the Sangha, are several. One is the backward state of the secular education of the Sangha, already discussed. The "new" layman may be a university graduate and one schooled in the ways of the newer and wider world. He finds his spiritual advisor out of touch with that world and not understanding its challenges. Hence he must begin to dig out his own answers for himself, if there are to be such. Besides there is good Buddhist precedent for each man to live by his own spiritual resources. And further, the modern layman, who is caught up in the faster-tempo life of the contemporary world, finds the Sangha so bound by its strict adherence to the traditional rules of the *Vinaya* that its effective interaction with the present social life is most difficult. We might say, in short, that contemporary Buddhism finds itself with a leadership vacuum which the layman rather instinctively has risen to fill.

The manifestations of this new leadership are varied. One type is that of the discussion group in which laymen, on their own initiative, meet periodically for the consideration of the Buddha's teachings and the classical doctrines of Buddhism. They are concerned both with their own education in the faith (perhaps neglected during a busy life) and with the active proclamation of the teaching of the Buddha among indifferent Buddhists or to non-Buddhists. From such groups there is issuing a stream of publications: pamphlets, booklets, and periodicals, some of them in English.[6] Others are concerning themselves with the practical application of Buddhist principles to economic, social, and political questions in a totally new way, and their pioneering efforts will be our concern in the next chapter.

-----

[6] Two laymen's periodicals of this sort are now being issued in Burma: *The Open Door* and *The Light of the Buddha,* the former published occasionally, the latter monthly. This is in addition to the official publication of the government department of Buddhist affairs (Sasana Council) publication, *The Light of the Dhamma.*

Another, and perhaps the most interesting, manifestation of
this new lay activity is the growth of meditation practice among
laymen. This is not the place to deal with meditation in detail
but we may briefly note that within the last fifty years the meditational path has been opened up to the Burmese layman. Though
not actually confined to the Sangha by any command of the Buddha nor completely unknown among laymen before, meditation
has for long been almost the sole prerogative of the monk. His
life pattern is set up with meditation practice as one of its central activities and traditionally meditation has been considered
impossible of accomplishment under the conditions of the house-
holder's life. But with the development (by a monk) of the Burmese method of Bare Attention, which is held to be the simplest
and most direct meditational method known to the Buddhist
scriptures, new hope is held out for the rapid attainment of the
higher spiritual states leading ultimately to Nibbana. And because it is more direct and simple—bypassing the complicated
technicalities and specialized conditions of monkish contemplation—this new method has been taken up widely by the layman. It
has become so popular in Burma that meditation centers, primarily for laymen, now number in the hundreds, some of them supported by the government. (A government employee may sometimes get special leave to retire to a meditation center for a week
or so.) And thousands of laymen are undertaking such meditation when and as they can, or even forming meditational associations of their own.

It is true that most of the official meditation centers are conducted by monks, though there is at least one important exception to this rule.[7] But even so, the layman has been religiously
up-graded as to speak in contemporary Buddhism. No longer is

---

[7] This is the International Meditation Center in Rangoon. Begun
unofficially in his office by U Ba Khin, then Accountant-General of Burma, it later was established on its own grounds with its own facilities.
U Ba Khin directs it in his spare time and on week-ends, and is its meditation master or *guru-gyi*. (There is some criticism of a layman's arrogat-
ing to himself the role of a spiritual teacher. But for the most part the
Sangha is tolerant of his effort, if not enthusiastic; and some well-known
monks have given it their blessing.) The center is operated by a Vipassana Association of which U Ba Khin is president.

he merely the supporter of the Sangha, who can only attain to the primary-school level of Buddhist instruction; he is a fellow traveler with the monk on the way to Nibbana, even though perhaps at a slower pace.

The ethical implications for the layman-meditator are most interesting. As a *layman* he is directly involved in the affairs of the mundane world; as a *meditator* he is seeking to achieve the higher and unworldly goods of the nibbanic quest for detachment from the world. In other words, he is seeking to bridge the gap between Kamma-Rebirth Ethic and the nibbanic Ethic of Equanimity which we have been at pains to emphasize. He is making a deliberate effort to synthesize the two sets of values, and to demonstrate that meditation has a *practical* worth of present use and significance even for the layman. Thus in the following interview with a lay-meditator:

Question: "Do you find the practice of detachment hinders a vigorous active attitude toward everyday duties?

U San Nyun's answer:

"No, I do not find it so. In fact I find I can work better after meditation. . . . A good Buddhist devotes himself to meditation for an hour or two at his home, either at night or at early dawn. When he is so absorbed in his meditation, he is detached from worldly matters even as a sleeping man is detached from all cares. . He has rested himself from worldly cares, he has raised his mental plane to a higher state of purity, and has developed his power of concentration, so that when he applies himself to his daily work . . . he does so with a greater zeal, greater concentration, and with a broader outlook, working for the good of all and not merely for selfish ends.

One thing I should like to add: Absolute detachment comes only at the last stage of perfection."[8]

What then is the quality of this new synthesis? In part it is

---

[8] Christopher Mayhew, *Men Seeking God* (London: George Allen & Unwin, Ltd., 1955), p. 51. This particular interview was with one of the meditators at the International Meditation Center mentioned in the previous note. The emphasis upon detachment being achieved only at the highest stage of perfection counters the Western charge that meditation means world-negation. This comment confines world-withdrawal to the very few, i.e., the saints.

obviously psychological rather than ethical. Meditation is an escape from the drive of the practical life into a realm where corroding daily cares cannot come. The meditator thus having thrown his mind "out of gear," comes back to his daily task refreshed and renewed in mind and body. And further he learns that sufficient unto each separate task is the worry connected therewith—not to be carried on to the next task. But this, be it repeated, is psychological rather than ethical, at least in the narrow sense. No new principle of *ethical* import is here added. The same old set of principles and ethical standards still apply, though the man himself is renewed. Will this "peace of mind" approach to ethical problems solve them justly, or in a *Buddhist* manner, or according to Buddhist ethical principles?

Here is where East and West diverge in judgment, perhaps. The West looks for some specific, objective standard or principle to apply to the social situation. The Buddhist believes that the renewed man himself is the more necessary; that all things being equal, the balanced mind, the calm, serene spirit will be able to do what is "right" in any situation. Perhaps the rightness or justice of any decision, in any circumstances, is not so much a matter of given principle, as it is of right personal attitudes. The "objective" rightness of a decision is relativistic; what is absolute is the personal situation. The right-minded person decides rightly.

But though this remains the basic Buddhist answer to all social problems, there is also a new stirring here. Not only is there the principle of psychological rhythm and the subjective serenity of the individual in the social situation; there is also the suggestion that this serenity may be interpreted in terms of a "broader outlook" and a concern for the general good as opposed to one's own narrow advantage. This we shall refer to again at more length in the discussion on the activation of the Buddhist vocabulary.

b. *The Call to a Unified Buddhist World Mission*

Another response of the positive sort on the part of Buddhism to the new world situation is its resurgent missionary impulse. In its earlier centuries, around the beginning of the Christian era, Buddhism was markedly mission-minded as its spread from India throughout Asia bears witness. But this spread was

in great part under the Mahayanist impulsion, not so markedly
by the more conservative Hinayanist ancestors of modern Theravada Buddhism. And as Buddhism became firmly established
in its Asian domain, both north and south, both Mahayanist and
Theravada, it settled into a centuries'-long non-missionary apathy.
In the various national Theravada traditions the general cultural
isolation and the passive interpretation of the kammic doctrine
nourished this unaggressive attitude, and so it remained until very
recently. But there is a new missionary-mindedness in Theravada
Buddhism today that looks both toward some sort of rapproche-
ment among divergent Buddhist traditions and toward a united
world-mission to non-Buddhists. It is difficult to judge the vitality
or significance of this new movement. One cannot overlook the
nationalistic impulsion to missionary effort. The following ex-
cerpt from a letter to the editor of *The Nation* (Rangoon), with
regard to the impending visit of the Venerable U Thittila to the
United States on the U Nu Lectureship, is revelatory:

> Burma, which is so poor and backward in still other respects
> that she is still a mendicant, is now through her great son U
> Thittila . . . repaying her debt by this greatest and noblest of all
> gifts to the people of the United States of America.
> If the Sayadaw's mission . . . can make a sufficient impact on
> the minds of the great leaders of thought, the world will be a much
> happier one to live in.[9]

The writer signed himself "A true Buddhist." The "greatest of
all gifts" is, of course, the Buddha's Teaching. And one here sees
modern Asia coming into her own by sharing her ancient spiritual
treasure with a civilization which has outstripped her temporarily
in political power and material status, but now has need of her
wisdom.

But to make this the only or basic motivation of the new missionary movement is too superficial a reading of the matter.
Buddhism is today possessed of two convictions about the world
situation. One is that other philosophies, religions, and moralities
have all broken down and are incapable of prescribing for the
world's ills. The West, says Buddhism, has turned away from its

---

[9] *Circa,* mid-January, 1959.

insufficient faiths to an aggressive, religionless materialism which is bound to destroy the world sooner or later.

Twin to this conviction of world break-down is that of Buddhist adequacy for world recovery. Having heard that the West is turning away from its predominant faith, Judeo-Christianity, Buddhism sees in that situation its own call to evangelize. Hence many Buddhists, both in Theravada and Mahayana circles, are girding themselves for this new task. They are seeking to learn the culture and language of the West (English) in order to carry their message to it. Funds are being raised to send such missionaries abroad. And at least one organization has been formed to carry on such reconciling and missionary efforts, the World Buddhist Fellowship, which held its fifth biennial meeting in Bangkok in 1958. It was represented by delegates from all Buddhist countries of the world, and also from Buddhist groups in the West, who encouraged each other in the faith and laid plans for the conversion of the world into a "practical paradise on earth." A number of monks are active in the Fellowship, and most committees have monks in their memberships. Yet the inevitable impression is that it is the layman, more internationally minded and often able to speak an international language, who furnishes the real leadership and who will carry on the Fellowship's work in the future.

c. *The Reinterpretation of Doctrine*

It may be noted at the very beginning of this section that its title would draw dissenting statements from contemporary Buddhist, indeed *especially* from those who are in the forefront of the "progressive" movement.They would affirm that Buddha Dhamma is the same "yesterday, today, and forever." And they would further affirm that their effort is to bring no new gospel, but simply to call the attention of the world to the ancient Buddhist truth which it needs to practice as never before.[10] The most that would be conceded is that perhaps some groups have sometimes misinterpreted the Dhamma, even in the Theravada tradition, and that the popular mind in particular has often distorted it.

---

[10] "People talk about new ideas to counteract other ideologies. We Buddhists do not need any new ideologies. We have enough in the teach-

It seems to the outside observer, however, that something new *is* occurring in the field of doctrinal interpretation. It is not that the scriptures are being altered or basically new doctrines being added. It is rather that the voluminous Buddhist literature is being searched for those elements that will fit it to meet the present situation and that some basic doctrines or viewpoints are being interpreted in a somewhat different context than formerly. Likewise there is the matter of proportion: some elements that have been recessive in the Buddhist tradition are now being advanced to a leading position, and others retired. In general we can describe this tendency in terms of *activating* and *socializing* the Buddhist tradition.

This is observable in the number of writings which are now being produced in this area: pamphlets on race relations, Buddhism and democracy, Buddhism and society, Buddhism and communism, and so forth,[11] as well as many scattered articles in various public prints on similar themes. And it is observable in the frequent statement that Buddhism is a religion fitted for successful and happy living in this world, as well as a discipline for the attainment of the final Nibbana. Two quotations out of many will give the flavor of such statements:

> Buddhism . . . is of all religions in the world the best suited to improve and elevate the character and manners of the people; awaken self-respect and feeling of self-responsibility of a people and stir up a nation's energy . . . self-respect, self-confidence, comprehension, tolerance, all-embracing kindness, soberness of mind, and independence of thought: these are some of the salient qualities created in a people by the influence of Buddhism. And in

---

ings of the Buddha." Venerable U Thittila, "Buddhist Metta," *Light of the Dhamma,* V, No. 1 (January, 1958), 49.

[11] Instances of this are as follows: Malalasekera and Jayatilleke, *Buddhism and the Race Question* (Unesco Pamphlet); *Buddhism and Society, Everyman's Ethics,* in the *Wheel Publications* (Buddhist Publication Society, Kandy, Ceylon); Francis Story, *Buddhism Answers the Marxist Challenge* (Burma Buddhist World Mission). Interestingly, Francis Story and the editor of the Wheel Series (or its moving spirit), the Venerable Nyanaponika, are Western converts to Buddhism. However in Burma there are appearing various editions of the Metta, Sigolavada, and Mangala Suttas with interpretations relating them to contemporary conditions, by Burmese writers.

the country in which such qualities preponderate, peace and happiness will reign supreme, and such a country will be a model to the whole world, will be a paradise on earth.[12]

The teachings of the Lord Buddha are so instructive that a person following them would find himself progressing in the life here and the life hereafter. Buddha often spoke of the value of renunciation and the attainment of Nibbana as the highest gain. But till such time as we attain final liberation we have to float in the life of Samsara and it was the Buddha's exhortation that this life should be lived in such a way that it would make this life happy while not impeding the progress in Samsara or continuity of existence consummating in Nibbana.[13]

Here is a complete reconciliation that makes the best of both worlds, kammic and nibbanic, by the same course of action!

But more fundamental even than this, perhaps, is the more general quality of *reinterpretation* throughout Buddhism at all articulate levels. We may best instance this by examination of what is happening to four key concepts or elements of the Buddhist tradition: *Nibbana, Equanimity and the Illimitables, Kamma*, and the *Bodhisatta*.

With regard to *Nibbana* there has, of course, been little outward change. It is still the ineffably Supreme Good which transcends all description and all time-space values and relationships. The difference is to be found in the *context* in which Nibbana is now· discussed. It is brought into the *present* life in increasing measure. There is of course perfectly good tradition for doing this. As we have noted previously (p. 83) there is the *kilesaparinibbāna*, or the destruction of mental-moral defilements *in this life*. This of course is the case of the arahat. But while arahats are scarce in contemporary Buddhism (as are saints in Christianity), contemporary Buddhists are stressing more than ever that Nibbana is not something far off but that which may be experienced here and now. The following quotation is one which could be multiplied, in essence, many times over:

---

[12] Venerable Nyanatiloka, "Influence of Buddhism on a People," *Light of the Dhamma*, I, No. 4 (July, 1953), 32.

[13] Thera A. Chandrairi, "Prosperity in This Life," *Buddhist Supplement* of *The Burman*, September 15, 1958.

Its [Buddhism's] truth can be proved. And in its proving lies the greatest objective of human endeavor, *the realization of Nibbana in this very life.*[14]

And in somewhat similar terms the same author goes on to say about the Dhamma in general, but with obvious nibbanic relevance:

The Buddha . . . declared that His Dhamma produced happiness *here and now:* He said that in this very life it is possible to achieve a state of bliss greater and more enduring than the bliss of heaven.[15]

There is an interesting variation on this here-and-nowness of nibbanic peace which has come to the author's attention. In the practice of meditation it is sometimes said that one directly experiences "Nibbana dhatu" or the nibbanic element. To be sure there is in the classic theory of meditation experience a direct perception of Nibbana itself by the saint, so different from other realizations or higher states of consciousness that it is absolutely distinct from any of them. And the tradition is that if this occurs four times in one's lifetime, he must in all certainty attain to Nibbana itself upon death. But here in the "new" interpretation, the possibility of some sort of actual contact with the Nibbana dhatu seems to be extended a bit below the arahat's high level of attainment, even perhaps to an ordinary lay-meditator. And there also seems to be imparted to it something of *activity*: it was said that the dhatu "came down into" a man's life—in a manner somewhat like the Christian's grace of God.[16]

Not only is Nibbana's quality experienceable here and now, it is also capable of a social interpretation in present-day thinking. To requote a passage used above in another context, Nibbana can be expressed as the ability,

to crave for nothing, to love all and pardon all, serve others without a desire for a reward or even appreciation, to live in peace and bliss as long as one's life lasts.[16]

---

[14] Francis Story, "Is Buddhism True?" *Light of the Dhamma,* V, No. 1 (January, 1958), 47.

[15] Francis Story, "Elementary Principles of Buddhism," *Light of the Dhamma,* I, No. 2 (January, 1953), 27.

[16] From "The Problems of Buddhism," quoted above.

As might well be expected, the interpretation of the *Sublime States* or *Four Illimitables*,—loving-kindness, compassion, sympathetic joy, with equanimity as their consumation—has likewise been activated. The current emphasis in Theravada Buddhism is that of an emphatic denial that these are mere armchair virtues, both because of their televolitional force and because, in the words of the Venerable U Thittila, "If the thoughts are intense enough, right actions follow automatically."

And there has also been a transmutation of the quality of complete detachment traditionally associated with the exercise of these dispositions on a universal scale. It is still held true in theory that the saint sends out his vibrations of loving kindness and compassion in an equanimous fashion that leaves him completely detached and unspent, emotionally immaculate. Yet this is now being translated into "disinterestedness" or "love without attachment," without the desire to receive anything in return. Or again, with reference to metta (loving-kindness) in particular:

> Love without a desire to possess but with a desire to help, to sacrifice self-interest for the welfare and well-being of humanity. This love is without selection and exclusion.[17]

Or it may be, as above, in terms of the meditator explaining the value of meditation for daily work, "working for the good of all and not merely for selfish ends."

Thus again we see the depth to which contemporary Buddhism is being stirred by the new situation. Once it would have been willing to remain undisturbed by the scepticism of the outside world about the reality and worth of the inward states of truth-realization and about the effectiveness of the radiation of moral virtues. But today it valiantly seeks to prove to the new world it faces and hopes to evangelize—and perhaps also prove to itself—that even the transcendent good of Nibbana and the outwardly detached states of higher consciousness have a social value and relevance.

We turn now to the manner in which the *Kamma* doctrine, that doctrine which especially connotes pessimistic fatalism and

---

[17] Venerable U Thittila, "Buddhist Metta," *Light of the Dhamma*, V, No. 1 (January, 1959), 49.

social passivity to the Westerner, is today being reinterpreted. The effect that it has seemed to have upon Buddhist societies in the past is well illustrated in the writings of Shway Yoe at the end of the nineteenth century. He is raising the question about the status of those pariahs of Burmese society—the pagoda slaves, the deformed, the lepers, the gravediggers—in a supposedly "democratic" religious tradition:

> How does all this agree with the theory of Buddhism that there is equality for all?
> The answer is that it is *kan* (kamma), it is the accumulation of merits or demerits in past existences. A man is rich, powerful, and great because aforetime he was pious and good. Therefore he now has a right to govern and look with contempt on the poor.
> The poor man must have been a bad man before he entered on this existence. He deserves to be miserable; he knows it himself, and submits fatuously. It is true that the tyrant does not do well if he oppresses him. . But in his present existence the great man has the fullest right to oppress and grind down the poor as much as he chooses. He enjoys the fruits of previous virtues. . .

The writer goes on to point out that even in terms of future Kamma-results the scales are weighted against the poor man. He has but little to offer to the monk and perhaps has to kill wild animals to keep alive "which infallibly dooms him to a few million years in hell." The rich man is able to give so richly, to plant so many seeds in that superior field of merit, the Order of monks, that his blessed and continuingly rich and powerful status is assured. And he further believed, on the basis of many years in Burma, that

> This doctrine of kan (kamma) also accounts for the equanimity and callousness with which Buddhists view human misery and the taking of human life, notwithstanding the law which forbids the killing of even the smallest insect. They recognize apathetically the working out of inexorable destiny, and watch a man drowning in the river with undisturbed tranquility.[18]

But this was long ago, when Burma was under control of a foreign conqueror and when the common man in Burma was not aware that he had any rights at all—certainly no splendid future.

---

[18] *Op cit.,* II, 149–150.

Today his lot is different. Burma is independent and both Marxism and democracy promise him a glorious political future, if only he will exert himself; and scientific technology promises to make him godlike in power. What then shall Buddhism do with its doctrine of Kamma which seems to bind each man irrevocably to his present social status and personal circumstances? Buddhism today emphatically denies that Kamma *is* a doctrine of despair. Again and again the loyal Buddhist rejects the Western implication that the doctrine of Kamma is fatalism or implies the passive acceptance of one's present lot. Rather is it mankind's supreme ground of hope for the future.

This alteration of the connotations of Kamma doctrine is not achieved by constructing a new or heretical version, but by means of a predominant emphasis upon *one* phase of Kamma to the temporary subordination of the other two. For in Buddhism there are three types of Kamma, in terms of temporal sequence. There is *past* Kamma which cannot be altered or evaded, though it may be "burned up" by Vipassana meditation. (See above pp. 163-4.) Thus the major aspects of one's *present* life are largely determined. Kamma as a principle of explanation of present inequalities or of unforeseen good or evil fortune, is thus always *past* Kamma, and past Kamma only. This has been its traditional use for the most part, especially for those humble people who had little hope of changing their lot in a static society; it was both rationalization and consolation, passive and fatalistic in connotation.

But there are two other varieties of Kamma: *present* and *future*. Future Kamma of course does not yet exist in actuality, though its seeds may have been sown in the past. For according to the Buddhist doctrine of momentariness and cause-effect, the present actually contains all the past. But this also actually puts it more within our power. For though we cannot by-pass evil Kamma entirely, and may not yet be able to burn it up by Vipassana meditation, we *can* produce good *present* Kamma out of which will grow the future. What good we do now must inevitably bear its fruit and somewhat balance or compensate for the evil we have already done. Thus it is that Buddhism in its present mood of activism strongly accents the inherent free will possessed by each man and the almost infinite possibilities of improving both this life's and his future lives' fortunes by present action. The very inevitability of kammic result, when not construed as an iron-clad determinism, enables the doer to depend upon the fruitage of his free deed. Therefore in current usage Kamma is not so much a principle of consolation and explanation as a rousing call to be up and doing.

But strangest of all, Kamma has also become a bulwark of democracy and fellow-feeling, rather than the guarantor of privileged position and autocracy! This transformation may be stated in philosophical terms. Kamma is only the individualized or personalized expression of the law of Dependent Origination, which is "the doctrine of the Conditionality of all physical and psychical phenomena." That is, each human being is only a group of psycho-physical elements conditioned by each other and having no existence or reality outside of that mutually conditioned existence. If there were not the body-factor there would be no mental factor, nor vice-versa—and of course no human being. And usually this doctrine of Dependent Origination is used in connection with the anatta doctrine of the insubstantiality of the self in order to destroy the illusion of permanent self-hood.

But, says the author of the above definition, Dependent Origination *also* may be viewed "*synthetically* by showing that all these phenomena are, in some way or other, conditionally related to each other."[19] And by other authors this dependence is translated to mean *inter*dependence. Thus the individual who knows himself to be an entity whose "existence" is a case of Dependent Origination conditioned by the Kammic law, and not of self-subsistent reality or independence, is both humbled in that knowledge and made aware of his involvement with every other creature in existence. *To be nothing in oneself is to be a part of every other self.*

But it may be expressed less philosophically as the spirit of cooperation that springs out of the conviction that he who stands should take heed lest he fall. Thus:

> If everyone understood the law of Kamma, there would be an end to the greed of the rich and the envy of the poor. Every man

---

[19] Venerable Nyanatiloka, *Buddhist Dictionary* (Colombo: Frewin and Co., 1956), p. 119.

would give away as much as he could in charity—or at least spend his money on projects beneficial to mankind.

On the other hand there would be no burning feeling of injustice on the part of the "have nots," since they would recognize that their condition is due to their own past Kamma, while at the same time its crushing effects would be alleviated by the generosity and social conscience of the rich.

The result would be a cooperative scheme of sharing, in which both would prosper. This is the practical plan of living that Buddhism suggests to us: it is sane, ethical and inspiring, and it is the one answer that a free world can make to the anti-religious materialistic ideologies.[20]

One cannot quarrel with the Buddhist if he chooses so to interpret Kamma. He does no technical violence to the doctrine itself, and if the doctrine of Kamma can be made to bear the weight of such an interpretation in a convincing fashion, so much the better. There are similar cases in Christianity where, for example, the Calvinist doctrine of predestination became an immensely energizing concept for a major strand of Protestant endeavor. Those who were persuaded that they had been predestined to victory under Divine Purpose let nothing and no one withstand them in accomplishing that purpose in their lives. Whether Kamma can be made to energize and democratize such endeavor is another question. To gain the spirit of co-operation from individualistic Kamma seems to be distorting it beyond recognition.

We may turn finally to one other long-buried, or long-dormant, concept of Theravada Buddhism, that of the *Bodhisatta* (Sanskrit *Bodhisattva*). So much has this been made a part of Mahayana Buddhism that many in the West scarcely realize that there is a Bodhisatta doctrine in Theravada Buddhism as well. There is in fact an astonishing amount of it there. Theravada Buddhism fully accepts the doctrine of a succession of Buddhas, of whom Gotama Buddha was the fourth in this world-age, with one (Maitreya) yet to come; and before him in other world-ages was an endless line of thousands of millions of previous Buddhas. And of course where there are Buddhas in

---

[20] Ledi Sayadaw, "Kamma and Causality," *Light of the Dhamma*, III, No. 2 (January, 1956), 51.

succession there must be Bodhisattas who have been perfecting themselves through countless ages of time for the achievement of Buddhahood. Indeed the *Jātaka Stories,* so popular in Theravada Buddhism, are presumed to be accounts of previous incarnations of Gotama on his way to Buddhahood.

Thus is the Bodhisatta concept amply present in the Theravada tradition. But on the whole it has not exercised any very important influence therein. The reason for this is not far to seek: the presence of the arahat ideal of perfection cancelled the Bodhisatta ideal so far as ethical potency is concerned. For if the central way to perfection is to press on to Nibbana as rapidly as possible, the arahat's route is the only practical one. The route of the Bodhisatta is perilously long and subject to many hazards; countless lives must be passed in which infinite stores of goodness and mental power are accumulated. Besides all this, and perhaps part and parcel of the same movement of thought, Buddhahood, though only "human," has been made so high and holy in the Theravada tradition that it seems pretentious for a man to say that he has taken a Buddha-vow, i.e. a vow to become a Buddha by endless lives of good works. And it is accounted sacrilegious for one to claim to be a "'living Buddha."

Nevertheless the way of the Buddha-vow is gaining some new interest in the Theravada tradition. Now and then one finds a Theravadin reminding his Mahayana brethren that he too has the Bodhisatta concept in his tradition. And there are those today who will take such a vow, though not in public nor as the usual rule. But almost inevitably the current temperament of wishing to find in the tradition a more active social emphasis is bringing the latent Bodhisatta elements to the fore, whether under that name or not. Thus it is quite common for a contemporary Theravadin to point out that the Buddha-to-be did many deeds of compassion and often sacrificed his life. (See above p. 59.) And this is usually said to point out that Buddhism, as well as Christianity, has in it the element of self-sacrifice and vicarious suffering. Others will say that it is more important today to have good Buddhist doctors or statesmen than for everyone to enter the monastic life and become *that* kind of saint. Now and again there are tentative suggestions that some pagoda-money ought to be turned to public welfare. And in Burma there is at least an incipient movement within the Sangha to turn itself to social service.

It is quite unlikely that the Bodhisatta ideal will ever be taken up in the Theravada tradition to the same degree as in the Mahayana, and almost certainly not in the same form. But it may well be, as suggested above, that there will be its *virtual* adoption, in content if not in name, and that it will in this hidden form play a large part in the reorientation of Theravada Buddhism.

CHAPTER VIII

Up to this point we have been considering the somewhat instinctive reactions of those in the Buddhist tradition to the new social, cultural, and political factors in the contemporary world. These have been in the nature of adaptations of method, vocabulary, and general outlook in an attempt to meet current challenges to the Buddhist way of life and to make a large place for Buddhism in world thought and life. But on the whole they have been a kind of cultural reflex action rather than a deliberate or planned advance.

In the materials dealt with in this chapter we come to a somewhat different situation. These too, of course, represent a cultural and religious reaction to new stimuli. But they are not mere reactions. They represent what are perhaps the first deliberate attempts to go beyond the bald assertion that Buddhism is what the world needs to solve its problems; or that if every man would achieve inner peace, peace would come to the world. They are attempts at a definite statement of Buddhist social and political principles applied to concrete situations. The examples chosen here are of various sorts. One is an attempt—by a Western convert—to define the position of Buddhism with regard to communism. His critique of the latter is somewhat sharper than the usual Theravada statement, but generally in keeping with major Buddhist principles. The next two are rather brief statements by native Burmans of a basic economic principle or of a touchstone of Buddhist correctness in economic matters, best expressed by a phrase in each case: Economy of Sufficiency and an Economics of the Middle Way. The last two expressions are those of deliberate attempts to frame a political philosophy according to Buddhist principles. In the case of the last one, that of the Honorable U Nu, there is a particular interest because he was returned to political power in 1960 (as Prime Minister) on a platform committing him to establish Buddhism as the State Religion. His statement therefore represents a contemporary attempt deliberately and consciously to implement Buddhist political priciples by actual governmental policies and procedures, perhaps the only attempt of its kind in recent years.

1. Buddhism and Communism

The attitude of Burmese Buddhism to communism has been ill-defined on the whole. This is explained in great part by Burma's internal socio-political situation and by her geographical location next to Communist China. As has been noted above, many of Burma's independence leaders used communistic ideology as a weapon against British control and joined forces with some genuine Marxists to that end. And though some of them have since abjured any loyalty to Marxist communism, they remain socialists in their political philosophy. (Both major parties are socialist). U Nu, as we shall see, finds indeed that Buddhism and socialism are almost identical in their basic goals and principles. Hence communism, as a species of socialism, was not heartily or roundly condemned until events in Tibet and the simultaneous publication of anti-Buddhist propaganda, carried on by Burma's own communist insurgents, produced a tremendous wave of anti-communist sentiment.[1]

---

[1] In the spring of 1959, the caretaker government of General Ne Win showed the press a notebook of a young communist indoctrinator captured from the insurgents. In it communists characterized Nibbana as nonsense; Buddhism as an opium of the worst kind because it had been "processed to square with science," yet remained religion; Buddha as deceived; the monks as unproductive idlers; the gold on pagodas as wasted. Further, tales were spread about some communists who said to reclining Buddha statues: "I say, Gotama, it is time to get up," and others who tore up the scriptures and broke down and defiled Buddhist shrines. Shortly thereafter the press was filled with accounts of anti-communist meetings attended by hundreds of monks and laymen protesting against communist "materialism and atheism."

Therefore Francis Story's booklet, *Buddhism Answers the Marxist Challenge,* is atypical for two reasons. The author is a European convert to Buddhism and approaches the matter of communism somewhat from the Western viewpoint.[2] And his criticism is consequently much sharper and more militantly anti-communist than was typical of the general Buddhist attitude at the time when the booklet was written, before the later disturbances. But since the main positions are soundly Buddhist they will serve to set forth the central Buddhist antagonism to communism. After a rather keen analysis of Marxist inconsistencies along the lines followed by Western democratic criticism, Mr. Story makes a series of pronouncements about Marxist doctrines from the specifically Buddhist point of view. Buddhism *rejects* Marxist philosophy, says Mr. Story for the following reasons:

(1) The Marxist doctrine that *all* religion of whatever description is false and injurious is sheer dogmatism. The author is second to none in decrying the weaknesses, inconsistencies, and evil superstitions of religions in general, but for him Buddhism is a religion apart from all others, having none of the weaknesses of those others.

(2) While Marxist and Buddhist agree on the denial of God, soul, and purposive world-process, Buddhism rejects Marxist materialism. This materialism, says the author, cannot be proved scientifically; and in any case Buddhism stands for a "spiritual" view of the universe, i.e. mentalistic rather than materialistic. Mind-states determine physical states rather than physical arrangements of matter or energy producing and determining mind.

This is a sentiment often echoed in Buddhist circles. We find the Venerable U Thittila saying something of the same sort:

The official philosophy of Communism is pure materialism. This means that nature and human history are interpreted from a

---

[2] Published by the Burma Buddhist World Mission which was headed by Francis Story in Rangoon for some years. The author removed to Ceylon in 1957 or 1958. His mission was suspect in part by Burmans because to them its strong anti-communist bias suggested that Buddhism was being used by it in the cold war. And Buddhists resent the use of their faith for political purposes, by outsiders in particular.

purely materialistic point of view. There is no place in the world for religion.

Thus Communism being against religion, which teaches universal love and the moral law of righteousness, is not suitable for Burma. . . . What is needed in Burma is not materialistic Communism, but the practice of the noble principles of Buddhism which has been the source of the peace, happiness and culture of the Burmese people. Recent events show that the moral concepts of some of them have been deteriorating rapidly.[3]

(3) Buddhism rejects the coercive character of Marxism, especially its attempt to level down all classes and make all individuals alike. Buddhism teaches the inherent differences of men due to past Kamma. This kammic "right to be different" should be preserved in a "good" society, for each man must have the liberty to work out his own personal destiny.

We may note that one or two of our other authors are less certain about the kammic "right to be different," than Mr. Story, and even hope for its limitation in fact. And it seems in one sense a rather curious and perverse argument for democratic rights to assert that each man ought to have the right to reap his just deserts—which have perhaps condemned one to poverty and another to riches. Usually democratic rights consist in the public freedoms that belong to every man regardless of his birth, i.e. his kammic inheritance; and such rights are thought of in the positive sense of opening the doors of opportunity as widely as possible to each person—not in guaranteeing his privilege to be inferior! Here again we have a very interesting result of the attempt to adapt traditional Buddhist doctrines to the new social situation in the contemporary world.

(4) "Good men make good social systems, but no social system on its own has ever made a good man." (pp.100-1) The first is the Buddhist viewpoint, of course, and the second (when affirmatively stated) the Marxist; and Mr. Story is on solid Buddhist ground in making this criticism. For as we have seen before, the Buddhist believes that society is but an agglomeration of individuals whose character, good or bad, determines the character of society, and whose individual reform will result in

---

[3] From a mimeographed paper entitled "Buddhism and Communism."

social reform. In view of the fact that Communism is an expression par excellence of the philosophy that social environment makes man (in the mass at least) and not that man makes society, we have here a most fundamental opposition between the two view-points. But it might also be noted in passing that this is likewise the ground of Buddhist criticisms of social and political planning of almost *any* sort.

(5) Marxism pins false and exaggerated hopes on material improvement. Actually man's desires can never be completely fulfilled; as fulfillment increases so does desire. Hence Marxism's promise of an earthly paradise brought about by materialistic means is delusory. Perfection is not outward and collective, but inward and personal. The Buddha "did not encourage wishful thinking in terms of worldly Utopias. Instead he told each one the way in which he could *alter his own world*—the inner subjective world that is everyone's private domain." (p. 100) In the final analysis the political-social world is transitory and unworthy of ultimate devotion.

(6) Marxism sets one class against another in a struggle for the world's goods, whereas Buddhism teaches harmony. This too is a basic Buddhist objection to Marxist methods which cannot well be softened as long as Marxism remains Marxism and Buddhism remains Buddhism. For Buddhism, as we have seen, favors permeation, infiltration, and evolution of a good society through good people, not reform, and most emphatically not revolution. The latter is violent, hate-breeding, destructive—all of which qualities are diametrically opposed to Buddhist love and non-violence. Better, in Buddhist eyes, to allow social gradations with their sometimes injustice and exploitation to continue, than to seek to destroy them by setting brother against brother, class against class, in bloody struggle.

2. The Economics of Sufficiency

For this concept the author is indebted to the Honorable Justice U Chan Htoon. And the intention of the phrase is clear. A "Buddhist" economy would be one which would moderate *its* plans somewhat as a Buddhist individual is called upon to do: avoid either indulgent or ascetic extremes and take a middle way. A Buddhist philosophy of economics would call for a moderation of those ambitious economic plans that would seek to make an enterprise or nation the biggest and best in the world, or aim at ever-expanding expansion and production. Presumably also it would limit personal wealth by means of taxes, though this is not so clear in what follows below. And on the other hand it would limit the lower range of income so that grinding poverty would be avoided or eliminated, presumably by State action if necessary. This is a pattern obviously fitted to a nation in Burma's situation: moderate resources, small size, one that finds its population restively calling for a higher standard of living yet must avoid rash and over-ambitious economic projects. Besides it has that good flavor of moderation characteristic of a Middle Way outlook. But what sufficiency actually means in this world of relativities, and whether it should or could apply to all nations of whatever size and resources, is not so clear.[4]

In a written statement the Justice spells out further his conception of an essentially Buddhist government and economy. Somewhat in the same terms as Mr. Story, he sets forth the generally democratic bias of Buddhism:

> Buddhism requires that the freedom of the individual to determine his own destiny and to choose the kind of life he lives must never be subordinated to group interests which seek to mould him to a standardized pattern. . . . For this reason the Buddha opposed caste distinctions, seeing in them an attempt to confine people in a rigid framework and prevent the full realization of their potentialities.

---

[4] In conversation we found it hard to define in practical terms how sufficiency worked as a principle. Should advertising and aggressive merchandising, which raise the consumer level of demand and thus create new industries, be considered wrong and be drastically limited? In a later quotation (see below) the Justice seems to favor competition in industry, not a state socialism. And how should science which voraciously reaches out to ever new fields of endeavor, often under commercial impulsions, be regulated in a Buddhist economy? "Sufficiency" appeared to indicate a Buddhist reaction against excessive materialistic craving, rather than a social "plan."

This emphasis on Buddhism's essential democratic and egalitarian viewpoint is not confined to the above author. Dr. Malalasekera in his UNESCO pamphlet on *Buddhism and the Race Question* sounds the same note. Buddha defined caste in terms of the individual worth of a person, not in terms of an accident of birth. All four caste levels as well as women were adjudged capable of salvation. One has no right to despise another because, like the robber-murderer Angulimali of the Buddhist scriptures, even the veriest criminal has the potentiality (perhaps) for a complete transformation of personal character. Again we must note that this represents a somewhat new use of Kamma doctrine. Those hidden potentialities of the kammic self are, in a democratic context, to be developed, and apparently represent a precious heritage. Yet in the *nibbanic* context of ultimate salvation, kammic individuality is a thing to be despised and destroyed because it is inimical to salvation.

But to return to Justice U Chan Htoon's further statements on the subject of Buddhist economics and society: A Buddhist society is *not* a classless society because of these same kammic endowments which differentiate one man from another. Such differentiations, i.e. inequalities, should not be glossed over or forcibly ignored:

> Buddhism is democratic but makes no attempt to achieve a classless society, considering this to be an impossible condition on account of the inherent inequalities between one man and another as the result of personal Kamma; but it classifies men according to their character and natural abilities. It is thus the antithesis of a totalitarian concept.

Still further, in a remarkable approximation to the "rugged individualism" of free-enterprise capitalism, he speaks of the "prizes in the school of life that each may strive for and obtain," but maintains that this is not cut-throat competition but a kind of competition against oneself only. Thus:

> If a man chooses to interpret this as free competition, it is still competition without rivalry, for victory to oneself does not mean the defeat of someone else. On the contrary every spiritual victory to oneself is one that should and can be shared with all. The Buddhist finds no difficulty in conceiving himself as a citizen of the world, a member of the great brotherhood of mankind. He

acknowledges his kinship with all that breathes, lives and hopes.[5]

At this point it is difficult to tell in which realm of discourse the discussion is proceeding. A kind of free competition that takes nothing away from anyone else may apply to one's improving his own golf score or to a spiritual ideal, but scarcely to the world of society and economic free enterprise. It does not even apply always to the realm of personal relationships for, as a well-known administrator once put it: Every decision *for* one man, i.e., to advance him, is also a decision *against* another man, i.e. *not* to advance *him*. There are only so many positions, so many goods, so much money—and not everyone can have all that he desires. One man's profit is another's loss, one man's victory another's defeat. That such competition can produce directly a sense of kinship with "all that breathes, lives and hopes" is not self-evident. Presumably this has meaning only in the long-run of kammic or nibbanic achievement, not in strivings on the ordinary social and political level.

3. Buddhist Economics of the Middle Way

In this version, as in the previous one, the concept of the Buddhist Middle Way is used, *here* very definitely and explicitly. The writer was a prominent Buddhist layman in Rangoon, U Tun Hla Oung by name, who had held various governmental posts during his life. He presented his views before a Buddhist men's discussion group in a very modest fashion as only a tentative approach, representing "a beginning made by some of us."[6]

The term "Middle Way" is used metaphorically rather than literally—a usage which was strongly criticized by some of the discussants. For it is not mid-way between luxury and poverty, indulgence and asceticism, as in the scriptures, but mid-way between capitalism and communism:

> In the Capitalist method the good points are the four democratic freedoms, which are national, political, personal and eco-

---

[5] An address presented before the International Association for Religious Freedom, Chicago, August, 1958. Privately printed. Pp. 9 and 11 respectively.

[6] Written in 1958 or 1959. The writer died in 1960.

nomic freedoms. In the Communist method the good features are:
(a) central planning (b) the stopping of un-economic competition and (c) the enthusiasm of the workers. In our journey
through *samsara* should we not avoid the extremes of these two
economic methods and take the best from each? The best is what
is rational and is exactly what the Buddha-Dhamma has outlined.
Therein lies the economics of the Middle Way—the scheme for
the salvation of my country. (p.6)

The specifics of this middle way suggest a relatively modest
economy for Burma within the limits of her national resources
and capabilities. Extreme laissez-faire capitalism is to be avoided
on the one side, as is rigid state regimentation on the other.
Every man, says the author, must have *some* capital of his own
if he is to be free and self-respecting—and if there is to be true
democracy. But there is a place for the state activity here too:
the state is to assist in this process by giving the poorer man
an opportunity to receive the monetary results of his own labor
by a system of "just distribution." This is to be accomplished
in part by an income-tax system, apparently scaled to respective
incomes, whose receipts will be used for an old-age pension
fund. And how can this be related to the doctrine of kammic
differences that our two previous authors have been concerned
to retain? This is one of the most interesting aspects of U Tun
Hla Oung's presentation:

> There will be no need to pull the rich down to the level of the
> poor; his *Kamma* will bring him down to the correct level. But
> the poor must be helped up and whether he stays put on the high-
> er level or not, despite the fair and just laws, is after all his *Kam-
> ma*. He will have thus assured the capitalist of fəir play and at the
> same time improved the living standards and dignity of the work-
> er. Enmity between the two will disappear and production will be
> increased. There will be employment for all and more consumer
> goods to buy at lower prices. (p. 6)

The implication is that the rich will be taxed only enough
to help the poor, but not enough to bring them down to their
level; or perhaps this would be corporate, not individual, income
tax. At any rate it appears that Kamma is in need of some
assistance in order to perfect its operation in modern society.
We may call it therefore, *state-aided Kamma*. For apparently

in its *natural* form Kamma unjustly handicaps many by poverty. Therefore in order for them to have a fair chance to rise—regardless of the justice of their present predicament—they must be given a financial assist by the state. Then, every man for himself, and Kamma, thus aided, will determine the outcome! It may also be noted that somewhat contrary to classic Buddhist doctrine, Kamma will *surely* take effective action in *this* life. Here is actually a Burmese New Deal: The weak, or the kammically handicapped, must be assisted to hold something of their own against the strong and rich, or the kammically blessed.

The expected results of this Middle Way sound somewhat utopian, as do the hopes of many pioneers. According to this Middle Way *every* man will be in some degree a capitalist, in the sense of holding retirement shares. The payment of income tax by the rich and the corporations "will become a pleasure" because one is thereby saving for his old age, and not subsidizing an extravagant government—surely a somewhat optimistic estimate of human nature. The nation will be united as never before, since it is economic inequality almost entirely that divides it. And, in contrast to the previous author who wants no classless society, "for the first time in the history of man a classless society will be found." If she follows in this way

> Burma can give the lead to the rest of the world and prove that the wisdom of the great Sage of the East and His moral influence can help save her and the world from the appalling disaster threatened by the conflict between Capitalist and Communist Powers which would lead us to be dominated once again by foreign powers. (p. 9)

4. A Buddha-Dhamma Commonwealth

There have been other more direct and more specifically political-economic versions of Buddhism in Burma, however. One of these is represented by the Buddhist Democratic Party which contested the 1959 elections on a platform of applying Buddhist principles and scriptures directly to national planning and policy. The main aim of the party, according to its constitution, was the reestablishment of the Buddhist moral and cultural values within Burma. At present they are threatened, says the constitution, in educational, economic, linguistic and religious spheres by the importation of foreign ideologies, the incompetence of the government, and the neglect of the way of Buddhism. The specific aims as stated in the party constitution are divided into several subheads including religious, racial, economic, educational, administrative, and foreign-relations matters. We shall note only a few high-lights here. With regard to *religion* the party favored the establishment of Buddhism as the State Religion of Burma, a note we shall hear again in U Nu's philosophy. The party platform is very unspecific as to what this means, but the party secretary, U Tun Sein, a self-made businessman, suggested two leading features: The study of Buddhism would be made compulsory in all state schools—which is also the main substance of the education section of the constitution; and the rights of religious minorities would be protected. He seemed to think that no special safeguards would be necessary to assure this latter, because Buddhism is by nature and history exceedingly tolerant.

With regard to *racial concerns* the constitution promises that the cultures of all the indigenous people would be protected.[7] There would be an attempt to "uplift their morals, prevent crime, cure disease," and "guard against foreign and imported political ideologies which are not only contrary to religion but also impair the unity of our national strength."

With regard to *economics* the party constitution recommends a combination of Burmese nationalism and new-deal policies. Burmese nationals are to be given priority in economic enterprises, but as between different citizens of Burma the state should act only as arbiter and not interfere unduly in the affairs of private citizens. Peasants and workers should be freed from the clutches of politicians—whoever *they* might be. The secretary of the party expressed himself as against socialism, because this

---

[7] Whether this included their religious beliefs is not discused in the constitution. Today a considerable effort is being undertaken, semi-official and governmently approved, to convert the hill-tribe animists to Buddhism. Is this an invasion of their cultural rights, or that uplift of their morals which the next section calls for?

was "anti-Buddhist" and quoted certain of the scriptures which opposed the "leveling down" of all men to one economic plane. He further said, after the analogy of one Buddhist scripture which tells how the beings in a degenerating earth found it necessary to appoint a "king" to settle their disputes and agreed to give him ten percent of their goods for his services, that anything above a ten percent income tax was "non-Buddhist." "It takes away a man's just deserts," said he. Yet he was opposed to capitalism because the profit motive was wrong. Somewhere in between socialism ("a gradual taking away of one's property") and communism ("a sudden taking away") he believed there was a non-capitalist Buddhist economic way. In general he would favor a welfare state—if not of an oppressive sort such as socialism represents. The "laws" of this welfare state, or its guiding principles, would be the application of the four illimitables. In this context Metta would be the objective (physical welfare) aid of destitute people lower than oneself; Karuna would be practiced in the care and support of all living things— though the prohibition of meat-eating would be too idealistic for practical application; the exercise of Mudita would signify contentment with one's lot, non-envy of those persons, classes, and nations more successful than oneself; and Upekkha would result in "neutrality between the moral and immoral." It was never quite clear what this would mean *within* a state, though it might mean positive neutrality in international relations.

The remainder of the constitutional articles of the party can be briefly described. Education, as we have noted, should include the compulsory study of Buddhism by Buddhist students. (The Secretary was greatly concerned over the gap between the Sangha and the younger generation because of the current secularized education.) Government servants should not affiliate with political parties; bribery and corruption should be eradicated from government administration; democracy, honesty, fair play, and efficiency should control all government operations. Land reform laws of the last ten years should be reviewed. And in foreign relations Burma should work for world peace and live in accordance with the principles of the United Nations Charter.

It may be added that this party was not able to elect even

one deputy to the national Assemblies in the 1960 elections despite the similarity of its platform to those of the major political parties.

5. The Buddhist Socialism of U Nu

The most interesting of all the contemporary attempts to relate Buddhism integrally to the new political and social forces that move the modern world, was U Nu's proposal to make Buddhism the State Religion of Burma should his "Clean" faction of the Anti-Facist People's Freedom League party win the election in early 1960, and he be chosen as prime minister. Both events did in fact occur. The "Clean" AFPFL won by a landslide victory, due to several factors, important among which were both the personal popularity of U Nu himself and the religion issue. (Indeed *some* campaigners were willing to say that "a vote for U Nu is a vote for the Buddha.") True to his promise U Nu as prime minister put all his prestige and party power behind the accomplishment of this goal, with the result that Parliament overwhelmingly enacted the State Religion Promotion Bill into law on September 15, 1961.

With regard to the particular provisions of this bill and the ensuing effects upon it of the coup d'etat of General Ne Win, overthrowing the government of U Nu, March 2, 1962, we shall speak later. But for the present we must turn to the ideas and motivations behind U Nu's move toward a Buddhist Establishment in Burma, and its rooting in his total philosophy of a Buddhist socialism.

U Nu came to his Buddhist-socialist, state-religion position by two converging routes. The Marxist-socialistic route was that followed by U Nu in his *early* political career. In the days of the Burmese struggle for independence from British rule, he forthrightly espoused Marxism as his political credo and flatly stated that Marxist socialism provided the only possible successful methodology of revolt and the only meaningful and practicable socio-political pattern for an independent Burma. (This is a statement which his political foes have never let him forget, but which his friends excuse on the grounds that in the British days Burmese leaders were using "any old club" of ideas to get rid of the British.) And of the continuing socialist flavor of his political thought there can be no doubt. Even though he may fight communist insurgents within Burmese borders and deplore some of the actions of great communist nations, socialist economics and the welfare state are for him the only valid or desirable political patterns for Burma's future.

But there is another factor involved here, and undoubtedly the more important of the two. An Indian journalist put it very well:

> Though a leftist by conviction, he [U Nu] believes that Karl Marx's knowledge of human affairs was 'not equivalent to one-tenth of a particle of dust beneath the feet of Lord Buddha.'[8]

Whether his Buddhism was always a factor in his espousal of socialism may be questioned; but there can be no doubt that in the years after the Second World War and Burma's achievement of independence in 1948, U Nu's Buddhist heritage has reasserted itself in every phase of his life and thought. Buddhism became the senior partner in his Buddhist-socialist thinking. Socialism was to be adopted because it was in keeping with *Buddhism,* rather than the reverse.

Part of this reassertion of Buddhism was no more than political common-sense. If any democratic-socialistic pattern of government by the chosen delegates of the people is to prevail in a country, it must have the backing of the majority of that same people. Therefore since the large majority of the people of Burma are professing Buddhists,[9] and Burma's culture pervasively and solidly Buddhist for the last 1000 years, socialistic democracy can be strong and integral to the nation only as it is powerfully and directly related to Buddhism. It might be hazarded that most of U Nu's thought since independence has been given to achieving some such synthesis.

---

[8] Rafig Zakaria, "Asian Notebook," *The Times of India,* July 10, 1960.

[9] It is often said that 85% or 90% of Burma's population are Buddhist. On other occasions many of the Burmese Union's hill peoples are considered animists, to whom missionaries (Buddhist) are being sent. Yet whatever variations there may be in percentage figures, there can be no doubt of the fact that Buddhism is the almost universal religious faith to which nearly everyone at least nominally adheres.

It would be erroneous to assume that U Nu's motives were only those dictated by political expediency, however. There can be no doubt that latterly, at least, Buddhism has become the single most important concern in his life as a person. It was a concern that permeated both his personal and public life throughout his premiership, and his convinction that religion and politics are deeply related to each other—so often stated publicly—must be held to be absolutely genuine. His own political life, whatever its other flaws, has been a consistently earnest attempt to combine religious and political leadership in himself and his government.

We may observe first how this Buddhist philosophy affected U Nu's personal activities and his approach to political situations. His devotion to meditation is well known. And this has been no mere personal foible or publicity-seeking device. For him it is of primary relevance to politics: the man who meditates is resultingly better able to avoid the pitfalls that threaten the politician, to discipline himself for the political struggle, and to formulate his basic policies. Indeed U Nu would hold meditation to be an absolutely indispensable "means of grace" for the sincere Buddhist statesman. Therefore when his party split in 1958 and he subsequently lost political power, he spent considerable time in meditation; and before beginning the 1959-1960 campaign that returned him to the premiership he also spent some five or six weeks in solitary meditation. To repeat: there can be no doubt but that he has consistently sought earnestly to relate Buddhist principles directly to political practice.

With regard to political activities we may characterize the Nu method with these two adjectives: *persuasive* and *personalized*. Persuasion rather than coercion is of course the Buddhist method in politics. U Nu has sought to apply this wherever possible even in the rough and tumble of ordinary political office-seeking. He is able to campaign with the best and has no equal in Burma in his understanding of his people and his ability to speak to them in their own language. Yet he never indulges in vilification of his opponents and upon his accession to power in 1960 made repeated peaceful overtures to his erstwhile opponents. He proposed that the out-of-power Opposition leader in parliament be given status equal in most respects to the Government leader, and even be invited to membership on some committees—a procedure quite at variance with the British political tradition that Burma has inherited. And in most situations involving differences of opinion he makes a strong effort to hear all sides of the matter. In fact this latter procedure is often carried out to such a degree that it becomes difficult to predict the result of such a conference or to find in his decisions a political policy based on discernible principles—unless the attempt to satisfy all different shades of opinion be considered a principle in itself. In any case this approach can be considered both democratic—if democratic be interpreted to mean conformable to and respective of all opinions—and Buddhistic, in that emphasis is put upon consultation rather than coercion.[10]

This same policy of persuasion rather than force may be, and has been, applied to economic regulation. After an era of rigid price-control under the military government, the government of U Nu lifted price controls immediately upon accession to office as a measure of economic relief. Yet the rising cost of living still remained a problem, and was indeed aggravated by the simultaneous banning of cattle-slaughter. As a solution to the problem, price-control committees were formed. But their powers were limited; they were to exercise control by *mettā*, not force. This apparently signified that little or no coercive action was to be taken against those who raised their prices; they would be persuaded, if possible, rather than prosecuted, into keeping their prices down.

This persuasive approach has been consistently followed by U Nu on the wider political horizon as well, even with regard to the insurgency that has caused Burma so much trouble. To be sure, there have been limits here. During the violent insurrections of the early days of independence, when it seemed doubtful whether the Union of Burma would hold together for

---

[10] As further specific examples of this policy: Just before his out-of-power period in 1958-1960, U Nu called in the representatives of different economic, political, religious, and social groups in great numbers to hear their complaints and promised to do something, if possible, for each of them. Again after returning to power he espoused the cause of protesting university students against the university senate in the matter of continuing the contemporary easy examination system for one more year.

more than a few months, U Nu vigorously backed the army and for publicity purposes had his picture taken in active encouragement of their warfare, handing out guns and ammunition. Yet, wherever possible, and beyond what some of his fellow Burmans think feasible, he always sought reconciliation with the insurgents as well as his other political enemies. Just before the Army take-over in 1958 U Nu tried diligently to bring the underground insurgents "into the light" by offering amnesty and aboveground political representation upon the laying down of their arms. What the relation of the amnesty offer was to the takeover may be disputed; but it is clear that for U Nu it was not mere "softness" toward leftist political groups, but a genuine attempt to reconcile rather than fight the enemies of the state.

With regard to the international situation in which Burma found herself, his methodology was predictable. Certainly it is true that U Nu realistically understood that Burma must get along with China, with whom she has hundreds of miles of common border, and finds it dangerous to ally herself with either of the power-blocs. Yet "positive neutrality" is also thoroughly Buddhist. Thus:

> Burma's policy of neutrality can hardly be said to have been soley guided by the Buddhist principles. It grows also out of the circumstances in which Burma finds herself. However, its policy agrees with the Buddhist principles in the sense that it is against war that will bring in its wake pestilence and famine, three great catastrophes that can befall mankind, and which the U. N. O. is trying to prevent. This positive neutrality may be interpreted as a logical expression of the Buddhist position in international affairs.[11]

So it was quite in keeping with Buddhist principles for the premier to exhort the joint Sino-Burmese border adjustment Commission to work together in the spirit of loving-kindness, i.e. metta. And it is also in keeping with Buddhist principles of reconciliation rather than war, to work with the U. N. O. as far as possible, seeking therein to maintain an independent non-aggressive policy.

---

11 From a dictated memo in response to author's question.

A *personalized* political methodology is, of course, also implied throughout this persuasive technique. For to persuade, one must negotiate with *individuals;* persuasion *is* negotiation on the individual level. And as we have before observed, the preferred Buddhist approach to even the complications of international politics, let alone the lesser social problems, is a personalistic one. In this respect also U Nu is thoroughly Buddhist. In a speech on Buddhism, given in the United States in 1959, he analyzed the basic social problem at all levels along these lines: What causes individual difficulties, family divisions, social and economic strife, and international tension, is the prevalence of the "I" consciousness in each individual involved. He concluded his introduction thus:

> This being so, if we want to turn this world into a better world, we must look for ways and means of rooting out this "I", ... "I" consciousness, [and] this "I" motif.[12]

From here he went on to recommend the Buddhist meditative way of rooting out all belief in or devotion to I-ness.

We may see another example of this personalized approach to political patterns and problems in some of U Nu's statements of political principle to his followers in the opening stages of his 1959-1960 campaign. Every man, particularly the one in public life, should practice metta (loving-kindness) as far as possible; its practice is a *minimal* requirement for the performance of one's public duties in true Buddhist manner. There are some sixteen rules for the practice of metta on the part of the public servant, summarized as follows:

1. Performance of duty for the benefit of all, with the pure peaceful consciousness of Nibbana always in mind;
2. Faithful performance of assigned duties;
3. and 4. Absolute honesty up to and including self-sacrifice if necessary;
5. Obedience to superiors;
6. Kindliness in deeds and words;
7, 8. and 9. Suppression of pride and cultivation of contentment with the result that one is willing to live on a scale befitting his position;

---

[12] As reported in *The Burman,* April 30, 1959.

10. Acceptance of responsibility according to ability;
11. Simplicity of life;
12. Calmness and self-possession;
13. Depth of knowledge and wisdom;
14. Avoidance of harsh language;
15. Avoidance of discrimination toward different classes;
16. Avoidance of all appearances of evil, even very minor misdeeds.[13]

The portrait that emerges here is quite clear: It is one of the dedicated public servant who in selfless non-political spirit works to the limit of his ability for the welfare of the state and people at large and lives according to his means and station. It might be taken as the description of the ideal office-holder in any nation of the world, with perhaps a few especially Buddhist features added, namely calm, possessed spirit and depth of knowledge and wisdom. Nor is there any doubt that this was indeed the ideal which U Nu himself consciously held up before himself in his own political life, and quite consistently practised; for however bitter have been the criticisms of his methods and policies, or his subordinates, there has been no one able to impugn his own personal financial honesty and integrity while in office.

In this same connection U Nu, in another one of the same set of policy speeches, outlined the way in which a Buddhist *Sotapanna,* or Stream Winner, can make his contribution to politics. A Sotapanna is the lowest grade of saint; he is one who has so perfected himself in virtue that he will nevermore be born in lower than human status, and may hope for Nibbana in the course of seven further existences as a maximum. To translate this into Western terms, though not fully, we could say that a Sotapanna was a person of absolutely incorruptible integrity of character. U Nu believes that this level of character among political leaders is almost essential for the establishment of a Socialist State.

In my opinion the Socialist State can be built by Sotapannas because they have the necessary qualifications; . . . . . They are

---

[13] From an unofficial translation. Unfortunately the official translation of the six speeches in which U Nu defined his basic political philosophy was not available at the time, nor have they since been made public.

not worldlings although they live in the world; their destiny is Nibbana. Once a person becomes a Sotapanna he believes with his whole heart in the three Gems [the Buddha, his Teaching, his Order of monks], and he is free from any deviations in the practice of the Five Precepts.

It will be seen that the Sotapanna-politician can serve his country with honesty and efficiency because he cannot be bribed or threatened. Dirty politics will be gone forever! People can trust the politicians in full confidence. . . . . By seeing the example of Sotapanna-politicians, other bad politicians or worldlings will imitate them. So everybody will be reformed. . . . .

In order to combat Communism and Fascism in our country, to preserve our independence, and to establish a socialist state, I urge all of you to practice the way to become a Sotapanna.[14]

But what if the way to Sotapanna-hood seems too hard for the ordinary politician?

If this seems to you very difficult, please start practising the Thirty-Eight Blessings [Mangala Sutta] taught by our Buddha. . . . For even if politicians fall short of the Sotapanna stage, they can still be a great help if they follow the ethical principles, or even practice loving-kindness towards all beings as taught in the Metta Sutta. [If they do this] the achievement of a Socialist world will not take very long.[15]

This completely personalitic approach to politics is a full exemplification of the axiomatic political credo of Buddhism noted above: reform the individual and all society will be reformed. Nor is this a mere public statement on the part of U Nu; he consistently followed this principle in all his political activities. The mid-1958 split in the major political party, of which he was leader, was primarily a matter of the direct application of this personalistic philosophy. Some of those who became his opponents were considered by him to be "somewhat moving away from the Sotapanna ideal"[16] of personal and public life; because they were thus not "good" men, they were not fitted to carry on in political office. His new party was subsequently named the "Clean" AFPFL to indicate in part at least its emphasis on

---

[14] *Ibid.*
[15] *Ibid.*
[16] As phrased by one of his confidants.

good personal character.[17] And the same opponents complained in the campaign that U Nu's party was running on
personalities rather than policy. It was a "Trust Me" platform,
with U Nu's picture on every "'Clean" ballot box, said they.

We may now turn to the more properly public domain of
stated political principle and policy. Two items call for attention
here. One is the matter of the establishment of Buddhism
as the State Religion of Burma. U Nu's philosophy of action here
remains unclear. In the early days of independence his government turned down the State Religion proposal in favor of a
constitutional recognition of the "special position" of Buddhism
as the majority religion—which meant substantial subsidies for
Buddhist activities but with full freedom for other religious
groups and also some slight financial aid to them. To have
made Buddhism the State Religion then would have led to strife
and disunity, said U Nu. But in his campaign of 1959 he indicated that he believed that "the people seemed to want it" and
seemingly on that basis alone pledged himself to the Buddhist
Establishment, to be effectuated after sufficient study by a responsible committee.

Whether there was in fact any more unanimity among the
Burmese for making Buddhism the State Religion in 1961 than
a decade before may be doubted. One of U Nu's own leaders, a
Moslem, protested against making Establishment a campaign
pledge. It is also true that many Burmese Buddhists themselves
were opposed to the move. Some feared the growth of intolerance and political pressure groups. Some also expressed doubt
that a national state could be honestly and consistently Buddhist,
i.e. avoid the taking of all life, animal and human. And following

---

[17] Some campaign literature of the "Clean" party adherents, though
not necessarily emanating from U Nu himself, portrayed the leaders of
the opposition as being drinkers, smokers, billiard players, and bettors on
the horse races. It was this type of failure in goodness which indicated
their unfitness for office, rather than public dishonesty or gross immorality.
No charges of malfeasance in office can be maintained against these
leaders any more than against U Nu.

The opposing or "Stable" AFPFL literature portrayed U Nu as a
monk whose mind was set on Nibbana rather than this world. This portrayal backfired to his advantage in the election, however.

the election, leaders of various religious minorities expressed full confidence in U Nu's own fairness, but fear of what some less tolerant successor might do to minorities in the future in the name of State Buddhism.

But there was at the same time a tremendous and apparently decisive popular sentiment for the Establishment among the masses of the people, brought to the level of active expression by contemporary agitation and occurrences. The soil out of which this sentiment sprang was a general, often unarticulated, sense of the "'decline" of Buddhism in Burma, or at very least of the dangers now threatening Buddhism's health and well being. A good part of this condition was blamed upon the British under whose rule Buddhist life and institutions had suffered by neglect if not by actual discouragement. But whatever the cause, the facts of decline were generally admitted. The younger generation, it was said, was woefully ignorant of the most elementary Buddhist teachings; there was evident a growing disregard for the Buddhist way of life and an increasing irreligiosity of life, or conversion of Buddhists to other faiths (though this latter has not markedly increased of late). There was also the decline of the monastery schools, increasingly moribund in the twentieth century, unable to face the competition of the government (secular) and missionary schools.

The Sangha (brotherhood of monks) was concerned in particular with this latter situation. Not only were there the dangers of a national apostasy, or purely nominal Buddhism, but the decline of the monastery schools had progressively deprived the monk of his role as the educator of the young and made him to appear a social parasite to many. And further, they asked: If children of Buddhist parents are no longer trained in the monastery, where will the next generation of monks come from?

Not only was there this general awareness of decline, but many monks and laity were also acutely aware of the dangers of communistic teaching for the Buddhist way of life, without knowing precisely how to combat them. This diffused anxiety over the anti-Buddhistic influence of communism was brought to sharp focus by the publication on the part of the caretaker government of General Ne Win (1958-60) of a pamphlet called

Dhammantaraya (Danger to the Dhamma) in which appeared photographs of insurgent-communist desecrations of Buddhist shrines and images, as well as the text of captured communist propaganda materials, strongly anti-Buddhist in nature. It had a fantastically large sale.

A contemporary statement, written after the time of the elections but before the actual adoption of the Establishment law, summarized the feeling of many Buddhists with regard to the situation, and proposed Establishment as the remedy:

> It is an undeniable fact that not only have the morals and culture emanating from Buddhism degenerated from day to day, but Dhammantarayas (dangers to religion) have increased since the dethroning of King Thibaw, the last Buddhist Monarch of Burma. This is because Buddhism has lost the status of the State Religion.
>
> When this lack has been remedied, the mere acknowledgement and glory of the status will increase the fervour and zeal of Buddhists who form the great majority of the citizens of the Union of Burma. Morals and culture will correspondingly improve and progress and enthusiasm will also be so great that Dhammantarayas will be resisted with the very lives [of the people of Burma].[18]

This statement contains several interesting elements. It lays the chief blame on British rule. It left-handedly acknowledges the decline of Buddhism in hoping for future improvement in "morals and culture." Undoubtedly communism is implicit in the general reference to Dhammantarayas. But most conspicuous is the naive assumption that the mere establishment of Buddhism as the State Religion of Burma will automatically cure all that ails contemporary Buddhism. Naive this is indeed; but it points us, particularly in its reference to King Thibaw, to the deep cultural tradition which lay beneath this strong desire for an Establishment.

This tradition is the tradition of the ruler of Burma as the Patron of its Religion. For many centuries (the 10th or 11th century until the time of Thibaw's deposition in 1886) the sov-

---

[18] From a mimeographed publication of the Organization to Establish Buddhism as the State Religion, Statement No. 2/60.

ereign of Burma was viewed as the Defender of the Faith, and its nourisher. Indeed this was his *chief* role, far more important than his role of tax collecter. For the health of Buddhism was the health of Burma; and loyalty to the sovereign as Patron and Provider for Buddhism (builder of pagodas, cherisher of the Sangha) was the *one* tie which bound *all* Burma's diverse peoples together with the throne. Not only so, but the royal palace was held to be the center of the earth, both geographically and religiously; it was full of the symbolism of Mount Meru the home of the gods, a "sacred space" which served as a conduit or contact-point for beneficial relations with spiritual potencies.

Now since the beginning of British rule and the dethronement of King Thibaw in 1886, the government has been purely secular, completely *de*-sacralized, with only fear or the hope of favor to hold the taxed, ruled and levied people to itself. Even a Burmese government, elected by the people themselves, might founder on the rocks of ethnic differences and regional ambition. Hence the hope of *re*-sacralizing the government, making it again the Patron and Provider for the Faith, as a means of strengthening it. While U Nu never spoke in precisely these terms, and did not formally approve the above statement of the Organization to Establish Buddhism as the State Religion, this factor seems implicit in all that he said and did concerning the Establishment.[19] At least we may call him the high priest of a *de facto* sacralization of the Government of the Union of Burma, and consider the passage of the State Religion Bill in September 1961 his first sacramental act. The tremendous political victory won by his party at the polls confirmed him in his conviction that the people did indeed want Establishment and had chosen him as the agent of its effectualization.

Whatever one's analysis of the motives underlying the popular enthusiasm for the Establishment, and the immediate forces which secured the passage of the State Religion Bill on September 15, 1961, the event did occur, and it may be of interest briefly to note its chief provisions.

---

[19] For a fuller discussion of this, see chapter by the author entitled "Buddhism and Political Power in Burma" in *Studies on Asia, 1962* (University of Nebraska), 1962.

According to the *Buddhist News Forum* the more important provisions were:

(1) Teaching of Buddhism to all Buddhist students in State schools, and making it a subject of study at Universities and Colleges if a sufficient number of students wish to take it,

(2) Study of Buddhism by Buddhist students compulsory in Teachers' Training Schools and Colleges,

(3) Opening of State primary schools at monasteries,

(4) Closing of Government offices, and offices of various Government Boards and Corporations and local bodies, on Buddhist sabbath days,

(5) Closing of bars on Buddhist Sabbath days,

(6) Teaching of Pali in State schools starting from the 8th standard, if there is a sufficient number of students wishing to take it,

(7) Grant of leave, in accordance with existing rules, to Government servants . . . if they desire to sit for any examination on Buddhism conducted by the Buddha Sasana Council and similar other statutory religious organizations.[20]

It may further be noted that by common consent the Sangha was to be kept carefully within the confines of its own scriptural rules, i.e. without votes and with no political role whatsoever allowed it.

The thrust of the provisions is obvious. The deplorable ignorance of Buddhist children about Buddhism is to be remedied; the monks are again to be given status and occupation in the educational system; a new set of *Buddhist* sabbaths (lunar) is to be instituted, in addition to the Sunday holiday. Said the minister of religious affairs with regard to the Bill:

> As regards the provision for compulsory teaching of Buddhist students . . . the aim was to let students cultivate an interest in and respect for religion. Such students would acquire good character and grow up to be good citizens of the Union. And the more scrupulously they observed the tenets of Buddhism, the more would they enjoy material and spiritual well being not only in the present life but in all lives hereafter.[21]

---

[20] Article "State Religion in Burma" (Rangoon, October, 1961), p. 13.

[21] *Idem.*

And what now was to be the position of non-Buddhists in a Buddhist State? Many were deeply concerned about the matter even before the State Religion Bill was put to the vote. The "Organization" referred to above urged (in another part of the document) that non-Buddhists need not be apprehensive, for, said the Organization,

> It is perhaps possible that in some foreign countries their State religion has been discriminatory and has imposed disabilities on followers of other religions. This would certainly not occur in Burma because Buddhism does not curtail the rights of other religions. . . . Buddhism is not a religion which strengthens itself by persecuting others. Because it has Metta as its basis, it can establish in strength the principles of Justice, Liberty and Equality and ensure peace and prosperity to all beings for all times. . . . The establishment of Buddhism as the State Religion will in itself make the Union of Burma an exemplary State to other nations.

When the bill was finally enacted it included third and fourth amendments which specifically guaranteed the right of the free exercise of their own faiths by non-Buddhists, and quite surprisingly, the right to *teach,* i.e. propagate, those faiths in Burma. These amendments received the full backing of U Nu himself.

But events attendant on the passage of the bill, and subsequent thereto, might well shake one's confidence in the absoluteness of the tolerance of Buddhism, particularly when it is teamed up with resurgent nationalism. Thus it was that no sooner had U Nu been chosen premier in April 1960 and announced his intention of framing the State Religion legislation, than it was publicly suggested that only Buddhists ought to be given posts at the upper levels in the new government. (However U Nu retained a Moslem member in his cabinet, the same Moslem who had opposed the State Religion issue in party councils.) So also a substantial number of monks picketed the legislature when it was about to consider the religious freedom guarantees, complaining that these provisions totally neglected the State Religion Bill and put Buddhism merely "on the same level" with all other religions. After its passage, U Nu was attacked in speeches, and his residence picketed, be-

cause he had been a "traitor" to Buddhism. Lastly, but significantly, when Moslems sought to build some new mosques in
the satellite towns about Rangoon, the building sites were
picketed (again by monks) and some violence ensued before
the government police bodily removed the picketers.

Before we turn to the death of hope for the re-sacralized
Buddhist State of Burma, after Ne Win's coup, we need to note
a matter that is perhaps of the greatest interest of all with regard
to U Nu's ideology of the ideal Buddhist society: his philosophy
of the consonance, yes, even the deep affinity, between Socialism
and Buddhism.[22] This ideological synthesis may be surprising to
the West. Some indeed have said that the connection between U
Nu's Buddhism and Socialism is only a politically expedient or
emotional one. Such a reading of the facts seems to be quite
superficial, however. As suggested above: U Nu's attempt to
join socialism with Buddhism is no mere expedient on his part,
even though it *was* politically astute to make such a connection.
It represents rather a synthesis growing out of his two deepest
convictions—the supremacy of socialism as political method and
form, and the absolute truth of the Buddhist Dhamma. To those
who criticize him for mingling politics with religion and sermon-
izing in his political speeches, he has this rejoinder:

> I wish to reply that whether a person is a business man or a
> politician, or whatever he is, one cannot separate religion from
> his occupation since religion is concerned with [all] the affairs
> of mankind. Religion is a restraining force among human beings,
> to bind peoples together, to wipe out injustice, and to lead all
> men to the good life.
>
> In short religion is the guide for all. If religious principles are
> involved in politics, I see many resulting virtues because politi-
> cians must then conduct themselves well. Bribery, sexual indul-

---

[22] What of the compatibility of Socialism with Buddhism as a *state
religion?* This was never discussed specifically by U Nu. Some Burmese
believe that the more the State is socialized the less money there will be
for the support of the non-productive Sangha and for Buddhist pagodas
and monasteries in general. This might be true of some forms of socialism. But in U Nu's brief synthesis (1961-62) there was envisaged
full state support for Buddhism and the Sangha, especially if the latter
took up the duty of teaching again. Indeed with the destruction of capitalism and private fortunes, there can be no other alternative.

gence, gambling, use of intoxicants, abuses of power—all these are due to the neglect of religion in politics.

Politics, as I understand the term, has no other purpose than to protect the people from danger, to guard democratic rights, to give economic security to all, to wipe out malnutrition and disease, to banish ignorance, to develop human character, and to prevent wars. Religion should therefore be the guide. Thus I see no error in my approach to politics.[23]

Indeed there is a kind of inevitability about the final synthesis of Buddhism and Socialism in U Nu's thought and life. For him the connection is integral and logical; it is no mere fortuitous historical relationship. Because socialist principles in their essence accord with Buddhism, there is only one genuinely proper political pattern for Burma: Buddhist Socialism.

What may be said about the teaching of the Buddhist *scriptures* with regard to socialism? Is any thing therein relevant to modern politics? This is a matter of great importance to U Nu, who seeks to find a scriptural authority for all that he does in every sphere of activity. We cannot here detail all of the many scripture quotations made in his speeches but may observe that U Nu finds that the scriptures do actually and emphatically suggest that socialism is the ideal Buddhist pattern. Thus with regard to the welfare state:

The Buddhist scriptures provide a considerable number of instances which show that Buddhism favours a Welfare State in which the government has assumed responsibility for the care of the poor, the unemployed, the sick, the aged, etc.[24]

This presumably refers to those scriptural portrayals of ideal kings as "fathers" of their people, caring for each subject as for a son. U Nu also refers to the suttas of the *Dīgha-Nikāya* in which the Buddhist theory of world cycles is set forth, as indicative of a primordial "socialistic" condition. According to the cyclic theory every world-age begins in Eden-like splendor; the earth is peopled by radiant beings, descended from higher spheres where their good Kamma has run out, who at first subsist on "radiance" alone. But progressively the world de-

---

[23] Unofficial translation of speech.
[24] From dictated memo.

teriorates until it descends to the level of the world we know today—short life, misery, sin, strife, imposition of governmental authority. And this, according to U Nu's interpretation, is a descent from an anarchical (but not chaotic) *socialist* perfection of peace and plenty to a *capitalist* order of things: "Keen competition now arrived. Kings had to be elected to maintain law and order."[25] Thus it is the presence of the competitive strife for material rewards, the free enterprise which officially licenses and approves greed, that constitutes the misery of the world. "Free enterprise" is only a governmental-approved sanction of the "I-regarding" instinct that is the root cause of all human woe. As such it is anti-Buddhist; and U Nu categorically rejects the profit motive as a dangerous venom that poisons the well-springs of life in every society which embodies it—for it enshrines greedy strife as a major "virtue." Therefore he condemns capitalism root and branch, and welcomes socialism as the perfect expression of the Buddhist economic way of life.

Buddhism and Socialism then form a harmonious team. They agree on the proper functions and goals of society. Buddhism, as religion, will supply the ideal pattern and the inspiration for the new state, while socialism provides the practical method of the implementation of the ideal. We may note some further statements which make this relationship explicit. With regard to the basic motifs of socialism U Nu, as a *Buddhist* politician, is in full accord:

> Present day problems of inequalities, exploitation, etc. should be solved by socialism which declares "To each according to his needs and from each according to his ability." Under socialism the fruits of labor will be equally distributed and unfair practices of the rich against the poor will be eliminated. The profit motive should be abandoned. . . . There will be no greed, no hatred between man and man. The miseries of the world are due to the lack of Socialist principles.[26]

He further specifies the ills which have arisen from the capitalist organization of contemporary societies:

> The world is rich enough to provide sufficient food, clothing

---

[25] As in 23 above.
[26] *Ibid.*

and shelter for everybody. The maximum standard of living is now enjoyed only by the few; but the majority of mankind has to live in extreme poverty. The producers do not produce their goods for the welfare of the masses. They exploit the natural resources of the world for their profit; they create personal ownership instead of aiming for the common utility.[27]

Thus far we have doctrinaire socialist gospel. But there is also a basic Buddhist reason for urging socialism. And it may be stated very simply: *A Socialist world would make it much easier to achieve Nibbana*. Thus in the first keynote speech of the series we read:

> The main aim of Buddhism, to my mind, is to gain liberation from the rounds of existence. . . . Yet I believe that only one percent of the Buddhist population of Burma can aspire for Liberation. This is because under the defective economic system which we see before our eyes, much time and energy has to be spent to earn the bare necessities of life. . . . So the significant teaching of the Buddha has to be neglected. The economic set-up of human society allows no way for the practice of the Noble Virtues.
>
> Even when the maximum standard of living is achieved, the competitive system compels the people to get more wealth, more power and [awakens] more desires. The more you get the more you want. We thus lose sight of the Path to Liberation.

Now in U Nu's opinion Socialism will cure all these evils. There will be no social distinctions, no avid pursuit of wealth, no competition for personal gain, no envy of someone else who has a better house or finer clothing, in a socialist society. Greed, pride and illusion of superiority based on wealth will be destroyed. The aged will have no anxiety for their old age. And violence will disappear from the land, because there will be no attachment to wealth, no undue inequalities in material status. Not only will such a society be pleasant to live in; in such a non-materialistic, non-striving atmosphere people may more easily turn to the pursuit of their proper spiritual destiny. No longer lured by the hope of material gain, no longer perverted by the profit motive, no longer enmeshed in the web of

---

[27] *Ibid.*

selfish striving, men may seek for that only true Buddhist good, Nibbana itself. There will be time and disposition for Nibbana-bringing meditation. Indeed in the New State (of Buddhist Socialism) the *whole communal* structure of mutual concern and sharing will itself serve to forward all men on their way to Nibbana:

> So under the new society people can spare their surplus money and property to set up a common pool for the establishment of a Socialist State. This is true Dana [charity]. I believe the Socialist Society has these four virtues: (a) Right view with regard to property; (b) the main emphasis can be put on the achievement of Liberation [i.e. Nibbana]; (c) Sila, Samadhi and Pañña may become dominant principles in daily life; (d) communal charity becomes possible, and the practice of Dana [alms-giving] leads to Nibbana.[28]

And how far off is the realization of this splendid dream? In U Nu's opinion the New Day is even now at hand:

> I believe the dawn of Socialism is not far off. We can establish this State in Socialism in our time.[29]

Historical Epilogue

As noted above, General Ne Win took over the government of Burma from U Nu on March 2, 1962, arresting him and numbers of his leaders because of the "deteriorating" situation. What will this mean for Buddhist Socialism and State Religion?

One can only presume to conjecture. General Ne Win is certainly not *anti*-Buddhist, though he might be called a *secular* Buddhist when compared to U Nu the devotional, meditating Buddhist. It was under Ne Win's earlier regime in fact that a study of the monastery schools was undertaken, and measures for their rehabilitation suggested. Likewise most of the members of his first cabinet were staunch Buddhists.

However, General Ne Win is primarily a practical, this-worldly man who thinks in terms of internal harmony, economic well-being, and national security for Burma. He may not indeed repeal the state religion bill in its entirety; but if not, he will

---

[28] *Ibid.*
[29] *Ibid.*

most certainly see that its enforcement does not stir up internal dissension nor aim at utopian Buddhism to the detriment of the practical welfare of the Burmese people. Almost immediately upon his return to power, for example, he repealed the cattle slaughter ban of U Nu's government, and will undoubtedly again reduce the stray dog population of Rangoon, whatever the Buddhist connotations of the act. He did find a two-sabbath week a luxury too rich for Burma's weak economic health. He will very realistically recognize the special position of Buddhism in Burma, as the religion of the vast majority of its people, and will no doubt make a larger provision for its support than most other secularist governments do for their religions. But he will never confuse the idealities of Buddhism with the practicalities of statecraft and realities of daily administration.[30]

Will there ever be another resurgence of Buddhist Statism in Burma? In view of such a resurgence in Ceylon an absolute denial of its possibility seems brash. Yet there are some signs that even those who initially favored a Buddhist State in Burma may be having second thoughts about its desirability. And in the two years of his power as the chief prophet and high priest of State Buddhism and Buddhist Socialism, U Nu was unable to bring these concepts effectively into focus or to lead his party from hungry power-grabbing and intra-party strife toward disinterested service to a Buddhist State. His political subordinates were not transformed into those Sotapannas that are necessary for the realization of Buddhist Socialism. Not only so, but in this same period Buddhist intolerance for the non-Buddhist appeared to be on the rise, given new encouragement by the state religion establishment.

It would seem that with U Nu's passing from power the second time, whatever the reasons for his overthrow, the golden hour for the effectualization of his Buddhist-Socialist state has

---

[30] The Buddhist lunar sabbath was abolished; and with the suspension of the constitution, State Religion was *de facto* disestablished also. The restiveness of non-Buddhist minorities under State Buddhism appears to have been an important inducement to the military take over. Even the Buddha Sasana Council, established in 1953 to hold the Sixth Buddhist Synod, and remaining as a kind of bureau of Buddhist affairs for scripture revision, publication, and promotion of Buddhism, was re-formed in 1962.

also forever passed out of the history of *this* world into the realm of those almost-maybe, might-have-been dreams which strew the life of man. Perhaps, in Buddhist terms, some such opportunity will be his again under some other identity in some future birth in some future universe.

CHAPTER IX   WHITHER BUDDHIST ETHIC?

The title of this final short chapter is misleading, perhaps. The author is neither a prophet nor the son of a prophet—nor has he any special revelation about the future course which Buddhist ethics will take. The course of development of a culture or religion is clear and inevitable only after it has taken place. And especially is this the case with contemporary Theravada Buddhism. What might seem to be the logic of its development is not bound to happen. Religious developments are seldom logical in terms of predictable results or inevitable effects following from specific doctrines or viewpoints. And in the present instance there are so many variable and unforseeable factors—political, economic, social, personal—which will strongly affect the response that Buddhism will finally make to the new world situation, that prediction is impossible. Therefore we shall content ourselves with some summary comments and the specification of some unresolved problems or tensions that are present in the ethical sphere.

It may be said in general that Theravada Buddhism must make up its mind in which world it expects to live and strive, before it can give a clear answer to its ethical problems. For there are two worlds here with their respective values and ways. We have called them the world of absolute transcendent value (Nibbana) and the world of relative mundane concerns (Kamma). In the past there *was* a solution of sorts: It was held that though most men necessarily lived in the world of Kamma, they were really only marking time in it. For this lower world was neither worthy nor capable of salvation or whole-hearted concern. As W. H. Sheldon puts it:

> Gautama saw no salvation in the worldly scene, in remolding human society, in reforming the state, in changing mundane things for the better as time goes on. Recall his teachings in respect to time, so widely accepted in Asia: There is nothing permanent in the physical or psychical, no lasting substance or perduring ego; time is but the continual destruction of everything that is born. This temporal world is not to be saved.

With this attitude he contrasts that of the West:

> Here then is precisely where the Western love of the world changes the whole perspective. This world is *worth saving,* in all its complexities and particulars. . . . If this world is to be perpetuated and perfected, it must still be *this* world; in brief, it must *change* what is bad or imperfect within it into something good, also within it.[1]

Now this is a fundamental matter about which Buddhism must make up its mind: Does it wish to live by the philosophy that the world is worth saving, and give to that saving a substantial effort by attempting the world's transformation for the better? Or does it wish to turn away to the higher world of transcendent inner values and largely ignore and deplore modern "materialistic civilization" which is firmly proceeding toward the goal of some sort of world betterment? Or can it find some way in which to combine the two in a new and dynamic synthesis? Obviously until Buddhism makes up its mind, or perhaps its heart, about the matter, no clear ethical philosophy or course of action can be charted.

There are factors tending toward all three solutions. The heavy traditional weight of Theravada Buddhism is with the second solution. Let the world go by; it is not worth saving, and is perhaps going to blow itself into pieces in any case—a very drastic form of "betterment." The only salvation is retreat to inner peace. But there is also the prod of unhappy circumstance and social-political disturbance that is increasingly invading this attempted seclusion. The quiet haunts of the meditator are threat-

---

[1] *Essays in East-West Philosophy,* C. A. Moore, ed., University of Hawaii, 1951, pp. 292–293.

ened by insurgents and invaders, and made noisy by modern technology. The society which protects the meditator is itself in crisis. The teaching of the doctrine of the Great Enlightened Meditator is in neglect and in danger. Something must be done about such a world!

And what shall be done? The natural reaction of Buddhists is to try to combine the values of the interior and exterior worlds, the world of eternity and the world of time, in a viable synthesis. We have seen the general pattern which this synthesis takes as the rule: an activation of the nibbanic vocabulary and its application to concrete social situations in the form of the ideal of disinterested and unselfish but active endeavor. Or we may see it in the attempted synthesis between meditation and the active layman's life. Thus the contemporary Buddhist assertion that Nibbana and Kamma can be reconciled both in ideal and action. The Buddhist answer to Professor Sheldon's above statement might be put in the words of the Honorable U Nu:

> Of course the main Buddhist goal is Nibbana and to reach it one must turn away from the mundane world. But that does not preclude taking any interest in the promotion of interests for one-self and for others in this very life. . . . The Buddha is not against the promotion of social welfare but against indulgence in sensual desires which cause the round of rebirths. Achieving a better material standard of living, care for the poor and distressed, maintenance of social order, etc. are quite in keeping with the teachings of the Buddha.
>
> A Burmese saying goes, "One can observe moral precepts only when his stomach is well-filled." Again, it is obvious that there can be no peace within when there is no peace without.[2]

Is this a satisfactory answer? The question will remain in the mind of the Westerner: Can a world-view that gives only negative approval or neutral consent to the promotion of social welfare, as a mere means for securing ultimate escape from the world of society, ever adequately deal with the aggressive counter-forces of contemporary world society? Can such a philosophy produce a social dynamism sufficient to create a vital new order; or will the nibbanic potency paralyze, or at least weaken, the vital

---

[2] From typescript answer to author's question.

nerve of active social involvement? It is impossible to answer such a question confidently, but the latter danger is present, whatever the final result.[3]

We may turn to a second question: *Where will Buddhism find its leadership for the new day?* Here again it is caught between its two worlds. Traditionally the monk, the Nibbana-farer by definition, has been the moral and spiritual leader in the Buddhist world. Insofar as religious counsel might be given to the ruler or a Buddhist society be built—though it was seldom conceived in those terms—the Sangha provided the wisdom. But as we have noted, Sangha leadership is being by-passed for a number of reasons. The Nibbana-farer, fascinated by the hope of the inner vision of world-transcendent truth, concentrating his mental powers on the ancient tradition of the scriptures, and ignorant of the political-social world about him, cannot give Buddhism the leadership it needs in its day of crisis. Indeed, there *are* stirrings even in the Sangha; but we may ask: Will the stirrings be sufficient for the situation? And again: Can the monk retain his spiritual leadership if he forsakes or modifies his traditional pattern of monastic seclusion and unworldliness? Much Buddhist sentiment is opposed to such modification and demands that he remain as he is, apart from, and above, all social welfare and political activity—the visible hope of Nibbana for the common man.

It appears likely (a cautious prediction) that the new layman will have to do any such working out of the practical Buddhist response to the current situation as will be done in the im-

---

[3] Ironically it may be the very power of Nibbana-seeking, and the corollary social apathy, that may turn out to be a better protection against communism than any social-gospelizing of Buddhism. For in the East it is in an oft-repeated pattern that social-gospel-Christian and Western-democratic talk of justice, human rights, and this-worldly concern for physical welfare have aroused the very forces that produce communistic sentiment. And on the other hand, the very "other-worldly" disinterest of Buddhism and other religions in the world of time and space and physical realities is the strongest bulwark against communist agitation, at least for the moment.

If Buddhism, then, becomes socially conscious, will it be able to resist communism as well as before? Or better: Will it be able to achieve such a consciousness in time to mount resistance of the long-term kind?

mediate future. The general lines of this leadership we have observed: a new interest in the study and exposition of the Buddhist teachings; a concern for missionary outreach on somewhat
ecumenical and international lines; deliberate attempts to work
out specific Buddhist political and social philosophy. Two questions may be asked at this point. Will this leadership secure a
significant following, significant enough to make a genuine
change in basic Buddhist attitudes? And what will be the resulting version of Buddhism?

Articulate Buddhist leadership on the lay level seems rather
scarce at the present moment, and largely confined to the older
generation, so far as Burma is concerned. The Buddhist periodicals, at least the English variety, are the products of middle-aged
and retired men on the whole. There seems to be a dearth of Buddhist leadership and scholarship, with a few notable exceptions,
in the younger generation that is now coming into active leadership in the nation. No doubt there is considerable thinking now
going on among such persons with regard to the practical role
which Buddhism should play in the world today. But the author's
impression is that most people of this generation tend to put
Buddhism in one compartment and socio-politics in another compartment of their thinking and acting. A living synthesis of the
two on the practical and effective plane scarcely seems to be a
major concern among them. It is because their worlds are divided: One is of traditional, childhood culture, and perhaps piety
of the strictly personal sort; and the other is the world of present-day science, technology, politics, and economics. Nor is there
yet a clear pattern for bringing them together.

But granted that something of significance will come from
the new lay leaders; what will be the composition and quality of
this new version of Buddhism? The specifics of such a new gospel
—or as the layman insists, the old gospel rediscovered—cannot be
foretold. But undoubtedly it will be of practical, this-worldly sort
in considerable part. Emphasis will be given to the value and
efficacy of Buddhist doctrine and practice, including meditation,
for every-day life. There will be a continuation of the "activating" of Buddhist doctrine, and a bypassing of some of the finer
distinctions of Buddhist tradition. And the Sangha will be subject to increasing criticism because of its indiscipline, worldliness,

or, on the other hand, for its inability to lead. Whatever type of criticism prevails among the laity will depend upon how lay Buddhism develops; but it will undoubtedly force the Sangha to define its role anew.[4]

This leads to a third question: *Will Buddhism be able to produce satisfactory answers and solutions to the new problems in time to have an effective part in their resolution?* This again depends upon many essentially unpredictable factors—the stability of the international situation, the personality of leaders, the pressure of social and economic forces. The attempt of Burma, under the leadership of U Nu, to provide a Buddhist philosophy of state and government now remains only as a historical curiosity. Whether any new Buddhist political philosophy and methodology is there in the making seems doubtful

It is precisely at this point that Buddhist social and ethical formulations to date demonstrate what seems to be a central weakness. This is their tendency to set personal character over against plan and technique, and to substitute it for the latter in actual procedures. Hence a "Buddhist" political campaign may be more like a religious preaching mission than a statement of political principles, and a party platform an exhortation to be pure rather than a statement of basic policy.[5] The controlling philosophy is that good men make good government.

This is true, of course, in a very important but also a very general sense. A man of good character may be a simpleton, or unable to control his unprincipled subordinates. Because there is no rigid legalistic system of standards and controls, a personal-relations way of carrying on government affairs may be in actuality only the best possible way to perpetuate a system of personal

---

[4] Burmese tradition will probably tend to keep the Sangha closely confined to its *Vinaya* pattern of life. Other national Theravada traditions are more liberal in some respects (e.g. in the type of education allowed the monk) but stricter with regard to some rules of conduct.

[5] The 1960 political campaign in Burma illustrates this. The Stable AFPFL campaigned on the basis of a clearly stated set of socialistic principles; the Clean AFPFL (U Nu's party) campaigned on the basis of making Buddhism the state religion and on the personal popularity of its leader. The latter's platform tended to be an exhortation to purity in personal life, particularly among politicians.

"pull", influence, and corruption. And emphasis upon "government by character" rather than government by principle, may well become only a camouflage for an indisposition or inability to plan and execute intelligently. In any event, this tendency to over-value the personal and discount the systematic and technical, seems to be the Achilles heel of all present Buddhist social-political philosophy and methodology.

One final item remains: *What thought-forms or terms are likely to play the most significant role in any new formulation of Buddhist ethic in the Theravada tradition?* Here again prediction is most difficult if not impossible; for a religious tradition tends to express those values that its devotees desire it to express. Therefore to say with certainty that this term and not that one will play a basic role in new doctrinal formulation, or become the vehicle of new meanings which are being poured into it, is unprofitable. What we can say is that whatever occurs here, there will be no radically new formulations nor any wholesale discarding of old terms. It will be rather in the shift of emphasis or interpretation that novelty will make itself felt; and it will be done under cover of reviving and rediscovering the ancient and original truth.

We may also say one more thing. Certain terms whose reformulation we have previously dealt with, seem capable of serving as the channels of the currents of change and revitalization. *Kamma* may be reinterpreted in terms of each man's power to change his future, both immediate and long-term—though conceivably the long-term (rebirth) factor may be less emphasized. *Nibbana*, and the meditational technique of attaining to it, may be interpreted to mean a dispassionate, balanced quality of judgment brought to bear upon social situations and mundane problems. The *Four Illimitables*, or Blessed Dispositions, may be given a more activist, man-centered implementation than formerly. And the *Bodhisatta* ideal with its almost unlimited potentiality for social-service motivation, may spring into new importance, either implicit or explicit.

But whether these potentialities will indeed be realized and the revitalization of Buddhist ethic be also realized through their instrumentality must remain the secret of Theravada Buddhism's unknown future.

1. Non-Killing

Writes a contemporary Buddhist:

> The first precept of non-killing may be taken as the most important one from the Buddhist standpoint, because by the careful observance of non-killing, such evil emotions as anger, greed, hatred, etc. may be gradually controlled, paving the way for the development of such good and noble feelings as kindness, love, mercy, compassion, etc. which Buddhism seeks to cultivate in the minds of people.[1]

Such a statement would be agreed to by most Theravada Buddhists: non-killing, with its attendant virtue of a gentle, harmless, non-violent spirit, seems to them central to the Buddhist view of a good life. One might say that the principle of non-killing is as near an absolute as one can get in practical Buddhist ethics.

But when we come to the application of this principle in actual circumstances, there is considerable difference of opinion. There is the difficulty for example with regard to the position of a public official in government: Does he not perforce disobey the First Precept in many of his official actions? In the election campaign of 1959-60 in Burma this matter of how absolutely a ruler of state could keep the Precepts became an election issue after the opponent of U Nu had been accused of saying that the Five Precepts could not and should not be observed by government

---

[1] U Ba Kyaw, "The Buddhist Conception of Moral Purity," *Light of the Buddha*, II, No. 10 (October, 1957), 22.

officials. He replied as follows in words which represent an honest facing of the problem:

> In connection with the Five Precepts, they are desirable precepts and I personally try to observe these Five Precepts in my daily life. But as a political leader it is really difficult to observe these precepts strictly at all times.
>
> Take the "No Killing" precept. The Government has to suppress the insurgents, sell airborne mutton, and distribute fish. These schemes all involve killing.[2]

This of course is a difficulty faced by all statesmen who try to live according to a principle of love or non-violence and yet rule over states. It is essentially insoluble in terms of its absolute observance, even for the Buddhist, and he must make a division between public and private conduct. Part of the Buddhist solution to this situation we have already alluded to (p. 79 above) —maintaining a minimum of evil dispositions and a maximum of private devotions on the part of the statesman or government official. Another way to deal with the matter, though in a less-than-absolute observance of the non-killing Precept, is to moderate official policies as far as possible in the direction of peaceableness and non-violence. And this was clearly the hope of U Nu. With regard to insurgents he has at times in the past found it necessary to prosecute the armed struggle against them with great vigor. But whenever possible he favored the policy of extending to them the invitation to voluntarily "come into the light" of above-ground, non-violent political action.

Obviously Buddhist sentiment is also against capital punishment, for this too is a deliberate taking of life. Sometimes the suggestion is made that the ideal Buddhist way to treat one who has committed murder, for example, would be to imprison him for life and then provide him with Buddhist instruction periodically while in prison in the hope that he would "repent" and

---

[2] Statement of U Kyaw Nyein to a group of monks as reported in *The Nation*, December 1, 1959. Despite this statement, U Kyaw Nyein never quite escaped the onus of having "spoken against" the Five Precepts. U Nu, his opponent, made no reply to this or to U Kyaw Nyein's further statement that U Nu had, as former Prime Minister, agreed to and enforced such violent policies, as well as licensed liquor sales.

change his heart. As a matter of fact punishment by death is still practiced in most if not all Buddhist countries. Some Buddhists see the dilemma involved in capital punishment as a conflict between the "mundane" morality of the state, which calls for capital punishment to keep order, and the "supra-mundane" moral absolutes of religion. And, writes one such author, "the two cannot be blended."[3] He apparently thus finds himself as a Buddhist still in a dilemma practically speaking. He goes on to quote with approval, or at least great interest, Gandhi's statement that "Circumstances can be imagined in which not to kill would spell himsa (violence), while killing would be ahimsa (non-violence) . . . The final test as to its violence or non-violence is after all the intent underlying the act."[4]

The same author further suggests a more sophisticated and extensive interpretation of non-killing than is usually found in Theravada Buddhism:

> Apart from an act of downright killing which is strictly forbidden by Buddhism, the following *actions or inactions which tend to endanger or shorten human lives,* may be taken as very serious though they may not come within the purview of killing, and should, therefore, be avoided by all Buddhists.
>
> They are, namely: crowded and ill-ventilated buildings, workshops and factories; slum conditions in big cities and towns; the overworking of children as well as adults; careless driving of steam boats, rail engines, planes, motor and other vehicles and engines; sale of spurious medicines and adulterated foodstuffs; unskillful use of syringes with or without license; treatment of sick people by quacks; sale of foodstuffs not fit for human consumption; careless sanitary inspection; treatment of patients in a half-hearted manner; careless nursing of patients; failure to give timely attention to seriously ill or wounded people; careless keeping of loaded guns, rifles, revolvers, pistols and other automatic weapons; . . .
>
> inspection of boilers without heeding public interest; unkind beating causing grievous hurt to boys and girls by teachers, parents and guardians; harsh treatment of menials; employment of labourers on starvation wages; manufacture of firecrackers and other explosive materials near human habitations; failure to give

---

[3] U Ba Kyaw, *op. cit.*, p. 24.

[4] *Ibid*, p. 27.

timely warning to surface craft, planes, etc. against impending violent weather changes; failure to give timely aid to people in distress due to flood, famine, fire, earthquake or other calamities; destruction of rails, bridges, etc. by any means; failure to withdraw licenses from reckless drivers; overfeeding of children; forced labour in unhealthy places; . . .

driving motor and other vehicles by drunk people; employment of labourers in dangerous places; careless keeping of sweets and sugar-coated pills together; careless or incompetent installation of electrical wires; certifying of motor trucks and lorries as fit, though unfit for public use; issue of license to unfit drivers; failure to make timely repairs to rickety bridges; failure to give timely warning to motorists and other vehicular travellers regarding unsafe bridges, etc. etc.

But knowing his own country the writer adds:

The theoretical understanding of these is one thing and the practical application quite another.[5]

This is a rather remarkable statement, coming out of conservative and somewhat literal-minded Buddhism. It is remarkable for the width and depth of its understanding of the concept of social responsibility; for its inclusion of all factors that tend to "endanger and shorten" human lives, as well as the avoidance of outright killing; and especially for its recognition that *in*action may be equally as reprehensible as action in some cases. It suggests the surprising social-gospel transformation which *might* occur in Buddhism. The fatalistic, individualistically selfish overtones of Kamma are totally absent; the neutralistic attitude toward the positive *saving* of life, so characteristic of traditional Buddhism, is completely overcome and a positive responsibility for life-saving and death-preventing measures is actively urged.

This latter contrasts quite strongly in spirit—though the author does not make the specific application—with the usual Burmese Buddhist attitude toward such matters as public health measures, for example. It has frequently happened that in Rangoon persons who were urged to destroy rats, because of their endangering food supplies and their disease-carrying propensities, would capture them alive and release them outside the city environs. The

---

[5] *Ibid*, p. 23, 24. Italics added.

Army campaign of 1958-9 to destroy pariah dogs and crows, as well as mosquitoes, was not received with enthusiasim. For the average Buddhist is much more certain that killing is bad, than that keeping alive or preventing the death of higher beings by the destruction of lower ones, is good. Hence he emphasizes the former and neglects the latter.[6] But practically speaking the distinction between lazy insanitation, regardless of the health and welfare of others, and the genuine desire not to destroy life, is very often blurred, with the former taking cover under the latter.

2. Meat Eating

The principle of non-killing carries over directly into the matter of meat-eating. And here opinion is even more varied and practice and theory often in conflict. Logically, of course, the principle of non-killing was carried to its final conclusion by the ancient Jains who strenuously avoided destroying the life of even the smallest insect by sweeping the paths in front of them as they walked during the rainy season, by straining their water, by wearing masks over mouth and nose, and even by refusing to eat the life-giving roots of plants—at least in strictest theory. While equally committed in theory to the absolute principle of non-killing, Buddhist practice has halted somewhat this side of Jain absolutism. And just where to halt is the difficulty.

Practically speaking the actual Buddhist pattern is a compromise. Most Buddhist laymen eat meat with relish; nor do all monks abstain. Some, indeed, do not eat beef or pork and count it a great virtue not to do so.[7] Yet again some will abstain from

---

[6] One Buddhist friend stated that undoubtedly the Army's killing of rats and dogs was wrong and would have kammic consequences of a bad nature. Yet the passive by-stander could console himself in Buddhist fashion with the reminder that these beings that were killed (rats, dogs, mosquitoes) were simply reaping the results of their past evil deeds. And *possibly* some good would result from their destruction.

[7] This special regard for cattle *may* spring from the Indian attitude on the same matter. However, in Burmese Buddhism it is (probably speciously) attributed to the special place which cattle occupy in the agricultural economy—Burma is an ox-economy, it is said. This was the reason given for the reimposed ban upon cattle slaughter in 1960. But it was also looked upon as kammically meritorious to save the lives of animals.

meat-eating during the meditation periods, sabbaths, or holy days. Fish eating has traditionally been given a special dispensation in Burma, as somehow less sinful. Is it because fish simply "die of themselves" when brought out of the water? Or because they have a lesser life-quality?[8] Most reasons given seem to be in the quality of *ex post facto* rationalizations of long-established habits.

But what did the Buddha say about meat eating? Here a debate rages even at the present time. Two contemporary quotations will serve to illustrate the conflicting views:

> Since killing of all sentient beings is prohibited by Buddhism, it may, in all probability, be assumed that a Buddhist must refrain from eating flesh, living only on vegetables; but it is not the case at all because Buddha does not forbid the eating of meat. . . .
>
> A Buddhist is permitted to eat either flesh or vegetable for the maintenance of his five khandhas [body-mind]. . . . He is taught that meat eating does not make him impure but only his evil actions by mouth, body and mind do defile him.
>
> Buddha says, "My disciples have permission to eat whatever food it is customary to eat in any place or country, provided it is done without indulgence of the appetite or evil desire."[9]

The general reference here is to a passage in which the Buddha, somewhat like St. Paul, tells his disciples to eat whatever is set before them without asking questions. Only if they *ask* specifically for meat, or know that their food-provider has killed the meat specifically for them, is meat-eating sinful. (Whether one who buys a pork chop in a public market has arranged for it to be killed specifically for him, is a point that admits of endless argument.) And still further it is affirmed by such persons, the

---

[8] A modern proponent of this view attributes it to the Buddha himself who spoke (in the *Anguttara-Nikāya*, or *Book of Gradual Sayings. Vol. III*) of a division of beings into fish, animal, and human. He further opines that it is less sinful to kill a harmful (to human beings) creature such as a snake, than a harmless and helpful (to human beings) animal like the cow, which is something of a father and mother to the human race. Letter to the editor entitled "The Beef Question," by U San Hla, in *The Nation*, mid-November, 1958.

[9] U Ba Kyaw, *op. cit.*, p. 23.

Buddha himself ate meat and indeed died as the result of one last meal of pork.

But this is not the end of the story. There are others, a small minority it must be said, who vigorously deny most of the above statements. That last meal of the Buddha was from a palm shoot or other vegetable that *tasted* like pork. (The Pali original is perhaps somewhat uncertain here.) Writes such a vegetarian:

> The fact is that the Buddha never ate any flesh during his ministry of 45 years and there is no reason to believe that He should have accepted pork as His last meal. Of course, strictly speaking, Buddhism is not synonymous with vegetarianism: nevertheless, a Buddhist is not expected to take any flesh that is the outcome of slaughter for consumption as diet.[10]

But there are even stronger statements than this. The venerable U Lokanatha, an Italian Roman Catholic convert to Buddhism since many years ago, speaks of "The Crime of Killing." He puts in flatly thus:

> Any Religion which allows Killing is false. And Why? Because it is impossible to kill with any trace of love left in the human heart. The first thing that dies in the act of killing is Love . . .
> A Religion which permits animal slaughter is based on Greed, Selfishness, and Hatred. . .
> How can you love animals by killing and eating them? Where is your Love? Are you not a human tiger. Your love is in your teeth, *not* in your Heart. You tell the animals, 'Your death is my life.' I am a Vegetarian Buddhist and I tell the animals, 'Live and let live.' Buddhism is the Religion of Boundless Lovingkindness through Renunciation.[11]

One other and even more emphatic voice raised in the interest of vegetarianism is that of the Venerable S. B. Okkata, a Bur-

---

[10] R. L. Soni, M.D., "The Last Meal," *Light of the Buddha*, V, No. 4 (April, 1960), 39. He goes on to say that the mere presence of the word "pig" as a component part of the name of the food eaten by the Buddha in his last meal, is no more convincing than "cat" in catnip, "fingers" in ladyfingers, etc.

[11] A typescript sent to the author. In conversation U Lokanatha extended his ban on killing to mosquitoes, flies, etc. He found in modern plastics a great help to the non-killer, who now need not wear leather sandals, or indeed use anything that costs the life of another being.

mese monk of somewhat radical opinions in general. In a little book called *Twin Paths* he musters arguments against meat eating from all fronts—scientific, humanitarian, and religious. Man is not fitted to eat meat physiologically, he says, and when he does so he becomes more subject to body-foulness and dangerous disease. Nature teaches us a lesson here in that vegetarian animals are more alert (young ones open their eyes sooner) and stronger. Further the fact that meat spoils more quickly than vegetables indicates its greater impurity.

And who is the real criminal here? The butcher—whose livelihood the Buddha proscribed as non-, even anti-Buddhist? No, it is the flesh *eater* who is the real criminal; he will not be raised to heaven while his butcher descends to hell!

And what will be the effect of continued meat eating upon the eater?

> If a man eats the flesh of dead animals perpetually, his sensory organs will in the long run be transformed to those of the animal whose flesh he has eaten. . . . His eyes, ears, nose, tongue, body and brain will as a matter of course be those of the pigs', if he be a perpetual consumer of pork. Hard it is for him whose eyes are pig's to see the right and wrong, to choose the way of good and the way of bad. . . . Harder still will it be for him whose brain is built up of the pork to know the truth and walk on the path chalked out by the Buddha. . . .

And in a somewhat apocalyptic vision he affirms that "the world minus the carnivorous habit will at once give birth to Nibbana."[12]

This vegetarian group is definitely atypical and a small minority. Yet their witness disturbs the average Buddhist somewhat. He will confess that though he does eat meat regularly, when he stops to think about the matter he has some inner discomfort of conscience. And no doubt this will continue to be the case—a minority witness and a sometimes unquiet conscience among the majority, but no wholesale vegetarianism. After all, perhaps only a saintly monk can really be expected to keep the First Precept absolutely.

---

[12] Lucknow: Ideal Technical Press, n.d., *passim* and pp. 69, 86 and 75 respectively.

BIBLIOGRAPHY

1. Books

Ambedkar, B.R. "Le Buddha et l'avenir du Buddhisme." *Présence du Bouddhisme*, France-Asie, Vol. XVI, Saigon, Feb.-June, 1959.

The Book of the Discipline (Vinaya-Piṭaka), (Sacred Books of the Buddhists Series) Vol. I, 1949; Vol. II, 1940; Vol. III, 1942; Vol. IV, 1951, (I. B. Horner, tr.) London: Luzac.

Book of the Gradual Sayings (Anguttara-Nikāya), (Translation Series), Vol. I, 1951; Vol. II, 1952, (F. L. Woodward, tr.); Vol. III, 1952; Vol. IV, 1955 (E. M. Hare, tr.); Vol. V, 1955, (F. L. Woodward, tr.) London: Luzac.

Collection of the Middle Length Sayings (Majjhima-Nikāya), (Translation Series), Vol. I, 1954; Vol. II, 1957; Vol III, in press 1960 (I. B. Horner, tr.) London: Luzac.

Collis, Maurice, *She Was A Queen.* London: Faber and Faber, 1937.

Dialogues of the Buddha (Dīgha-Nikāya), (Sacred Books of the Buddhists Series), Vol. I, 1956; Vol. II, 1951; Vol. III, 1957; (T. W. Rhys Davids, tr.) London: Luzac.

Harvey, G. E. *Outline of Burmese History.* Calcutta: (Indian Edition), Longmans, Green, 1947.

————, *British Rule in Burma.* London: Faber and Faber, 1946.

Jātaka Stories, Vols. I–VI. London. Luzac, 1957.

Kashyap, Bhikkhu J. *The Abhidhamma Philosophy.* Buddha-Vihara, Nalanda (Patna), 1954.

Minor Anthologies of the Pali Canon, Vol. 4 *(Vimāna-vatthu and Peta-vatthu),* Kennedy and Gehman, tr. London: Luzac, 1942.

Maung Maung, Dr. *Burma in the Family of Nations.* Amsterdam: Djambatan, Ltd., 1956.

Mayhew, Christopher. *Men Seeking God.* London: George Allen & Unwin, 1955.

Nyanatiloka, Mahathera. *Buddhist Dictionary*. Colombo: Frewin and Co., 1956.
Nyanamoli, Thera (tr.), *Path of Purification*. Colombo: R. E. Semage, 1956.
Okkata, S. B. *Twin Paths*. Lucknow: Ideal Technical Press, n.d.
Panikkar, K. M. *Survey of Indian History*. Bombay: Asia Publishing House, 1956.
Pe Maung Tin and Luce, G. H. *The Glass Palace Chronicle of the Kings of Burma*. London: Oxford University Press, 1923.
Questions of King Milinda, (Sacred Books of the East, Vol. XXV). London: Oxford, 1925.
Rahula, Walpola. *History of Buddhism in Ceylon*. Colombo: M. D. Gunesena, 1956.
Sangharakshita, Bhikshu. *A Survey of Buddhism*. Bangalore: Indian Institute of World Culture, 1959.
Shway, Yoe. *The Burman and His Notions,* Vols. I, II. London & New York: Macmillan, 1882.
Sen, Amulyachandra. *Aśoka's Edicts (Institute of Indology* Series, No. 7). Calcutta: Indian Publicity Society, n.d.
Story, Francis. *Buddhism Answers the Marxist Challenge*. Rangoon: Burma Buddhist World Mission, n.d.
Warren, H. C. *Buddhism in Translations*. Cambridge, Mass.: Harvard University Press, 1953 ed.
Yule, Capt. Henry. *Court of Ava*. London: Smith, Elder and Co., 1858.

2. Periodicals

Light of the Buddha, Vols. I-IV (1956-1959). Mandalay: Buddhist Publication Society.
Light of the Dhamma, Vols. I-VI (1953-1959). Rangoon: Union of Burma Sasana Council.
The Open Door, Vols. I-II (1959-1960) Rangoon.
Newspapers listed in footnotes only.

3. Pamphlets & Miscellaneous

Chan Htoon, U. "Buddhism—The Religion of the Age of Science," Rangoon, 1958.
————, "Address to Sixteenth Congress of the International Association for Religious Freedom," Rangoon, 1958.
Lokanatha, Venerable, "The Crime of Killing," unpublished typescript, n.d.

Malalasekera and Jayatilleke. *Buddhism and Society*. UNESCO pamphlet.

Moore, C. A. (ed.). *Essays in East-West Philosophy*. University of Hawaii, 1951.

"Statement No. 2/60," Organization to Establish Buddhism as the State Religion," mimeographed.

Tun Hla Oung, U. "The Buddhist Middle Economic Way," mimeographed pamphlet, 1959.

Vijara, Sister (tr.), *The Sutta Nipata*. Sarnath (India): Maha Bodhi Society, n.d.

Wheel Series, (Wheel Publications), Buddhist Publication Society, Kandy, Ceylon, 1958 to present.

SUBJECT INDEX

AUTHOR INDEX